Peacekeeping in South Lebanon

Syracuse Studies on Peace and Conflict Resolution
Robert A. Rubinstein and Çerağ Esra Çuhadar, *Series Editors*

Peacekeeping in South Lebanon

Credibility and Local Cooperation

Vanessa F. Newby

Syracuse University Press

For a listing of books published and distributed by Syracuse University Press,
visit www.SyracuseUniversityPress.syr.edu.

ISBN: 978-0-8156-3571-0 (hardcover)
       978-0-8156-3589-5 (paperback)
       978-0-8156-5437-7 (e-book)

Library of Congress Cataloging-in-Publication Data

Available from the publisher upon request.

Manufactured in the United States of America

Contents

Illustrations

Maps

Tables

Figures

Preface

I first stumbled upon the United Nations Interim Force in Lebanon (UNI-FIL) mission in January 2012 when I traveled to South Lebanon as part of a symposium I was attending in Beirut. I was immediately intrigued by the work of the mission and the lives of the people who live in the area of operations. On that first drive along the Blue Line that divides Lebanon from Israel, all was quiet; all was calm. But knowing the pain and suffering that have occurred in the past forty-odd years made it a surreal experience. The story of the people of South Lebanon has not been told enough, and this book provides glimpses of what they have lived through: roaming militia groups, no fewer than five invasions, and a twenty-two-year occupation. The work of UNIFIL, while ostensibly about maintaining peace on the Blue Line, is actually so much more than that; it is about helping the local population to rebuild their lives and to create an environment where it is possible to live a normal life.

There are a great many people I need to thank who helped me write this book. First and foremost, I need to thank the staff of UNIFIL to whom I am indebted and who so generously donated their time to help me with my research. Their patience with my endless questions and constant badgering to come and talk to them was remarkable. In addition, I deeply appreciate the trust they placed in me by allowing me to interview them so that I could record my impressions of the mission. Without their assistance, this book would not have been possible, and words cannot express my gratitude for their insights and honesty regarding the work of the mission. Over the years of my research I have come across a great deal of criticism of UN peace operations in the academic literature and in the media. While honest critiques are important and necessary in democratic society, it is important to note that there are many good people working extremely hard to make peace operations a success. What I witnessed at UNIFIL in many staff was a remarkable dedication and passion for their work and for the local community among whom they worked.

I would also like to thank the many other people in Lebanon who gave interviews about their perceptions of the UNIFIL mission. These include Timur Göksel, whose stories about the early days of the mission are invaluable; local civilians from all walks of life who kindly agreed to speak with me; and former members of the Lebanese Armed Forces (LAF).

I would also like to thank Karim Makdisi and Samar Ghanem at the American University of Beirut who assisted me in making initial contact with UNIFIL and for kindly allowing me the position of visiting researcher at the Issam Fares Institute for Public Policy and International Affairs in 2013. I would like to thank Griffith University, Brisbane, Australia, for providing me with the funding to conduct research in Lebanon, and Professor Andrew O'Neill, who supported my application to travel. I would also like to thank the Department of International Relations in the Coral Bell School of Asia Pacific Affairs at the Australian National University (ANU) for its support and funding assistance that enabled me to revisit UNIFIL in 2016 and update my findings.

In writing this book I have many people to acknowledge. I am grateful to Jason Sharman and Sara Davies for their comments on the initial drafts of the book proposal and their ongoing support. Ben Day, Bina D'Costa, Luke Glanville, Jeremy Youde, and Ben Zala also provided advice and help as I was working on this book.

A special note of thanks needs to be made to the following people. Jack Corbett looked at endless drafts of my book proposal and mentored me through those dark post-PhD days where you feel like you have fallen off a cliff. Jack provided me with research work that has kept me afloat while on the job hunt. I am in awe of his productivity as a scholar, and I will not forget his kindness and generosity to me during tough times. Jeremy Youde has been a patient sounding board for my random thoughts and ideas about the book and helped me make sense of my argument. No one should have to endure reading early chapter drafts of academic books, but Jeremy did, and I am eternally grateful for his help. Mary-Louise Hickey provided invaluable comments and advice on my writing style. It has been a privilege working with such a professional editor, and I thank her for her support and friendship during my time at ANU.

I must also thank my mother for her endless encouragement of my academic career, even at times when it looked as if I didn't have one. I must also posthumously thank my best writing companion, YoYo the cat, also known as Porky Paws. All writers and academics know the loneliness of this world, and having him near me in companionable silence, punctuated by the odd cat snore, was very comforting.

I also want to acknowledge the people who have been lost to us since I began my research journey in 2012. Anthony Shadid, one of the finest journalists on the Middle East who came from South Lebanon and did a great deal to show the world what the Middle East is really like, died while reporting in Syria, and his loss is keenly felt by those of us who work on the region. I met him only once, but he helped me with my research with a great generosity of spirit just before he passed. I hope he would have approved of this book. My friend Peter Kassig, who died a senseless death at the hands of ISIS on November 16, 2014, dedicated his life to helping the less fortunate in the region, and he did not care what religion they were. I know had he lived he would have gone on to do so much good, and losing him so young has been painful for all of us who knew him.

Finally, I dedicate this book to the people of South Lebanon who have lived through so much. I am in awe of their resilience and determination to remain on their land. This part of the world continues to hold my heart, and this book is not the only one I will write about South Lebanon, as there is so much more to be said.

Abbreviations

APC	armed personnel carrier
CIMIC	civil military cooperation
DPKO	Department of Peacekeeping Operations
IDF	Israel Defense Forces
LAF	Lebanese Armed Forces
OGL	Observer Group Lebanon
UNDOF	United Nations Disengagement Observer Force
UNFICYP	United Nations Peacekeeping Force in Cyprus
UNIFIL	United Nations Interim Force in Lebanon
UNMOGIP	United Nations Military Observer Group in India and Pakistan
UNSC	United Nations Security Council
UNSCOL	Office of the United Nations Special Coordinator for Lebanon
UNTSO	United Nations Truce Supervision Organization

3700'00'N

L E B A N O N

Shouaiya

Hasbaiya

Marj 'Uyun

Ebel es Saqi

Shab'a

3690'00'N

Al Qulay'ah

Al Khiyam

Kafer Chouba

S Y R I A

Shhur

Kafer Kela

Itt Taibe

Metulla

Rhajar

Majdal Shams

Sur
(Tyre)

Ma'rakah

Ed Aadeise

Misgav'am

Kefar Gil'adi

Dan

Mas'adan

Ar Rashidiyah

Qana

Markabe

HaGosherim

Dafna

3680'00'N

Ramin

*Mediterranean
Sea*

Hula

Kiryat Shmona

Tibnin

'Shaqrah

Marat Al Aqabah

Yatar

Mays al Jabah

3670'00'N

Bint Jubayl

Yiftan

Aytarun

Naqoura

Yann

Ayta ash Sha'b

'Alma ash Sha'b

Zar'it

Yarun

Avivim

Khirbat Miri

Shetula

Hanita

Adamit

Shomera

Rumaysh

Yir'on

Shelomi

Eilon

Ba'am

Nahariyya

Mifshtat

Dovev

Alma

3660'00'N

I S R A E L

LINE OF WITHDRAWAL
of Israeli Forces from Lebanon
June 2000

The line of withdrawal as shown on this map
has been identified according to the
Secretary-General's report to the Security
Council of 22 May 2000 for the sole purpose
of confirming the withdrawal of the Israeli
forces from Lebanon pursuant to Security
Council resolution 425 (1978). It is based on
the best cartographic and documentary
material available to the United Nations. The
line of withdrawal is without prejudice to
future border agreements between the
Member States concerned.

0 1 2 3 4 5 km

0 1 2 3 mi

Geodetic datum: WGS 84
Ellipsoid: WGS 84

Projection: UTM 36 N
Height datum: MSL

The boundaries and names shown and the
designations used on this map do not imply
official endorsement or acceptance by the
United Nations.

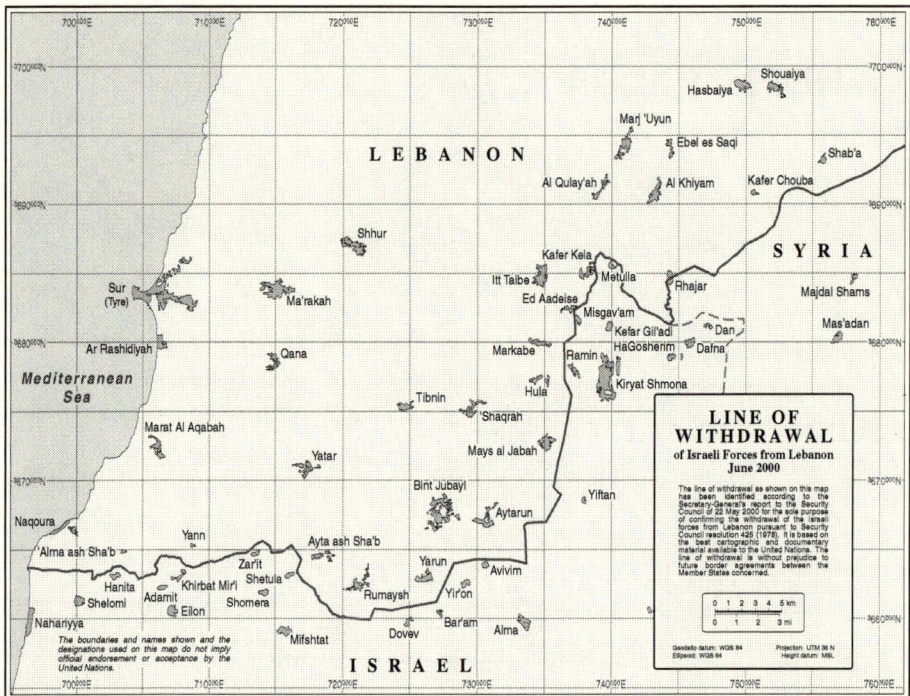

Map No. 4143 Rev. 1   UNITED NATIONS
July 2000

Department of Public Information
Cartographic Section

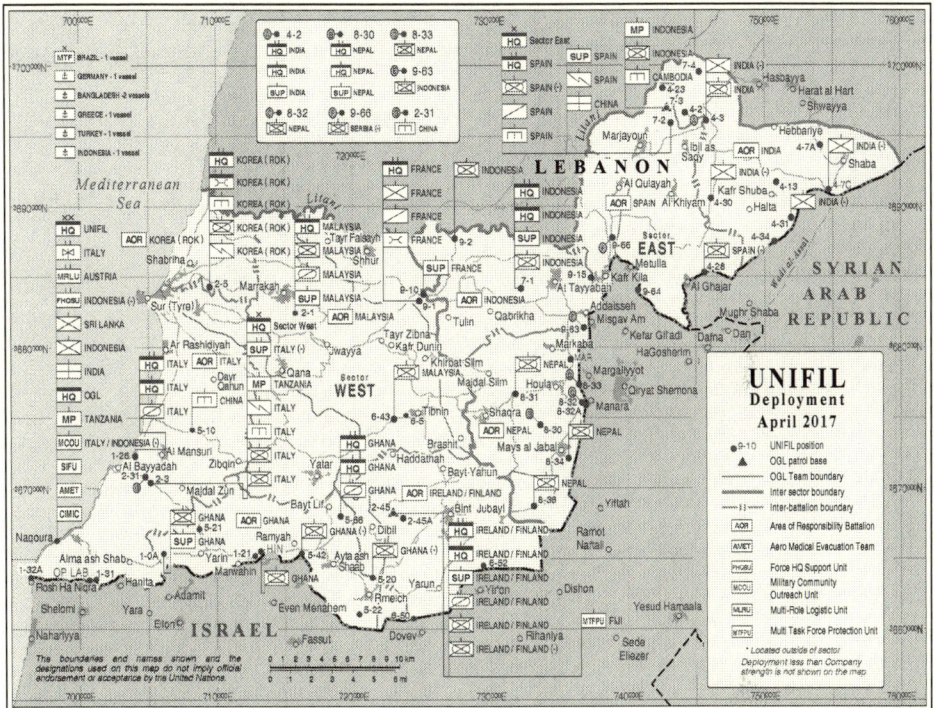

UNIFIL
Deployment
April 2017

Mediterranean Sea

LEBANON

SYRIAN ARAB REPUBLIC

ISRAEL

Sector WEST · Sector EAST

Legend / units:

- MTF BRAZIL - 1 vessel
- GERMANY - 1 vessel
- BANGLADESH - 2 vessels
- GREECE - 1 vessel
- TURKEY - 1 vessel
- INDONESIA - 1 vessel

- HQ UNIFIL
- AOR ITALY
- MRLU AUSTRIA
- PHQSU INDONESIA (-)
- SRI LANKA
- INDIA
- HQ OGL
- MP TANZANIA
- MCOU ITALY / INDONESIA (-)
- SIFU ITALY
- AMET ITALY
- CIMIC INDONESIA

Team markers: 4-2 INDIA, 8-30 NEPAL, 8-33 NEPAL, 9-63 NEPAL / INDONESIA, 2-31 CHINA, 8-32 NEPAL, 9-66 SERBIA

KOREA (ROK), FRANCE, MALAYSIA, INDONESIA, SPAIN, CAMBODIA, CHINA, GHANA, IRELAND / FINLAND, FIJI, TANZANIA, NEPAL, INDIA

Place names (selection):
Naqoura, Shabriha, Sur (Tyre), Marrakah, Ar Rashidiyah, Dayr Qanun, Qana, Al Bayyadah, Zibqin, Maydal Zun, Bayt Lif, Ramyah, Ayta ash Sha'b, Dibil, Yatar, Haddathah, Brashit, Bayt Yahun, Bint Jubayl, Rmeich, Yarun, Marwahin, Alma ash Shab, Yarin, Manwah, Hanita, Rosh Ha Niqra, Adamit, Shelomi, Yara, Nahariyya, Even Menahem, Elon, Fassut, Dovev, Sede Eliezer, Yesud Hamaala, Yiftah, Ramot Naftali, Dishon, Yir'on, Avivim, Rihaniya, Manara, Margaliyyot, Qiryat Shemona, Misgav Am, Metulla, Dan, Dafna, Mughr Shaba, El Ghajar, Kafr Shuba, Halta, Shaba, Harat al Hart, Shwayya, Hebbariye, Shaba, Marjayoun, Ibil as Saqy, Al Qulayah, Al Khiyam, Kafr Kila, At Tayyabah, Addaisseh, Qabrikha, Tulin, Houla, Markaba, Kafr Giladi, HaGoshrim, Majdal Silm, Shaqra, Mays al Jabal, Tibnin, Khirbat Silm, Kafr Dunin, Tayr Zibna, Shhur, Tayr Falsayh, Swayya, Ayun as Siyan

Scale: 0 1 2 3 4 5 6 7 8 9 10 km

Legend (right panel):
- 9-10 UNIFIL position
- ▲ OGL patrol base
- OGL Team boundary
- Inter sector boundary
- Inter-battalion boundary
- AOR Area of Responsibility Battalion
- AMET Aero Medical Evacuation Team
- PHQSU Force HQ Support Unit
- MCOU Military Community Outreach Unit
- MRLU Multi-Role Logistic Unit
- MTFPU Multi Task Force Protection Unit

* Located outside of sector
Deployment less than Company strength is not shown on the map

The boundaries and names shown and the designations used on this map do not imply official endorsement or acceptance by the United Nations.

Department of Field Support
Geospatial Information Section (formerly Cartographic Section)

Peacekeeping in South Lebanon

Introduction

Writing about the United Nations Interim Force in Lebanon is extremely problematic. Having lived and conducted research in Lebanon for more than six years, I find people who love to hate the mission, people who love it, and people who hate that they love it. Furthermore, their feelings toward UNIFIL appear deeply interconnected with their feelings toward peace in Lebanon:

> But I tell you whenever any UNIFIL soldier wants to come into any house he will be welcome. . . . We get used that UNIFIL is here, and we relax and we feel that we are now the most secure area. The South is more secure than the North. That's why, and we don't feel the danger now.[1]

> So the confidence that people have in UNIFIL is a temporary confidence. But if something occurred, if an incident occurred, people know very well that UNIFIL will not be in the middle. They will escape; they will leave; they will not confront the Israelis. And who will confront Israel is the resistance. . . . Let us deal with them as tourists.[2]

> And then they know that UNIFIL are not going to make the peace, because even the politicians is not going to make the peace. So what they feel is if they are there, then it's better than if they are not there. . . . So peace is not real peace; peace is just feeling peace.[3]

Over the years I have heard many stories from civilians who for some reason or another had a fleeting encounter with UNIFIL that left them with a lasting impression of the mission that they retain to this day. No one is more aware of this phenomenon than UNIFIL, and so the money, time, and effort that go into ensuring positive civilian encounters are immense.

Lebanon is a highly politicized nation, still recovering from numerous foreign interventions and the trauma of a fifteen-year civil war that left Lebanese society deeply divided along sectarian lines. These conflicts affect their thinking about everything: politics, the economy, where they socialize, even whom they choose to marry. They have also affected societal perceptions of international politics and international political actors based on their foreign policy toward the region. When Lebanese people think about politics, they think nationally and internationally because international crises affect the Lebanese on a surprisingly regular basis. Therefore, as an international intervention mandated by the international community, the UNIFIL mission has to navigate both interstate and intrastate conflict and division.

Since 2006 UNIFIL has stationed up to fifteen thousand troops in South Lebanon to act as a buffer between the states of Israel and Lebanon, which remain technically at war. The security challenges that confront UNIFIL can at times seem almost farcical:

> One day, a cow came from the Israeli side, found a gap in the Israeli technical fence, pushed the gap here and there and succeeded to come inside to come and drink water from the pond. On the first day it was one cow, the next day it was five cows, and so on, until it was sixty cows! Now you can't say the cows were Israeli; they were just cows from the Israeli side. Now who got upset? The shepherds, the Lebanese shepherds! They keep the drinking water in the summer for their cattle, and with this big flood of cows from the Israeli side, they will lose water. So they complained to the LAF [Lebanese Armed Forces]; the LAF transferred the problem to UNIFIL. UNIFIL asked the Israelis to stop allowing the cows to come in. They said we cannot stop the cows—they are cows. Come on, they are not people. You ask the cow to stop going outside? If the Lebanese side doesn't want the cows to come there, let them build a technical fence. But if the LAF builds a technical fence here, the Israelis will consider it as a border, and they will swallow about two kilometers [of land]. So the LAF said no, we are not going to build anything. It is Israel's responsibility to prevent this violation; otherwise,

we will let the shepherds kill the cows. The Israelis said if you kill the cows, this is aggression against us! There was rising tension.[4]

One day it can be wandering cows, and on another, random rocket attacks from pro-Palestinian militias, violent civilian protests, or a confrontation between two militaries. These incidents always have the potential to trigger another regional war and highlight the sensitivity to territorial violations felt by both the named parties to the conflict—the Israel Defense Forces (IDF) and the Lebanese Armed Forces (LAF).

The UNIFIL area of operations in South Lebanon remains suspended largely in what is termed a "negative peace": that is, the absence of conflict.[5] The Blue Line that divides the territories of South Lebanon and northern Israel is merely a "line of withdrawal"; it does not constitute a border in international law, as neither side has agreed to a cease-fire. In the absence of a peace process at the political level, the two states remain locked in a permanent state of war, officially termed "a cessation of hostilities." South Lebanon is also host to Hezbullah—one of the world's most powerful substate militias—and its Shi'ite-dominated support base. While Hezbullah has given its tacit agreement to the presence of UNIFIL, it is not a named party to the mandate and as such is not answerable to its terms and conditions. Ultimately, Hezbullah's raison d'être lies in resistance to Israel, not making peace with Israel.

The UNIFIL mission is one of the oldest UN peacekeeping missions in the world. It was created in response to the Israeli invasion of South Lebanon in 1978. Established by United Nations Security Council (UNSC) Resolution 425, the mission was tasked with "confirming the withdrawal of Israeli forces, restoring international peace and security and assisting the Government of Lebanon in ensuring the return of its effective authority in the area."[6] The mission remained in the area during subsequent Israeli invasions in 1982, 1994, and 1996 and during the Israeli withdrawal from South Lebanon in 2000. The most recent Israeli intervention—"Harb Tamooz" (the July War)—began on July 12, 2006, and ended on August 14, 2006. Since the implementation of a new mandate in 2006 (UNSC Resolution 1701) in the UNIFIL area of operations, peace has endured, and UNIFIL continues to monitor the Blue Line.

UNIFIL is classified in the literature as a "traditional" mission, which refers to peacekeeping missions that hew closely to the traditional principles of peacekeeping: consent, impartiality, and a minimal use of force.[7] These missions were established before the end of the Cold War and often involved the imposition of a neutral force between the armies of two states at war.[8] Traditional peacekeeping usually takes place in the period between a cease-fire and a political settlement and is composed of activities that are suited to a holding phase or the creation of "a political space that will facilitate a political resolution of the conflict."[9] Since 2006, however, operating under a revised mandate, the UNIFIL peacekeeping mission now includes a great many peacebuilding operations that go well beyond the activities usually attributed to a traditional peacekeeping mission. As such, UNIFIL presents the interesting case of an older mission with considerable experience (having been present for thirty-eight years) that deals with very modern peacebuilding activities. The most politically charged aspects of UNIFIL's modern mandate are that it has been tasked with clearing the area of operations of all unauthorized weapons and establishing "an area free of any armed personnel, assets and weapons other than those of the Government of Lebanon"[10] and maintaining peace on the "border" with the state of Israel.

When I began researching UNIFIL, I assumed I would at some point need to think about the issue of the overall effectiveness of the mission. I also assumed that I would reach a conclusion that would become obvious, intuitive, and logical. This never happened. The UNIFIL mission continues to confound me today as much as it did when I stumbled upon it in early 2012. The reason for my conundrum is quite simple. The UNIFIL mission is a case that causes us to reevaluate what the terms *success* and *failure* mean in the context of peacekeeping and peacebuilding. Despite much of what has been said and written about it over the years, I found no use for terms like absolute success or absolute failure when describing UNIFIL. As a researcher who has spent many years researching and thinking about the mission, I conclude that these blunt descriptions do not capture what UNIFIL has achieved. Those individuals who have worked in the mission for years can identify the changes that UNIFIL has brought about in its environment as clearly as they can identify where things have not gone as they would have liked.

To clarify this point, I will briefly outline the arguments that surround the concept of the success and failure of UNIFIL. On the side of failure, there are many criticisms that can be made. UNIFIL has failed to rid the area of operation of Hezbullah and its weapons, incidents between Israel and Hezbullah still occur, and weapons belonging to Hezbullah are believed to remain. UNIFIL has not managed to prevent or forestall any of the five Israeli invasions or the twenty-two-year Israeli occupation. It has not managed to negotiate an official cease-fire between Israel and Lebanon.

On the other hand, since 2006 UNIFIL has prevented accidental outbreaks of armed confrontation in the area of operation from escalating into war. It has reduced the overt presence of Hezbullah and has provided an environment conducive to economic development. It has helped to rebuild local infrastructure and provides myriad public services for the local population necessary for everyday peace. In the South it has helped to rebuild and reestablish the presence of the LAF, which is the most trusted national institution in Lebanon. It has supported the smooth running of local elections and, where requested, has provided material and technical assistance in local governance. If UNIFIL were not present, South Lebanon would be more vulnerable to conflict, owing to poor infrastructure and a weak economy, more frequent transgressions of the Blue Line, and a bolder Hezbullah presence on the Blue Line itself. In the absence of a political solution to the stalemate that exists between the Lebanese and Israeli governments, UNIFIL has carved out an important role for itself, building positive local relationships and preventing the escalation of incidents that have the potential to trigger another regional conflict. In short, since 2006, were UNIFIL not present, it is very possible war may have broken out.

The answer to writing about the mission therefore lies not in evaluating the overall success or failure of UNIFIL, but rather in understanding the process of how UNIFIL has managed to get things done. It is not about counting stories of success or failure; it is about understanding how, in such a challenging environment, UNIFIL has negotiated the politics of peacekeeping in South Lebanon.

Credibility in Peacekeeping

This book is about the concept of credibility in peace operations. The question it seeks to answer is one that has thus far not been addressed in the international relations literature or the literature on peacekeeping specifically: What is credibility in peacekeeping? Questions that follow on from this are as follows: How is credibility fungible? What does being credible in a peacekeeping operation actually mean on the ground? Finally, once credibility has been obtained, what benefits does it afford a peacekeeping mission?

Credibility in a peace operation (discussed in more detail in chapter 1) is defined in this book as *the capacity of an actor to present as an honest and believable provider of knowledge and services in a sustained and highly responsive manner that wins confidence and cooperation.*

Credibility manifests as four main types: responsiveness, technical, material, and security; however, actors may not be able to win all four forms, owing to local or national constraints. By disaggregating credibility into four different types, I show that it has been possible for UNIFIL to deliver in some of these areas but not all. For example, responsiveness credibility refers to the responsiveness of the force to military and civilian concerns, technical credibility refers to a commitment to good governance, material credibility refers to the mission's provision of aid, and security credibility is the ability to protect civilians and civilian property from security threats.

Credibility is important to peacekeeping missions for several reasons. First, it is listed as a success factor for peacekeeping operations by the UN (2008).[11] As such, surely we should understand what it is and when a mission has it or not. Second, as I show here, credibility can serve as a tool that enables a peacekeeping mission to function in hostile environments where there is weak legitimacy or none at all. Third, by unpacking credibility, I show how it differs from legitimacy, an important distinction that will also help to develop our understanding of legitimacy, particularly local legitimacy in peace operations.

Using the case of UNIFIL, I present a new definition of credibility and disaggregate the concept into four different types. I show how security is only one way that credibility manifests itself in practice and how credibility can comprise other forms that work in an environment where a military force must obtain cooperation and where threats of violence (deterrence) have no utility. I show how, unlike legitimacy, credibility engenders not trust but rather confidence, which requires the constant provision of evidence in order to be maintained. I argue that credibility differs from legitimacy in three key ways: as noted above, it needs to be constantly sustained with evidence, it can be won in specific areas but not across the board in every area, and it cannot be obtained up front but must be earned over time. By investigating the concept of credibility, I illustrate the benefits it affords a mission, which are confidence and cooperation.

This book explains how building credibility serves UNIFIL and how it has enabled the mission to exercise a large part of its mandate in the face of significant political challenges on the ground. In this book, I also discuss how until now, credibility has been conflated with legitimacy in the peacekeeping literature, and I argue that it should be regarded as an independent construct when considering how a peacekeeping operation functions and survives. I do so by illustrating how material interests drive credibility, whereas ideas drive legitimacy.

The case of UNIFIL is useful in highlighting what credibility is and how it functions as an independent construct. Because its mandate cuts across local, regional, and international political divides, UNIFIL suffers from weak local legitimacy and among some audiences has no legitimacy whatsoever. UNIFIL sits at a localized coalface of the friction between those actors propagating or supporting the status quo (the United States, Israel, the United Nations, and the European Union) and the ones opposing or challenging it, sometimes termed the axis of resistance (Iran, Hezbullah, and occasionally Russia). UNIFIL cannot be the servant of two masters at once; in order to please one political constituency, it automatically displeases the other. As such, even though UNIFIL's mandate is not contested within the UNSC at present, the way that the mandate is exercised on the ground is highly contentious.

UNIFIL has been asked to patrol and safeguard the Blue Line that divides the states of Lebanon and Israel. While the international community broadly supports this objective, within Lebanon many argue the UNIFIL mandate is not legitimate for three reasons: First, the state of Israel is not recognized by many local residents, being regarded as the illegally occupied state of Palestine. Second, UNIFIL patrols only on the Lebanese side of the Blue Line, and therefore many Lebanese perceive the mission's role as protecting Israel from Lebanon rather than the other way around. Third, between 1978 and 2006, UNIFIL was unable to prevent or repel any of the Israeli invasions of South Lebanon that devastated infrastructure and took many civilian lives. Thus, UNIFIL is perceived by many among the local population as ineffective in the security space and biased toward Israel.

The next challenge that UNIFIL faces is that it has been awarded a mission that might be termed "Chapter VI and a half": it has been asked to create a weapons-free area in South Lebanon, which requires a proactive approach to the disarmament of local substate militias, including, in principle, Hezbullah's weapons. Many in the local population do not want UNIFIL to search for Hezbullah's weapons, however, because they view Hezbullah as the only deterrent to another Israeli invasion. This issue constrains UNIFIL in two main ways: it prevents UNIFIL from proactively searching for weapons and from patrolling in certain parts of the area of operation because of local resistance.

The concept of credibility helps us describe UNIFIL's achievements in South Lebanon precisely because political legitimacy is weak among some audiences. By building credibility in key areas, UNIFIL has ensured that the mission can function in the local community. Credibility has won UNIFIL cooperation from the local population and enables UNIFIL to operate with minimal threats to its security on the ground. It has enabled UNIFIL to work effectively with local government and the national army, which helps reduce the political and security space for substate actors such as Hezbullah. Credibility also affords UNIFIL some cooperation in managing security on the Blue Line, particularly when liaising with the

IDF, the LAF, and local civilians. Finally, building credibility has enabled UNIFIL to create a predictable security environment, which is conducive to the normalization of peace.[12]

This book also describes the process of peacekeeping and illustrates the strategies UNIFIL employs to depoliticize its role as much as possible. In the course of earning credibility through the types of assistance described above, UNIFIL employs a technocratic approach. In other words, UNIFIL presents as a creator and provider of "objective" knowledge that enables it to act bureaucratically rather than politically.[13] For example, when preventing incursions of the Blue Line, UNIFIL strives to make the Blue Line an objective fact instead of a politically contested issue. UNIFIL uses the latest global positioning technology to show where the Blue Line lies and, where possible, in agreement with the IDF, has visibly marked the Blue Line on the landscape with blue barrels. Other strategies UNIFIL uses are liaison, negotiation, reassurance, and reporting to obtain compliance and cooperation from the parties to the mandate and civilians. Showing how these techniques are employed on the ground by the mission is another contribution of this book.

By providing detailed insight into the practice of a UN peace operation at different functional levels, including political affairs officers, civil affairs officers, and the peacekeepers, as well as by integrating views from some members of the local population, I explain how an international institution can navigate tricky political ground and function in relative security.

Why Is the UNIFIL Case Important?

The UNIFIL mission sits in the crosshairs of a changing global political order. Understanding how that plays out on the ground is important to political scientists and anyone interested in the international relations of the Middle East. The UNIFIL mission also comprises some unusual qualities, born of being an older mission dealing with recurring and modern forms of conflict.

First, length of time is an important factor in peacebuilding, and debates continue over the pros and cons of long-term versus short-term missions. Peace operations often have insufficient time to develop the local knowledge that facilitates successful engagement with local popula-tions to determine what works best in which situation.[14] As an older mis-sion, UNIFIL can teach us a lot about peacebuilding and peacekeeping from its accumulated institutional memory.

Second, Lebanon occupies a special position in the Middle East in that it has been described by many scholars of the region as the mirror of the Middle East—what happens in Lebanon is usually a reflection of the wider political issues that are playing out in the region.[15] It is possible to find a microcosm of every political issue that the Middle East faces somewhere in Lebanon, whether the effects of the Israel-Palestine conflict; the regional competition between Iran and Saudi Arabia; the activities of substate mili-tias, such as al-Qaeda and ISIS, that threaten to destabilize states; or the political machinations of sectarian politics. Compounding the importance of the UNIFIL area of operations is the fact that a conflict in South Leba-non could quickly escalate into another proxy war between Israel and Iran or even between American and Russian interests, such as the current Syr-ian conflict. Whatever constraints peacebuilders experience in Lebanon, they are quite likely to encounter them elsewhere in the Middle East.

Finally, there has been minimal literature on the mission since the 2006 war and UNIFIL's revised mandate. Only a small body of literature on South Lebanon has examined the effects of the war, the revised man-date, and peacebuilding efforts.[16] Scholarship that has examined the work of the UNIFIL mission specifically has focused on the legality and poli-tics of the mission as well as the impact (or lack thereof) of the Strategic Military Cell established in August 2006.[17] The character of the UNIFIL mission, specifically the peacekeepers and the differences between differ-ent nationality troop contingents, has received the most focus. Janja Vuga, for example, investigated the effect of cultural differences between troop contingents in multinational peace operations. Michael Liégeois used the example of Belgian peacekeepers to examine whether francophone peace-keepers deployed to francophone areas were more efficient. Chiara Ruffa analyzed the drivers of perceptions of security among different nationality troops in the UNIFIL mission and how those motivations affected their behavior toward the local population.[18]

Within the Middle East, two other UN missions exist, both of which are observer missions—the United Nations Truce Supervision Organization (UNTSO) mission in Israel/Palestine, and the United Nations Disengagement Observer Force (UNDOF) in the Golan Heights. While these missions are important for regional peace, they do not carry out an active peacebuilding program. As the Syrian war rages, Yemen continues to suffer the ravages of war, and the specter of civil war continues to haunt Iraq, furthering our understanding of which techniques work best in a peacebuilding program in the Middle East is important. The case of Lebanon therefore offers a good example of how tensions manifest themselves in this environment.

What Is Peacekeeping?

UN peacekeeping has existed in some form since 1948, with the creation of UNTSO in (then) Palestine; however, it was never part of the original mandate of the United Nations. The enormous changes that have been made to peacekeeping since the early missions reflect how the organization was "learning on the job." Many of the oldest peacekeeping missions are still operational today, situated as they are in the buffer zones of unresolved conflicts: Cyprus, Kashmir, Lebanon, Palestine, and Syria.[19] Peacekeeping operations have changed over time, and the level of civilian staff in peacekeeping missions has increased, as have police forces and other specialists in justice and governance.

There is no definition of peacekeeping in the UN Charter. Two articles, however, refer to the concept of the maintenance of international peace and security—Chapter VI and Chapter VII. Chapter VI provides for the peaceful settlement of disputes by, among other things, negotiation and adjudication, and Chapter VII contains collective security provisions that were intended to be the foundation of its policy on the maintenance of global peace.[20] While the UN has largely avoided providing strict definitions of peacekeeping, in 2003 it provided a taxonomy of the tasks that comprise peacekeeping that help to provide clarity on the many varied roles of peacekeepers (see table 1).

Table 1
United Nations peacekeeper tasks

Military	*Civilian*
Assist in implementing peace agreement	Help former belligerents implement complex peace agreements
Monitor a cease-fire of cessation of hostilities	Support delivery of humanitarian assistance
Provide a secure environment	Assist in the disarmament, demobilization, and reintegration of ex-combatants
Prevent the outbreak or spillover of conflict	Supervise elections
Lead states or territories through a transition to stable governments based on democratic principles	Build rule-of-law capacity
Administer a territory for a transitional period	Promote respect for human rights
	Assist economic recovery Set up transitional administration as a territory moves to independence

Source: Alex J. Bellamy and Paul D. Williams, *Understanding Peacekeeping*, 15.

As table 1 shows, peacekeeping operations no longer simply comprise a military force on the ground acting as a buffer between two states at war. Peacebuilding activities have been incorporated into most peace operations with key roles for both military and civilian actors. Further development of the UN's definition of peacekeeping has been the creation of five categories under the heading of "peace and security activities"—conflict prevention, peacemaking, peacekeeping, peace enforcement, and peacebuilding.[21]

While the academic literature includes a variety of definitions of peacekeeping, a review by Alex Bellamy and Paul Williams argues that any definition should comprise the following components: it must take into account the fact that peacekeeping operations are not always run by the UN, it must explain the underlying purpose of a peacekeeping operation, and it must be explicit enough to explain what a peacekeeping force consists of.[22] The 2008 manual *United Nations Peacekeeping Operations* provides a useful definition of peacekeeping: "Peacekeeping is a technique designed to preserve the peace, however fragile, where fighting has been halted, and to assist in implementing agreements achieved by the peacemakers. Over the years, peacekeeping has evolved from a primarily military model of observing cease-fires and the separation of forces after inter-state wars, to incorporate a complex model of many elements—military, police and civilian—working together to help lay the foundations for sustainable peace."[23]

The above helps clarify the potential scope for a peacekeeping operation, but the activities undertaken by a peace operation have developed over time. As mentioned earlier, UNIFIL is classified in the literature as a "traditional" mission. Owing to the dynamics of the bipolar international system during the Cold War, a number of other traditional missions are based in the Middle East. At this time, certain areas were considered by Russia and the United States to be "off-limits" for peacekeeping missions, as they lay too close to their spheres of influence.[24] The Middle East was considered not firmly placed in either sphere, but conflicts that took place there had the capacity to escalate and draw both great powers into a war, which neither side wanted. These missions remain in place today in the absence of a resolution to the conflicts that triggered the interventions in the first place.

Aside from traditional peacekeeping, two further typologies have been created since the end of the Cold War—second-generation or "wider peacekeeping"[25] that evolved after the Cold War and involved "painting a country blue."[26] This shift meant heavy involvement in all the domestic institutions of the state and included but was not limited to "reforming or strengthening deficient structures and institutions of governance (judicial, constitutional, electoral, and bureaucratic); disarmament and demobilization of warring factions; restoration of public order and the rule of law, for example training/creating police forces; de-mining activities; provision of technical assistance for independent media; building space within civil society for political mobilization; monitoring, organizing, or supervising transitional elections and plebiscites; and support for rehabilitation and reconstruction of infrastructure."[27]

Modern peace operations nowadays always comprise an element of peacebuilding that the UN defines as an activity that "aims to reduce the risk of lapsing or relapsing into conflict by strengthening national capacities at all levels for conflict management, and to lay the foundation for sustainable peace and development. It is a complex, long-term process of creating the necessary conditions for sustainable peace. Peacebuilding measures address core issues that affect the functioning of society and the State, and seek to enhance the capacity of the State to effectively and legitimately carry out its core functions."[28]

Most scholars agree that peacebuilding can take place at all phases of a conflict and not simply in the postconflict stage.[29] Key debates center largely on critiquing the liberal penchant for intervening in states and question the quality of peace obtained from these interventions. They also include the type of intervention that should be employed[30] and whether peacebuilding efforts should be focused at the local level or should employ a top-down approach.[31] These debates tend to fall into two camps—problem solving and critical—with some scholars straddling the divide.

Since the creation of more complex peace operations, there has been a debate about how involved peace operations should be in the political and institutional structures of the states in which they intervene. This debate has emerged as a result of the failure of more complex peace operations to achieve their goals. The main issue is the dilemma of whether a peace operation should be heavily invested in a state in order to avoid "the problems of incomplete reform and premature departure" or retain what is termed a light footprint, to avoid international intrusion in the domestic affairs of host states.[32]

The UNIFIL mission is in some ways hard to classify. As an older mission with a modern mandate, UNIFIL can be said to have a light footprint, even though it has one of the largest European troop contingents of any current mission operating in a very small area. While UNIFIL is based specifically in South Lebanon and does not operate nationally, some of its peacebuilding work has national and international effects.

The Case of UNIFIL

The case of UNIFIL can be classified as a deviant case, which is one that "by reference to some general understanding of a topic (either a specific theory or common sense), demonstrates a surprising value,"[33] and UNIFIL differs considerably from all other traditional missions that are still operational.[34] It is an old mission with a completely revised modern mandate; the mission mandate has weak legitimacy, owing to the political effects of both inter- and intrastate war; it comprises more European troops than any other current UN mission; and it is much larger than all the other older missions that are its logical comparators. Ultimately, UNIFIL is a new "old" mission: its revised mandate includes "old" interstate buffer-zone responsibilities alongside modern peacebuilding activities in line with the developments that have occurred in peacebuilding praxis since 1996.

One consideration that is specific to the UNIFIL mission and relates to security is, as mentioned earlier, the high number of EU troops in the mission, with 32 percent coming from EU member states.[35] This situation is highly unusual in peacekeeping, where the top twenty-four troop contributing countries are non-EU states and the majority of troops serving in UN missions today are from the developing world.[36] EU troops currently contribute worldwide only 5.9 percent of the total number of troops to global peacekeeping operations.[37] The anomaly of UNIFIL is owing to the history of the creation of Resolution 1701 (discussed later in chapter 2).

The purpose of using a deviant case study as an exploratory form of analysis is to understand whether the case is genuinely unique or whether findings from this case can be generalized to other case studies. The findings generated from this research at the micro level have identified some traits consistent with the ones found in the literature on other peace operations as well as a new theoretical approach to international interventions that may have applicability beyond UN peace operations. As I note above, this case study offers ideas about how to research the concept of credibility in peacekeeping operations more broadly.

The choice of a single case study does mean that I cannot claim my findings necessarily tell us about credibility in all peacekeeping missions. Furthermore, I have chosen here to focus on credibility in a single peacekeeping operation largely at the local level. It is beyond the scope of this book to surmise how my findings apply to credibility at the international level. This research does, however, raise questions about the nature of credibility that could fruitfully be explored at the international level, specifically the need to maintain credibility with evidence, its basis in material interests, its fungibility, and the different types of credibility I identify here.

Framework and Methodology

In this book I draw on sixty-five face-to-face interviews with a variety of respondents. It is essential to note that I write this book largely from the perspective of UNIFIL, drawing heavily on interviews with UNIFIL staff, and less so on information from local civilians and other stakeholders. This approach was taken in light of the access I received to key staff at UNIFIL and the limited access I had to the local population in the area of operations, which is a highly securitized environment where the local population and local security organizations are very suspicious of foreigners asking questions. This is not to say I did not obtain a variety of local perspectives, but rather that I present here a view of what works in a peacekeeping mission largely from the perspective of the peace operation itself. As such, I can make no claims to represent the entirety of local views about the mission in the way that other works have.[38] However, obtaining local views was valuable and provided a more balanced perspective on the achievements of the mission. It was these interviews that afforded me the realization that UNIFIL has obtained credibility and not legitimacy, and without this input I would not have drawn the same conclusions. As such, my interviews with the local population provided me with valuable and nuanced insight into UNIFIL's achievements.

Given that this research obtained the perceptions of UNIFIL officers and local key stakeholders, it required a qualitative approach that made use of some ethnography. This method is described by Zoe Bray as "a naturalistic approach whose main data-gathering and analyzing techniques consist of participant observation and open-ended interviewing."[39] The purpose of ethnography is to understand interactions, power relations, and micro processes in the environment as they occur. The aim here is not to conclusively prove something; rather, it is to explore and understand the "why and how" of processes in order to formulate a hypothesis for testing across multiple case studies.[40]

Conducting research using qualitative methods means that the researcher must be reflexive and aware of the influence of their presence on proceedings. Mark Neufeld defines reflexivity thus: "[Reflexivity] can be understood to entail three core elements: (i) self-awareness regarding underlying premises, (ii) the recognition of the inherently politico-normative dimension of paradigms and the normal science tradition they sustain, and (iii) the affirmation that reasoned judgements about the merits of contending paradigms are possible in the absence of a neutral observation language."[41]

My main impressions in terms of observing my influence on the ground as I conducted the research was that all respondents appeared to feel comfortable telling me what they thought of UNIFIL, good and bad. They did not appear to be shy or nervous in my presence. I never felt that respondents were reluctant to share their feelings on the topic. As time passed, I realized I may have engendered a stronger reaction from some participants than they might ordinarily express, possibly because they believed that perhaps what they said would be relayed back to the international community. I also encountered many contradictions. It has been noted by others that this kind of research generates "inconvenient truths,"[42] whereby no matter how many interviews one conducts, it is impossible to simplify views into discrete categories because for every person who expresses one opinion, someone else will have a different view. I have tried to incorporate the myriad voices into this research without being too contradictory. There was, as I note later, a plurality to be found in the views of all respondents. Official views differed from personal views, religious views clashed with the desire for personal security, and political views about the UNIFIL mission clashed with personal views about individual UNIFIL staff, some of whom were well liked.

I should also note here that my interviews were sometimes in the presence of UNIFIL civil affairs, as at times it was the only way I could access respondents in the area of operation given my resources. As I conducted an equal number of interviews with respondents on my own, I did not notice any major differences between the two types of interviews. As noted above, all interviewees appeared to want to be frank in their views of UNIFIL, and I believe this openness goes to the heart of the credibility UNIFIL has won that contributes to an environment where people feel they can be honest about their views on the mission. Conversely, I am aware of the many people who would not speak to me and who may have had very different views from those individuals who consented to be interviewed. Of note is that the population I interviewed formally came into contact with UNIFIL on a regular basis. Their views corroborate what I found, which is that UNIFIL has credibility in certain areas. While the untapped population may have had different views, it may be simply because they did not have as much contact with UNIFIL, confirming my observation that constantly sustaining relationships through regular contact and supplying material benefits builds credibility.

To conduct this research I spent a year in Lebanon interviewing respondents and observing the UNIFIL mission at work in the area of operations. Within that time, I lived for six months in the Shi'ite neighborhood of Dahiyeh, which is a suburb south of Beirut known to be predominantly occupied by southern Lebanese who migrated to Beirut in waves as a result of the successive conflicts in South Lebanon. It is also a known Hezbullah stronghold. I was able to live there because I was married to a Lebanese Shi'ite from the area. From a work perspective, I was also keen to observe the type of civilians with whom UNIFIL interacts, the majority of whom are Shi'a. Owing to personal and security reasons, it was not possible for me to live in the area of operations, and residing in Dahiyeh was a good way of interacting informally with Shi'a from the South of Lebanon, many of whom retain property in the South and visit frequently.[43] While I would not go so far as to describe myself as embedded in the local culture, I was able to observe the local culture. This experience also enabled me to verify my findings and clarify informally that what I was told by civilians in the area of operations corresponded with what people said informally about UNIFIL. As an Arabic speaker, this experience provided me with insight into local southern culture and some reassurance that people were being truthful with me. I have since lived in Lebanon for more than three years, and until now the informal discussions I have had about UNIFIL with Lebanese people have not caused me to change the views I express here.

The techniques I employed in this research were participant observation and semistructured interviews.

Participant Observation

I observed a variety of interactions between UNIFIL and stakeholders in the UNIFIL mission whom I classify as members of the Lebanese public and the parties to the conflict.[44] I was afforded many opportunities to observe UNIFIL in the area of operations, interacting with the local population: conducting border patrols, medical and veterinary outreach visits, national day celebrations, and the social calls of civil affairs officers. This experience enabled me to understand more about the "why and how" of the interaction between UNIFIL and the local population in terms of what UNIFIL did and how the local population responded to them.[45]

Interviews

I conducted sixty-five face-to-face semistructured interviews with a cross-section of stakeholders, including UNIFIL military staff (civil military cooperation [CIMIC] officers and peacekeepers from the Irish, Indian, and Ghanaian battalions) and the current force commander. Within the UNIFIL mission I also interviewed civilian staff (political affairs officers, public information officers, and civil affairs officers). Other interviewees included senior LAF officers, international journalists who specialize in reporting on the South of Lebanon, local academics, UNIFIL's former spokesperson (1978–2006), and a wide variety of local civilians (agricultural workers, villagers, local business owners, local municipality politicians, former local politicians, and local journalists). Some respondents (for example, female tobacco workers) had limited interaction with UNIFIL and provided their impressions more through observations. Others were more involved with UNIFIL (for example, local politicians) and had more to say about their dealings with them on a regular basis.

Informal interviews or discussions were also conducted with people from the South of Lebanon. Other researchers using ethnographic methods have used the same approach to canvass as wide an opinion as possible and as part of the observational, "in situ" aspect of this type of research.[46] In general, these individuals were people who had property in the area and had spent a fair amount of time in the South during their lifetime. I used this material to inform my work and to corroborate views that I heard in my formal interviews with civilians.

All the formal interviews were recorded, transcribed, and coded to identify the dominant themes. All formal interviewees gave their consent to participate in the research, and their identities have been kept anonymous with the exception of two interviewees.[47] Interviews were sourced on a rolling basis, termed *snowballing*, whereby a respondent would recommend another person who might be suitable for interviewing.

Finally, I share the view of other field researchers in that I do not claim that this work represents all local or UNIFIL views in their totality; rather, it aims to discuss an understanding obtained from the views expressed to me.[48]

Why Read This Book?

This book provides a number of insights for scholars and students of peace and conflict or international security, scholars and students of the Middle East, practitioners in peace operations, and international relations scholars interested in theorizing about credibility and its relationship with legitimacy.

Taking each group in turn: The empirical detail offered in this book is useful for scholars engaged in research on the micro processes of peace operations, a research area that is steadily increasing. Chapter 1 provides a fresh examination of what credibility means in a peacekeeping environment, a topic that has thus far remained unexamined. Chapters 3–5 provide specific details about how a peace operation functions on the ground and the many different aspects of the work of a peace operation. These chapters provide some insight into both local and peacebuilder/peacekeeper perceptions of how a mission operates on the ground. For students in particular, the many stories provided in this book about "real-life" peacekeeping should provide a level of context that is engaging. In addition, those individuals studying peace operations more broadly may find a new book on one of the older traditional missions a useful addition to the literature. Equally, scholars of international security will find rich detail on the specific security practices of a peacekeeping mission at the international, national, and local levels of operation.

There is currently no book available on the UNIFIL mission since the revised mandate of 2006, so scholars interested in Lebanon, Middle East conflicts, Middle Eastern society, or Hezbullah and its constituents will find this book a useful reference tool for recent information on South Lebanon. Chapter 2 in particular provides the historical context of the mission and some detail about South Lebanon during the civil war and the Israeli occupation. Furthermore, as the mission sits at the coalface of some of the key regional disputes, this book may provide Middle East scholars or students useful insight into how these disputes manifest themselves on the ground in the Middle East.

The discussion between practitioners and scholars is more vibrant in the field of peace and conflict studies than in other areas of international relations. I hope, this book provides practitioners with a useful external view of their everyday work in the field. The insights this book provides on the concept of credibility will be useful to practitioners both in the field and at UN headquarters. By introducing a fuller definition and conceptualization of credibility, this book will inform thinking among practitioners about how to harness credibility effectively in peace operations. For those individuals who have served in the UNIFIL mission (a not inconsiderable number, as it has been present for thirty-eight years), this book may be of interest in terms of its up-to-date assessment of the mission and its work.

Finally, the concepts of credibility raised here have broader implications for the international relations literature. Scholars interested in theoretical questions about legitimacy may find the unpacking of credibility provides useful insights into other areas of international relations. This book provides some information about the relationship between credibility and legitimacy; the question of how credibility functions at the international level has yet to be fully addressed.

The Structure of the Book

In explaining how UNIFIL builds credibility, this book examines UNI-FIL's engagement at three levels: the international, the national, and the local. While UNIFIL is an international actor operating at a subnational level, UNIFIL engages at an international level with the IDF, at the national level with the LAF and local government, and at the local level with civilians. This distinction is made to help the reader easily navigate the wide variety of work that UNIFIL undertakes. Of course, these levels of engagement can and do overlap—for instance, monitoring the border involves engagement at all three levels—and local issues are bound up with national and international politics, so there is no clear delineation between these levels, but for the sake of clarity I have chosen to use this structure in describing UNIFIL's work.

Chapter 1 provides an in-depth discussion of credibility. It begins with a review of the literature on credibility at the international level and notes that until now it has been used to further theories of deterrence and coop-eration but remains unexamined as a stand-alone concept. I present an analysis of the existing literature on credibility and a discussion of what credibility is in peacekeeping. I posit that credibility has been conflated with legitimacy in peacekeeping and argue that they are two separate concepts: credibility is underpinned by material interests, while legiti-macy is underpinned by ideas. I then discuss the international relations literature on institutional legitimacy and show how it fails to adequately explain how local legitimacy in peace operations is won or lost. Despite very real attempts to overcome the conundrum of whose voice matters in peacebuilding, I show there are limitations to the current literature on local legitimacy and local ownership and thus far the concept of cred-ibility has been ignored. I then present a model of credibility that sets out the framework for understanding how UNIFIL has won cooperation and confidence.

Chapter 2 provides a history of UNIFIL's involvement in South Leba-non since 1978, describing the relationship that UNIFIL has developed with the local population, and shows how despite generating positive relations with the local population, UNIFIL has been unable to protect the local population from five successive Israeli invasions. It also provides details of the UNIFIL mandate and explains why UNIFIL has been unable to fulfill all the criteria set out in the revised resolution that came into place in 2006.

Chapters 3–5 reveal how UNIFIL builds credibility with illustrative examples. Chapter 3 illustrates how liaison, intervention, negotiation, and reporting build technical and responsiveness credibility that win UNIFIL confidence and cooperation from the named parties. I discuss how kidnapped goats, wandering cows, cleaning a river on the border, and pro-Palestinian protests have been the cause of standoffs between Israel and Lebanon and how UNIFIL resolved these problems peacefully. In this chapter the important role of time is discussed in relation to the influence it affords long-serving staff and how this dynamic helps to illustrate the difference between winning trust and winning confidence.

Chapter 4 explores UNIFIL's peacebuilding work at the national level and shows how UNIFIL wins technical and material credibility through its work with national and some local institutions in Lebanon. The chapter starts with a description of how UNIFIL assists with local governance by working closely with the municipal government in the South. In addition, UNIFIL works hard to bring other ministerial departments to the South of the country to shore up the state's presence in the area of operations. The second part of the chapter discusses how UNIFIL works to close the space for other actors to provide security by engaging in security sector reform with the LAF.

In chapter 5 I show how UNIFIL builds material and responsiveness credibility by being a responsive provider of goods and services and maintaining relationships with the local population. I describe the myriad forms of material assistance provided by UNIFIL and illustrate the creative ways in which UNIFIL assists the local population and how local agency places limits on UNIFIL's freedom of movement. UNIFIL's responsiveness and material credibility earn UNIFIL cooperation on the ground, which helps to provide a secure environment for patrolling troops. This chapter discusses the work of both civil affairs and civil military cooperation and highlights the instrumental nature of the relationship between the local population and the UN peacekeeping force.

Chapter 6 concludes that building credibility in specific areas is a useful strategy for building local cooperation and confidence with the mission that enables it to function. In doing so, the UNIFIL mission has created a predictable security environment that has helped to normalize peace for local civilians. UNIFIL has achieved this result by carefully preventing accidental flare-ups on the Blue Line and actively working to bring state institutions back into the area, which in turn has brought greater stability and encouraged increased economic activity. Understanding the utility of credibility also enables peace operations to conduct a more nuanced assessment of what can be achieved through the use of material and technical assistance in terms of mission scope, both on the ground and at mission headquarters. In the absence of any political peace process, the UNIFIL mission has had considerable success in helping to generate stability and predictability in the area of operations and in negotiating the tricky political terrain of inter- and intrastate conflict. This book concludes that credibility should be regarded as an independent construct when considering how a peacekeeping operation functions and survives.

The next chapter discusses the nature of credibility at the international level and the local level. Here I compare legitimacy and credibility and establish the theoretical framework for the empirical chapters that follow.

1 The Role of Credibility in Peacekeeping

The most useful way to conceive of credibility in peacekeeping is to consider an apt comment expressed to me by a UNIFIL officer early on in my research because of the way it captures the case for credibility: "You know the expression 'You're only as good as your last game'? That's here. You're only as good as your last game."[1]

The United Nations has three established pillars of peacekeeping: impartiality, consent, and minimal use of force. As the complexity of peace operations increased, the United Nations Department of Peacekeeping Operations (DPKO) identified three additional or second-order success factors in 2008: legitimacy, credibility, and the promotion of national and local ownership.[2] While literature that has looked at the second-order success factors in UN peacekeeping has focused heavily on legitimacy and local ownership, the concept of credibility has been ignored. To date no studies have examined the part that credibility plays in the success of a peace operation.

In this chapter I unpack the concept of credibility. I discuss how, until now, credibility has most often been invoked to support theories on deterrence and cooperation but up until now has rarely been examined as a stand-alone concept in international relations. I then progress to the question of how credibility functions in peacekeeping operations.

Credibility in International Relations

Credibility in the international relations literature has, until now, most often been used to advance theories on deterrence and cooperation. It is discussed in the realist literature on threats, deterrence, and military capability and has been used in liberal theories of cooperation, most often in relation to international financial regimes and institutions. Very little effort has gone into deeper examinations of what credibility is.

In realist theories of deterrence, the principle of anarchy, that is, the absence of an overarching government regulating the behavior of states,[3] underpins discussions that utilize the concept of credibility. After the Second World War and the invention of nuclear weapons, the concept of deterrence became the intense focus of literature that weighed the costs of conflict and examined how states could deter each other from going to war. Credibility in this literature rested on a state's capacity to fight a war and its willingness to do so.[4]

Reputation emerged as a major factor that informed states' calculations about when and how they believe threats emanating from other states. It is informed, according to one early scholar, by a record of past performance: the statements and behavior of its government and the attitudes of public opinion, both domestic and allied.[5] Schelling used the concept of "face," or a country's image, to describe how a state could present itself as a credible actor determined to face up to threats of war. Firmness was regarded as a key attribute that facilitated credibility in these scenarios.[6]

These early theories have been criticized for not taking context into account; rather, they asserted that assumptions of credibility were stable and generalizable. Later works argued that the specific conditions of a threat impact both how a state will act and the perceptions of the other state on how it will act, that is, its credibility in that particular context. Past behavior then was not seen as a key determinant in this literature, and factors other than material capability and willingness to fight were brought into the discussion. These factors included the level of democracy in the state, the actual level of interest a state has in a particular issue, its proximity to the other state, and perception.[7]

In later work, Downs and Jones argued that a state's reputation is not one size fits all and that a state's reputation cannot cover all issue areas. Drezner noted that reputation is a fuzzy concept and asks the valid question: "Countries should cultivate a reputation for what, exactly? Can a reputation for toughness in a crisis be reconciled with a reputation for compliance with international law? Do countries have reputations, or just leaders? Does a reputation in one issue area—say, aid generosity—spill over into other issue areas?" Press argues that in a crisis of war, reputation has very little effect on credibility and that the global military balance of power matters more. In a somewhat circular turn, Crescenzi reverts to past behavior and argues that when countries have similar capabilities, they will assess the past actions of states to assess credibility.[8]

In the deterrence and reputation literature, then, credibility refers to the idea that to be "credible," a state has to demonstrate it has the capability and resolve to make good on its threats. The extensive literature on this concept discusses the details of how states make calculations about the costs and benefits of going to war with another state.

Credibility has also been used to advance theories of cooperation, largely in the institutionalist literature. This literature is more concerned with how states cooperate in an anarchical system and has also been subject to heavy use of game theory.[9] Transparency, repeated interaction, and the provision of information are considered key to the success of international cooperation.[10] Here credibility is regarded as important, because otherwise states would have no faith in each other's commitments to one another. Past behavior too is regarded as an important indicator that states will make good on their commitments.[11] However, the rationale for cooperation provided in the institutionalist literature rests on the idea that social punishment—ostracizing, withholding favors, future cooperation, and friendship—is what keeps states in line rather than the threat of war. The role of credibility in the cooperation literature is based on the idea that institutions foster the conditions that enable states to be seen as credible actors.[12]

Taking a constructivist perspective for a moment, we can see there is a relationship between credibility and ideas. Krasner's definition of regimes or institutions relies heavily on the concept of shared norms: "as sets of implicit or explicit principles, norms, rules, and decision-making procedures around which actors' expectations converge in a given area of international relations." Mearsheimer, a committed realist, uses the phrase "a higher state of norms" when describing institutions as a set of rules.[13] The concept of norms and legitimacy will be discussed later in this chapter, but what emerges from the literature in international relations that utilizes the concept of credibility in cooperation is that ideas about the legitimacy of institutions and accepted norms of state behavior play a role in assessments of credibility. In other words, by cooperating on a given issue, states accept there is an inherent legitimacy in these actions. Therefore, states are not just behaving out of purely selfish interests; they are also cooperating in accordance with shared norms, and that plays a role in assessments of the willingness of states to make good on their promises. As such, credibility does not appear to have been fully untangled from the concept of legitimacy at the international level.

In sum, literature in the international system has used the concept of credibility extensively to justify theories of deterrence and cooperation. It has not, as yet, been unpacked to show what credibility means in different contexts as a stand-alone concept.

Credibility as a Stand-Alone Concept

Credibility has rarely been examined as a stand-alone concept in international relations, but more recently the relationship between emotion and credibility has received some attention. If we return for a moment to the idea of reputation, one state's belief in the willingness of another state to make good on its promises, we can see that this belief is underpinned by some underlying assumptions. Some authors have tapped into this notion and expanded the concept of credibility to include an emotional aspect. Stein makes the point that "credibility, a fundamental component to theories of action in international politics, is emotional as well as cognitive." Mercer argues that credibility is not simply a function of rational choices, such as the cost of the signal or past behavior. It is an emotional belief that is held by its intended receiver; the belief that another's commitment is credible depends on the selection and interpretation of evidence and on the assessment of risk, both of which rely on emotion.[14]

A few scholars have attempted to examine credibility more closely as a stand-alone concept. Sartori discusses how credibility functions in diplomacy and concludes that honesty is deeply connected to credibility in deterrence. She argues that countries in general try to speak honestly because developing a reputation for honest diplomacy is more useful in solving disputes without having to resort to force. From this idea we can deduce that credibility has a relationship with honesty and believability.[15]

One author who has examined credibility as a concept is Alvin Tze Tien Tan, who highlights that there are two main components of credibility at the international level. The first is structural, which he states is the ability of a state to fulfill its commitments, and this capacity includes capability and material interests. The second component he terms *behavioral credibility*, which is the willingness of a state to fulfill a promise. This willingness, in his view, is underwritten by three variables: past behavior, political instability, and the degree of democracy. Tan argues correctly that the structural components of credibility have been utilized a great deal when used in the cooperation and deterrence literature, but behavioral credibility has not. He provides a definition of credibility as "the belief by outside observers of the ability and willingness of a state to fulfil its promises."[16]

What emerges from an examination of the literature on credibility at the international level is the fact that credibility, unlike legitimacy, *needs to be constantly sustained*. It cannot exist without either constant reassurance (repeated interaction, past behavior) or evidence (military intelligence, material capability). If a state stops signaling its intent through the provision of truthful information, or is caught bluffing about its military capabilities, it will lose credibility. By identifying this aspect of credibility, we can see how it functions independently as a construct and attempt to clarify how it differs from legitimacy. If we accept the premise that credibility requires constant maintenance and across different issue areas, is it possible, then, that credibility can take different forms? If so, this insight helps to resolve the issues raised by Drezner about reputation. States may use different types of credibility at different times, depending on the issue. A state might want to be viewed as a credible security deterrent in one case, but in another it may choose to be viewed as a responsible and compliant international citizen. When it does so, it uses a variety of tools to indicate its credibility according to the issue area. So, for example, while China might have a very large army, it may not be interested in presenting itself as a military threat and may be more interested in being viewed as a responsible global citizen. Instead, it will indicate its credibility by acting as a regional aid provider after natural disasters or as a provider of troops to regional and UN peacekeeping missions.

By conceiving of credibility as multifaceted, we can see how it can be utilized by actors in different ways at different times. But what happens in a scenario where both deterrence and cooperation are required simultaneously in the same context? Peacekeeping operations are such an environment where deterrence and cooperation are required at the same time. This tension exists because, on the one hand, cooperation is extremely important to obtain local acceptance for the mission and, on the other, the mission needs to act as a deterrent to those actors wishing to return to conflict. This environment then exposes how different types of credibility can exist because a peacekeeping force necessarily needs to employ different types in different scenarios.

Furthermore, as I will discuss later in this chapter, the UNIFIL case is useful because the legitimacy of the mission is weak or even absent among some audiences because of a lack of national consensus on the mission's goals. In this case, it is possible to examine how credibility works as a stand-alone concept and understand its fungibility in practice.

Credibility: A Reassessment

Credibility is one of the three newer second-order success factors that the UN has listed as important to the success of a peace operation. As I discuss later in the chapter, unlike local ownership and local legitimacy, credibility has been ignored in the extensive scholarship on peacebuilding and peacekeeping. I attempt to redress this balance by unpacking and redefining the concept of credibility and showing how the UNIFIL mission has won it. Furthermore, in doing so, I discuss the fungibility of credibility, which is not something that has been considered until now. Simply put, what does credibility do for a peacekeeping mission, and how does it work when there is limited or no legitimacy?

Credibility is similar to legitimacy in that it provides an institution with cooperation and some compliance, but it differs in three key ways: it needs to be constantly sustained with evidence, it is context dependent and can be won in specific areas but not across the board in every area of its work, and it cannot be obtained up front but must be earned over time. The benefits of winning credibility are cooperation and confidence.

Credibility in peacebuilding is defined here as the capacity of an actor to present as an honest and believable provider of knowledge and services in a sustained and highly responsive manner that wins cooperation and confidence. Credibility can be manifested in four main ways—responsiveness, technical, material, and security—but actors may not be able to win all four forms owing to local or national constraints.[17]

To understand how credibility differs from legitimacy, we first need to understand more deeply what has been said about legitimacy in the international relations literature and specifically the literature on peace operations.

Institutional Behavior and Legitimacy

While the UNIFIL mission is part of a larger institution—the mother ship being the United Nations in New York—UNIFIL behaves like an institution in its attempts to legitimize itself and depoliticize its actions as it exercises its mandate. By drawing on sociological institutionalism theory from the international relations literature, I will highlight why this is the case.

Sociological institutionalism focuses on the social aspects of how institutions behave and the way "organizations often adopt a new institutional practice, not because it advances the means-ends efficiency of the organization but because it enhances the social legitimacy of the organization or its participants. In other words, organizations embrace specific institutional forms or practices because the latter are widely valued within a broader cultural environment."[18] Sociological institutionalism examines how institutions are affected by culture within and without the institution and "emphasize the highly-interactive and mutually-constitutive character of the relationship between institutions and individual action."[19] This scholarship has examined in particular how authority or "persuasion by status or expertise is pervasive in social life."[20]

This approach to understanding institutions argues that in order to survive, organizations depend on legitimacy. Dowling and Pfeffer provide useful clarity on the rationale of organizations in this pursuit:

"Organizations seek to establish congruence between the social values associated with or implied by their activities and the norms of acceptable behavior in the larger social system of which they are a part. Insofar as these two value systems are congruent we can speak of organizational legitimacy. When an actual or potential disparity exists between the two value systems, there will exist a threat to organizational legitimacy."[21]

Organizations or institutions attempt to obtain and maintain legitimacy by responding to "new normative demands or requirements from outside."[22] The point here is that social norms can change and constitute both a motivation for organizational change and a source of pressure for legitimation. Legitimacy can act as a constraint on an organization, which forces institutions to adapt to changed conditions, and scrutinizing legitimacy can provide "a useful empirical focus for examining organizational behaviors taken with respect to their environments."[23]

Legitimacy in the international system is listed alongside two other factors believed to motivate actor behavior: coercion and self-interest, which are deeply intertwined with notions of power.[24] Legitimacy is regarded as important in motivating actor behavior even if coercion and self-interest are present. Ian Hurd invokes the Weberian concept of legitimacy, describing it as "the normative belief by an actor that a rule or institution ought to be obeyed." This belief can come from "the procedure or the source by which it was constituted,"[25] and there is broad agreement that legitimacy is a subjective assessment by the actor.[26] A useful definition of legitimacy is provided by organizational psychologist Mark Suchman, who defines legitimacy as "a generalized perception or assumption that the actions of an entity are desirable, proper, or appropriate within some socially constructed system of norms, values, beliefs, and definitions."[27]

Scholarship that has focused on legitimacy at the international level argues that legitimacy wins organizations authority. This is described by John Ruggie as "a fusion of power with legitimate social purpose." Ultimately, once an actor has internalized the legitimacy of an organization, compliance becomes unproblematic and is no longer dependent on coercion. Hurd equates this compliance as being similar to the dynamic of a parent and child, or how government attempts to socialize its people, which is "It is right to do as I say, because I say so."[28] This dynamic implies that once obtained, legitimacy releases an organization from scrutiny of its every move and enables it to be forgiven even when it makes the odd mistake. Legitimacy affords the source authority but also efficiency, which is why the powerful often seek to legitimize their actions. The reason is that legitimacy is co-constitutive. Once an individual or community has internalized a source or procedure as legitimate, the actor "reconceives his or her interests" in line with the interests of said source or procedure,[29] which in turn makes compliance habitual and automatic. It is noncompliance that causes psychological disequilibrium.

In the case of UNIFIL, there is no national consensus on the legitimacy of the goals of the mandate, and at the local level a significant slice of the population does not regard the removal of Hezbullah's weapons from the area of operations as a legitimate task of the peacekeeping operation. Conversely, at the international level, Israel and the United States in particular perceive UNIFIL's main role to be the removal of Hezbullah's weapons from the area of operation. These complex politics mean UNIFIL's mission goals are contested to the extent that if UNIFIL pleases one audience, it will almost certainly displease another. As such, how does UNIFIL function? How does it avoid being rendered useless and paralyzed? The answer partly lies in the fact that UNIFIL depoliticizes its actions as much as possible to neutralize the political nature of its mandate. According to Michael Barnett and Martha Finnemore, this depoliticization is typical of international organizations (and international institutions) because at times "there is often no neutral stance one could take in many of the situations IOs [international organizations] confront, yet IOs need to find one in order to maintain the claim that they are impartial and are acting in a de-politicized manner."[30]

The use of technocracy is one way for an organization to depoliticize its activities. In UNIFIL we can see how the use of technocracy is both regulative and constitutive at the three levels of engagement: the international, the national, and the local. At the international level, UNIFIL has been responsible in part for constituting the Blue Line and then regulating it. At the national level, UNIFIL provides training to local government officials on good governance and acts as a creator of knowledge and provider of "objective" knowledge. One of the main ways, it is argued, that institutions legitimize themselves is by "transforming information into knowledge by giving it meaning, value, and purpose."[31] In building the capacity of the Lebanese Armed Forces, UNIFIL is also involved in training and development, in this instance behaving as the literature expects an international organization to behave by defining "problems and appropriate solutions in ways that favor more technocratic impartial action, which, of course, they are uniquely able to supply."[32] With civilians, technocracy is found in the quick impact projects that are again constituted and regulated by UNIFIL. The approach to approving the quick impact projects is technocratic—the selection criteria has been standardized and is applied in a manner that enables UNIFIL to avoid being accused of favoritism, hence again avoiding local politics.

At times UNIFIL assists with matters that go beyond its mandate, which shows the dedication of many of its staff, but also highlights how organizational culture has influenced some staff into believing that the mission can be successful with the right amount of effort. This belief can be attributed to bureaucratic culture, whereby members of an institution generate a shared vision of how to achieve the goals of the institution. Despite the efforts of UNIFIL staff, without political engagement from the Israeli and Lebanese governments, nothing will change. But staff continue to go out on a limb in the belief that their actions will make a lasting difference. As Barnett and Finnemore state, "While bureaucratic cultures always draw on cultural elements from the environment . . . all bureaucracies develop cultures that are distinct from the environment in which they are embedded."[33]

Hence, we see how sociological institutionalism provides a useful framework by which to explain how UNIFIL, as an institution, behaves. It shows how UNIFIL uses institutional strategies to depoliticize its mandate; specifically, it employs a technocratic approach and acts as a generator of knowledge and a dispenser of "objective" knowledge. This theoretical approach also helps to explain why some UNIFIL staff go above and beyond their mandate in a relentless quest for solutions that ultimately they cannot arbitrate.

Sociological institutionalism also goes a long way toward explaining how international institutions obtain legitimacy at the international level. According to this theory, by exhibiting the above behaviors, institutions generate legitimacy and therefore authority. But in the case of UNIFIL, we see that while these behaviors help to depoliticize UNIFIL's mandate, they do not afford UNIFIL legitimacy.

Despite its best efforts at depoliticizing its own role, UNIFIL itself engages in political lobbying. This activity is essential for international organizations, because ultimately they need to sell their message to the audiences from whom they require cooperation.[34] In this way, we can see that legitimacy can, like credibility, also be context dependent. The literature in international relations on this topic highlights how needing to appeal to different audiences for legitimacy can affect the behavior of state leaders and international organizations themselves.[35] Hurd, in a discussion of the symbolism of the UN Security Council's legitimacy, makes the valuable point that when an institution has legitimacy, there will always be those individuals who resist it precisely by deeming it illegitimate.[36] To an extent this situation is what UNIFIL faces in the form of criticism from a variety of different audiences at the national, subnational, and international levels. It responds to this criticism by reminding everyone that they agreed to the mandate in the first place. But as I show here, this reminder still does not generate sufficient legitimacy from all its audiences; different audiences prioritize different actions. What I find is that while UNIFIL has international legitimacy in some quarters, it does not translate to legitimacy on the ground.

If UNIFIL is unable to win legitimacy for its mandate among varied audiences, what is the impact on the ground and how does UNIFIL exercise its mandate? A reasonable assumption would be that it would be prevented from carrying out its duties owing to a lack of cooperation and compliance at the international, national, and local levels. But my research shows that UNIFIL is still able to fulfill a reasonable portion of its mandate. But how can this be the case if there is contested legitimacy? Simply put, it is not legitimacy that UNIFIL has earned, but credibility.

What Is Local Legitimacy?

As noted previously, legitimacy is a co-constitutive mechanism whereby actors' interests change because of their belief that a source or procedure is legitimate. The benefit of obtaining legitimacy for an organization is that compliance with a legitimate source becomes natural and unchallenged. However, as also noted previously, in international interventions at national or local levels, legitimacy may not be obtainable using the mechanisms outlined in the international relations literature on bureaucracy and legitimacy. So what is local legitimacy, and why does it differ from international legitimacy?

If we return to the three UN second-order success factors of legitimacy, credibility, and local ownership described earlier in the chapter, we find that local ownership and local legitimacy are the two factors that have received the most attention in the literature on grassroots peacekeeping. Discussions of local ownership come largely from the critical literature in peacebuilding and argue that there is a need for greater local participation and local ownership of projects in any peacebuilding initiative.[37] Oliver Richmond advocates for more money to be disbursed on welfare as well as social and civic projects, as opposed to purely infrastructural ones,[38] and for a more contextualized approach that uses local knowledge and avoids working from generalized "blueprints."[39] Roger Mac Ginty argues for a hybrid peace whereby both liberal and critical models of peace can coexist and also for greater agency at the local level. Thania Paffenholz suggests that civil society can contribute to peacebuilding in limited ways: through protection, monitoring, advocacy, socialization, social cohesion, facilitation, and service delivery as an entry point for peacebuilding.[40] Scholars have also asked how the liberal peacebuilding project can better incorporate local cultural traditions.[41] However, there remains contestation over what constitutes "the local" in relation to local ownership,[42] one of the main debates being whether it is the national versus subnational, formal institutions versus informal, or local elites versus ordinary citizens.[43] Approaches to the study of the local have differed; some focus on the subnational arena, others discuss the everyday events in the life of local recipients of peacebuilding or "the everyday peace,"[44] and yet others focus on the everyday activities of the peacebuilders themselves to illustrate how peace operations can improve local relationships.[45] Critiques of this literature fault it for viewing the international and local as binary opposites, which romanticizes local solutions;[46] and the conclusion remains bleak, in that liberal peacebuilding is regarded as having failed to generate genuine local ownership or even define what it means. This failure is regarded as symptomatic of "the distance between its 'global' objectives and the local conditions for their realization."[47]

Within the literature on local peacebuilding, one of the more recent developments has been a discussion of what are termed *hybrid solutions.* Hybridity is the idea that the local and international become intertwined to generate new solutions through the agency of both. Mac Ginty and Richmond define hybridity as "a constant process of negotiation as multiple sources of power in a society compete, coalesce, seep into each other and engage in mimicry, domination or accommodation." Put simply, hybridity in peacebuilding describes how activities are created, operationalized, and experienced by the local and the international. Mac Ginty defines hybridization as "how individuals, groups, structures, and ideas evolve and adapt" as part of the peacebuilding process.[48]

Recent work on hybridity has been critical of the prescriptive nature by which some international actors have employed the concept.[49] This approach has led to a situation whereby local practices are instrumentally employed by peacebuilders to achieve top-down, internationally sanctioned outcomes within the liberal peace framework. Hybrid solutions have also been critiqued for producing unpredictable,[50] or even negative,[51] outcomes; for legitimizing hegemonic power;[52] for producing unintended outcomes that preserve the status quo rather than being "emancipatory";[53] and for being a problem-solving tool used to advance the "liberal peace."[54] Another criticism of the hybrid turn in the literature is that the concept is vague and does not always help clarify what is occurring.[55] Kate Meagher, Tom De Herdt, and Kristof Titeca argue that the value of hybrid governance depends on clarifying the aim of international engagement with the local and call for more empirical studies.[56]

In sum, hybridity in peacebuilding refers to the creation of practices in the peacebuilding environment that have evolved, and continue to evolve, out of the experience of the international and the local coming together. Political, cultural, environmental, and social considerations impact both sides, and these normative expectations help to shape these hybrid practices that act to provide "solutions" to tensions between the objectives of the local and the international. This book acknowledges the relevance of hybridity because in some areas of UNIFIL's work, hybrid solutions have become part of how UNIFIL builds credibility with the local population at the international, national, and local levels: for example, by engaging politically with local mayors who are affiliated with Hezbullah (whom the international community largely disapprove of) or by ensuring that the LAF takes the lead in clearing illegal weapons to avoid the risk of being seen to take sides in what is a national debate about Hezbullah's right to bear arms.

Winning local legitimacy has, until now, been regarded as the holy grail of peacekeeping. The idea is that if a UN peace operation obtains local legitimacy, the mission wins compliance and explicit cooperation from the local population. It is also less susceptible to the effects of peace-keeper mistakes or poor behavior and is able to fulfill the goals of its man-date in a secure environment. Even if peacekeepers cause accidental or deliberate harm to members of the local population, the local legitimacy of the mission should carry sufficient local capital to insulate it from ret-ribution or local rejection. But is this outcome really possible in a foreign intervention? Scholarship on peacebuilding suggests it is possible, yet the concept itself remains unclear.

A great deal of the critical literature argues that peace operations should transcend current liberal norms and that a "postliberal peace" is possible. As noted previously, this literature has tended to focus on local ownership, but those individuals who take what Robert Cox would describe as a "problem-solving" approach as opposed to a critical approach have tried to engage empirically with the concept of local legitimacy and how interventions might obtain it. David Roberts argues for what he calls a "popular peace," whereby global governance actors collectively work toward the provision of public goods.[57] He bases his theory on the premise that the vast majority of recipients of the peacebuilding project do not have the basic requirements of life, such as potable water. As such, rather than work to install institu-tions that serve the interests of a narrow few in the metropolitan areas of postconflict states, peacebuilding efforts should be directed at encouraging the provision of services that enable the local population to live. Doing so will contribute to the improvement of the everyday conditions of recipients and legitimize the presence of the peacebuilding effort. Roberts's point is important, and he notes, "Peacebuilding does not cater for the everyday, imminent needs of millions of people. This is central to understanding how and why people may not view prevailing peacebuilding priorities as legitimate."[58] Roberts's argument is relevant to this book, which also argues that when the practical everyday needs of the local population are seen as being met by the peacebuilders, there is likely to be more local cooperation. However, Roberts's argument does not take into account the role of politics in local decisions to accept or reject the peacebuilders. I contend that the actions he describes build credibility but not legitimacy.

Another confusing aspect of scholarship on local legitimacy is that often scholars will not specify a definition of the concept but will present an argument about how it can be obtained.[59] Concepts like custom and culture are referred to as being the most useful local sources for building a positive peace, but the literature fails to directly address what happens when these local sources do not match up with Western human rights norms, in particular around gender.[60] Roland Paris has argued that those scholars in the critical vein of the peacebuilding literature should be considered "liberals in disguise," because he notes that they often use liberal terminology to critique liberal peacebuilding ideology. For example, Richmond discusses the importance of making a "social contract" between international interventions and local civilians on the ground. What a social contract would look like in the local context is left to our imagination. Equally, his suggestion of establishing a welfare state is still suggestive of an imposition of Western ideas onto the local. Roberts makes the point that an emancipatory peace is unlikely "as long as neoliberal hegemony endures, and the character and content of the social contract is determined by the extent to which its foundations reflect neoliberal preferences." In other words, the current system so dominates that we need either to radically reconsider what we mean by peace or to accept that peace initiatives cannot truly be radical. Elisa Randazzo also makes the point that the critical literature is as guilty of cherry-picking acts of local resistance to the liberal peace as the liberal peace is of choosing whom to engage with on the ground.[61] The fact is that there remains a desperate need for scholarship coming from recipients of peacebuilding to help us establish what the term *local* really means and to help us reframe the concept of what peacebuilding at the local level should look like.

Thus, the literature on local legitimacy is heavy on suggestions about how to obtain local legitimacy but very light on what it is as a concept and the benefits that it affords a peace operation. A great deal of scholarship discusses the need for local legitimacy and still more critiques the UN for not obtaining it in specific case studies.[62] Nonetheless, there remains a mystique around the general rules that can be applied to afford missions local legitimacy and what obtaining it will do for the mission. This confusion exists possibly because trying to design a standardized set of techniques may be another flaw of liberal peacebuilding—its claims to universality[63] informs its perspective that all aspects of the peacebuilding project can be reduced to a one-size-fits-all mentality.[64] Most research on peacebuilding has acknowledged that context matters in assessing strategies for building local legitimacy and asks whether these strategies have been successful.[65]

Within the academic scholarship, there is one author who has attempted to unpack the definition of local legitimacy in peacebuilding, and we will turn to this work next in conjunction with another authority on legitimacy, which is the UN's definition of the concept.

The UN's Definition of Legitimacy

The UN's definition of legitimacy is long, somewhat convoluted, and composed of three parts. The first articulates the international legitimacy of a peace operation: "The international legitimacy of a United Nations peacekeeping operation is derived from the fact that it is established after obtaining a mandate from the United Nations Security Council, which has primary responsibility for the maintenance of international peace and security. The uniquely broad representation of Member States who contribute personnel and funding to United Nations operations further strengthens this international legitimacy."[66]

The second part of the definition articulates the behavioral aspects of UN missions, which, it is argued, affect local perceptions of the legitimacy of the mission: "The firmness and fairness with which a United

Nations peacekeeping operation exercises its mandate, the circumspection with which it uses force, the discipline it imposes upon its personnel, the respect it shows to local customs, institutions and laws, and the decency with which it treats the local people all have a direct effect upon perceptions of its legitimacy."[67]

The third part of the definition is particularly interesting because it argues that poor behavior on the ground will erode the legitimacy of the mission: "Experience has shown that the perceived legitimacy of a United Nations peacekeeping operation's presence may erode over time, if the size of the United Nations 'footprint' and the behavior of its staff becomes a source of local resentment; or if the peacekeeping operation is not sufficiently responsive as the situation stabilizes."[68] This definition assumes that international and local legitimacy are one and the same thing, or that the mission has what Hurd terms *source legitimacy*.[69] Furthermore, it is assumed that as long as a peace operation exercises its mandate fairly, it will remain legitimate. Finally, the UN definition argues that poor behavior will erode the overall legitimacy of a mission.

This last part of the definition highlights the challenge in understanding what benefits local legitimacy confers on a peace operation. As noted above, the concept of legitimacy as defined in the literature is that it is co-constitutive and therefore informs actors' beliefs about how the world should work that are in line with the beliefs of the legitimate source. From this standpoint we can surmise that once won, legitimacy provides the legitimate source with some form of social capital[70] that would in principle enable it to make mistakes and remain legitimate. However, as we have seen at the international level in the case of the United States since the Second World War, legitimacy can be eroded if the behavior of a state wanders too far from the norms or expectations of international society. Equally, the United Nations has made endless errors in peacekeeping missions yet retains significant global legitimacy and authority. Ultimately, then, we can say that international legitimacy probably does have limits, although the literature is not yet clear on what they are, and at the local level it is even less clear.

Jeni Whalan is a rare scholar who has unpacked the UN's definition of legitimacy in peace operations in an examination of the Solomon

Islands and Cambodian missions. In doing so, she has made two important contributions. First, she has clarified the important point that international legitimacy and local legitimacy are not one and the same thing. This divergence is what she refers to as the local-international legitimacy gap, which can be defined broadly as the space or the difference between the perceptions of the international community and the local community about the legitimacy of an international intervention. Particularly relevant to the UNIFIL mission is that the local-international gap is most difficult to overcome when perceptions not only differ but conflict—that is, when legitimizing an intervention internationally actually delegitimizes it locally, and vice versa.[71] The local-international legitimacy gap can have myriad impacts on the ground, but its main effect is to constrain international actors in the local environment decreasing their ability to build local relationships, maintain security for troops, and therefore fulfill the obligations of the mandate. This gap affects different types of international interventions—peacekeeping, peacebuilding, statebuilding, and counterinsurgency—to a greater or lesser degree. As noted previously (and in more detail in chapter 2), UNIFIL suffers greatly from this phenomenon.

Second, and also important, Whalan has helpfully provided a definition of local legitimacy that is lacking in much of the scholarship purporting to deal with the concept: "Local legitimacy refers to evaluations by local actors about a peace operation's rightness, fairness, and appropriateness—that is, whether its practices rightfully cohere with the relevant framework of rules and values, are fair, and produce appropriate outcomes."[72] To further elaborate on the concept, she disaggregates legitimacy into three distinct types: source legitimacy, procedural legitimacy, and substantive legitimacy. Source legitimacy finds its roots in the first definition of legitimacy provided by the UN noted above, that is, international legitimacy, and is described as "the given structures of the peace operation . . . its mandate, design, and conflict setting."[73] However, Whalan includes a form of credibility in source legitimacy, citing the importance of material factors: "Source legitimacy is also derived from an institution's ability to signal its credibility to achieve its mandated goals and purposes. . . . [A] peace operation may be legitimized through its display of material resources, which justify its presence to local actors by demonstrating that it is adequately equipped to achieve its purposes."[74]

Procedural legitimacy can be located in the second aspect of the UN's definition of legitimacy, which refers to how a UN mission exercises its mandate and is described as being derived from "judgements about the fairness of procedures for making decisions and exercising power."[75] Thus, these two types of legitimacy can be traced back to the UN's definition of legitimacy that also refers to the "firmness and fairness with which a United Nations peacekeeping operation exercises its mandate."[76]

Substantive legitimacy is "the process by which an operation's outcomes justify it in reference to its goals and purposes, based on the desirability of its effects."[77] This definition refers to the mission's ability to deliver on goods and services that are part of its overall mandate. Whalan argues that if substantive legitimacy is not backed up by the other two kinds, it will be eroded: "Substantive legitimacy without procedural or source legitimacy can be expected to produce diminishing returns."[78] Whalan notes that substantive legitimacy has to be built up over time and cannot be won on arrival and that if substantive legitimacy fails to meet local expectations, it can cause a mission to be delegitimized.[79]

In this book I argue that there is a conflation between legitimacy and credibility in Whalan's definitions of local legitimacy, particularly in her definitions of source legitimacy and substantive legitimacy. Local legitimacy should refer only to the shared view between the local population and the mission that the goals of the mission are legitimate. While this form of legitimacy can be eroded by poor peacekeeper behavior, it should not need to be constantly sustained in the way that credibility does. As Chapman notes, "Although views differ on whether legitimacy stems from perceptions of procedural fairness, policy neutrality, or inclusiveness, once this relational characteristic is established, this perspective suggests that it should be relatively fixed, or at least slow to change."[80] In my view, the provision of goods and services should not be a key driver of legitimacy because according to the extensive literature on this topic, legitimacy refers to ideas, not material interests.

My work builds on Whalan's research but argues that legitimacy, once won, should not require constant maintenance in the same way that credibility does, because unlike credibility, it is not built purely on material gains but rather built on ideas, norms, and expectations. While (as noted above) legitimacy does act as a constraint on an organization, the fact that it is co-constitutive and forms actors' beliefs about how the world should work means it should not depend regularly on the more unreliable concepts of material or self-interest. Whalan describes the benefits of legitimacy as providing "a reservoir of support" to help withstand shocks, setbacks, and substantive failures in a power relationship and as exacting compliance that is sustained "even when the flow of desired outcomes is disrupted."[81] From this description of local legitimacy we can deduce two things: first, one of the key differences between legitimacy and credibility is that legitimacy affords an actor the ability to make mistakes and be forgiven for them; second, credibility requires sustaining precisely because it does not provoke a reservoir of support. It is pertinent here to remember that legitimacy can be eroded by a lack of procedural fairness, which has been discussed thoroughly in the criminology literature on policing and by Whalan herself.[82] Worth noting also is that the literature on local legitimacy has thus far been unable to explain the level of elasticity that local legitimacy can afford peace operations. How far does legitimacy provide cover for peace operations to be able to make mistakes? How much stock of goodwill does local legitimacy provide?

I believe local legitimacy as defined here by Whalan in part captures credibility and in part the UN's definition of legitimacy. There is also an inherent assumption that source legitimacy is present to some degree, which it may or may not be, and especially not when we consider other types of interventions such as the "coalition of the willing." Whalan herself notes this issue when she speaks of the local-international legitimacy gap. Her definition of legitimacy assumes a level of source legitimacy is present, and in her definition of substantive legitimacy she conflates credibility with legitimacy by including the provision of material resources. This inclusion suggests that legitimacy can be eroded by a lack of material goods and services, which again suggests that her definition is underwritten by both material and ideational factors. But I argue that legitimacy and credibility are two separate concepts underwritten by different factors.

Where there is no legitimacy or weak legitimacy, credibility can still be obtained. This is not to say credibility and legitimacy can't function alongside each other; if an institution has legitimacy, having the resources to achieve its goals will help to bolster its legitimacy among audiences with whom it is legitimate.

One can see the difference between legitimacy and credibility when one examines how UNIFIL behaves on the ground and the problems it faces. It is the contingent nature of UNIFIL's relationship with local and international actors that helps to reveal the difference between credibility and legitimacy. My work raises the question of whether the literature on local legitimacy has often been a proxy for what is really a form of credibility. Practitioners need to ask themselves whether they can make mistakes and be forgiven for them. Is the mission under constant pressure to provide evidence that it is delivering on what it has said it will? If not, does it mean legitimacy has been obtained or something else? The UNIFIL mission shows us that if there is a need to continuously provide evidence of good deeds to maintain local confidence in the mission, it indicates the presence of credibility and that the mission is not immune from loss of support because ultimately compliance is born of self-interest and not internalized norms induced by legitimacy.

Unpacking Credibility

Credibility ultimately means delivering on a promise. The dictionary definition of the word *credible* is "the quality or state of being credible; the capacity to be believed or believed in."[83] I posit that a peace mission is better off attempting to obtain acceptance and support for its presence by building credibility instead of trying to legitimize itself across a diverse range of local interests and local power brokers. As noted earlier, the definition of credibility I provide in this book is "the capacity of an actor to present as an honest and believable provider of knowledge and services in a sustained and highly responsive manner that wins confidence and cooperation." However, maintaining credibility means that a peace operation must continue to maintain a high level of service so as not to lose cooperation and sustain its relationships. It is underwritten by the need to provide evidence and material benefits.

Hurd provides insight into how we might conceive of the motivations behind local acceptance for missions with the concept of "self-interest." He describes self-interest thus:

> A society where compliance with rules is based principally on the self-interest of the members will exhibit several characteristic features. First, any loyalty by actors toward the system or its rules is contingent on the system providing a positive stream of benefits. Actors are constantly recalculating the expected payoff to remaining in the system and stand ready to abandon it immediately should some alternative promise greater utility. Such a system can be stable while the payoff structure is in equilibrium, but the actors are constantly assessing the costs and benefits of revisionism. . . . Second, and following from that, long-term relationships among self-interested agents are difficult to maintain because actors do not value the relation itself, only the benefits accruing from it. Such long-term relations may exist, and indeed persist, but only while the instrumental payoff remains positive. . . . As a result, a social system that relies primarily on self-interest will necessarily be thin and tenuously held together and subject to drastic change in response to shifts in the structure of payoffs.[84]

This concept goes some way in helping to explain the rationale for cooperation with the UNIFIL mission by groups such as Hezbullah or ordinary citizens who do not regard its goals as legitimate.

Table 2 shows the key differences between credibility and legitimacy. The other key difference between the two is that while legitimacy in principle acts as a political cover for all the activities of a peace operation and should provide the mission with authority across the board, credibility can be built in some areas but not others. As noted previously, I define credibility as having more than one aspect. The distinction between types of credibility is important because it illustrates how it is possible to win or lose credibility on one or more aspects. By disaggregating credibility, I show that UNIFIL has earned some types of credibility but not others (see figure 1).

Table 2
Key differences between legitimacy and credibility

		Features	Benefits	Limits
Credibility		• Underwritten by material interests • Requires time to build • Context dependent • Constant need to provide evidence	• Confidence from the named parties in managing security incidents and institution building • Cooperation from local civilians and therefore security for patrolling troops on the ground	• Inability to accomplish all mandate objectives • Cannot be a disruption to goods and services without risking negative repercussions
Legitimacy		• Underwritten by ideas and shared norms • Does not require constant provision of evidence • Can be won up front • Should not be context dependent	• Ability to fulfill the mandate • Ability to make mistakes and be forgiven for them • Norm internalization can generate trust • Flow of goods and services may be disrupted without negative repercussions on the ground	• Poor behavior may eventually degrade overall legitimacy • May be contextual if legitimate among only some audiences

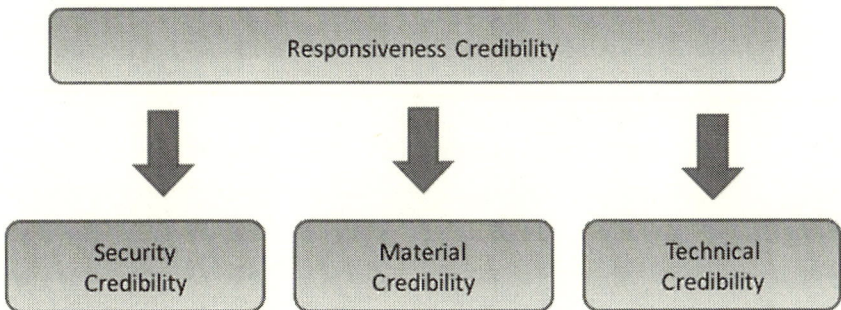

1. Types of credibility

• Responsiveness credibility: a demonstrated ability to respond quickly to military and civilian concerns in a predictable and reliable manner.
• Technical credibility: a demonstrated observable commitment to good governance.
• Material credibility: the provision of funding for local projects and other material benefits such as health care, services, infrastructure, and equipment.
• Security credibility: a demonstrated ability to deter conflict and provide human security.

This expanded definition of credibility illustrates the limitations of the current definition of credibility provided by the UN. According to the UN, "The credibility of a United Nations peacekeeping operation is a direct reflection of the international and local communities' belief in the mission's ability to achieve its mandate."[85] When a peacekeeping force is unable to fulfill all the tasks of the mandate, it loses credibility:

> Credibility is a function of a mission's capability, effectiveness and ability to manage and meet expectations. Ideally, in order to be credible, a United Nations peacekeeping operation must deploy as rapidly as possible, be properly resourced, and strive to maintain a confident, capable and unified posture. Experience has shown that the early establishment of a credible presence can help to deter spoilers and diminish the likelihood that a mission will need to use force to implement its mandate. To achieve and maintain its credibility, a mission must therefore have a clear and deliverable mandate, with resources and capabilities to match; and a sound mission plan that is understood, communicated and impartially and effectively implemented at every level.[86]

This definition is underwritten by three assumptions. The first is that it refers to credibility as something that can be established up front. The DPKO guidelines state that a UN mission obtains credibility upon arrival, but my work identifies credibility as being something that occurs after the mission has been present for some time. As noted earlier, a force can turn up well equipped, but to do what? Local civilians need to learn how the force will use its resources. Indeed, earlier research has pointed out that local reactions are often negative when a highly equipped peace operation comes into town with an overtly confident posture, as there is no assumption on behalf of civilians that these resources will be used for their benefit.[87]

The second assumption is that a peace operation needs to "strive to maintain a confident, capable and unified posture. Experience has shown that the early establishment of a credible presence can help to deter spoilers and diminish the likelihood that a mission will need to use force to implement its mandate."[88] But bottom-up studies have illustrated that while security, and human security in particular, is important in winning local support, it is not the only factor that local populations consider. Often peacekeepers are unable to provide security to local civilians in the way that civilians want them to, and peacekeepers often appear more engaged with their own security than the safety of the local population.[89] The danger here for interventions is that they may appear well equipped, and raise expectations, but then suffer more fallout when invariably civilians are disappointed. Furthermore, the role of emotion is important here: a show of military force may be perceived as threatening as opposed to comforting.

In fact, a heavy security presence when the goals of the mission are not supported among many in the local population can do more harm than good. When UNIFIL troops were increased directly after the 2006 war, the European troop component was largely composed of special forces, as they are the military units best able to mobilize in a short period of time. They arrived after the war with tanks and sophisticated equipment, which quickly made them extremely unpopular, not least because their behavior on the ground was aggressive toward all civilians. They were so unfamiliar with their environment, and so enthusiastic about security, that they even intercepted and questioned a very senior UNIFIL officer as he was driving to work![90]

After six weeks of war, surely the local population would have wanted to see a show of force by a peacekeeping mission. Yet this approach was very unpopular, signaling to UNIFIL that it required a different posture. This experience tells us that the UN's definition of credibility is biased toward security and that ultimately it is not the only type of credibility that a UN mission can or should work toward.

Finally, the third assumption of the UN's definition of credibility is that the mandate should be clear and deliverable with the necessary resources. This criterion immediately excludes UNIFIL, whose mandate is extremely unclear and contested at the local level. In fact, all UN mandates are known to be unclear; UNIFIL is not the only mission that suffers from this problem. As Severine Autesserre notes, "Mandates provide the broad guidelines for a given mission, but offer little detail."[91] The UN definition of credibility glosses over this issue, and according to its own definition, if a mission's mandate is unclear, this ambiguity renders it not credible.

How Does UNIFIL Demonstrate Credibility?

As noted previously, this book breaks down the concept of credibility into different types to understand what the term *credibility* means in the field of peacekeeping and to show how it can be won. It identifies how a peace operation can deliver on some but not all elements of credibility. It argues that credibility can be disaggregated and illustrates more directly how and where missions succeed and fail.

Responsiveness Credibility

Establishing a reputation for being responsive helps UN troops position themselves as being there to serve the needs of the local population. Therefore, responsiveness credibility is very important to material, security, and technical credibility—for example, when a member of the local population requires medical assistance or when a Blue Line violation has the potential to explode into a major security incident that could trigger renewed conflict. Regular liaison and negotiation play a crucial role in generating responsiveness credibility, and the swift provision of accurate information provides reassurance to the parties that all acts are being objectively recorded. Within the four types of credibility, responsiveness credibility sits slightly above the other types, as it can ultimately be located in all the other three. Responding to the needs of locals in a timely fashion provides a sense of reliability and predictability that is valued in a highly volatile and insecure environment. In this way, UNIFIL is viewed as a reliable and believable companion that is always there, even if it cannot deter another Israeli invasion.

Technical Credibility

Technical credibility lends itself to supporting state institutions—for example, the LAF and the local councils. By providing technical assistance to the LAF, UNIFIL achieves several goals. It patrols alongside the national force, which improves the quality of its relationships with national institutions. It works within the local political system and where requested provides training on government to local councils. It also regularly invites representatives from other national institutions down to the South, to tacitly assist these institutions in reestablishing a presence on issues such as infrastructure, policing, and other state functions. These activities show the local population that UNIFIL is working toward the long-term goal of helping Lebanon function independently of international assistance. It also works to reduce the space for substate actors to legitimate themselves by the provision of services that the state cannot currently provide.

Material Credibility

Material credibility affords UNIFIL goodwill when providing goods and services that the state is currently unable to provide and helps UNIFIL carve out a practical role for itself in the area of operations. Material credibility is more easily won because it largely comes down to the provision of resources, although, as chapter 5 reveals, material credibility is connected to responsiveness credibility.

Security Credibility

Simply put, I define security credibility as the demonstrated ability to deter conflict and provide human security. In the case of South Lebanon, security credibility is perhaps the most complex of all the types of credibility to explain because it speaks to the issue of audiences for legitimacy.

As noted previously, deterrence is an important aspect of a peacekeeping operation, but when the nature of that deterrence is contested, how does a peacekeeping operation accomplish this goal? In the case of UNIFIL, many in the local population seek security from Israel, not from Hezbullah, which they regard as a deterrent to Israeli aggression. UNIFIL faces pressure from the local civilian population that asks why the international community (represented by UNIFIL) is unable to prevent an Israeli invasion.

As Israel wants Hezbullah removed from the area, it regards UNIFIL's deterrence duties as being the removal of Hezbullah, not in providing a strong presence on the border willing to fight Israeli troops should they wish to invade. Furthermore, UNIFIL might be viewed by Israel as protecting Hezbullah's activities, which would also be unpopular with many in the international community. Not only is this aspect of UNIFIL's duties contested at the international level and local levels, it is too at the national level, where different political groupings have different views on Hezbullah's military activities.

This is not to say that security credibility alone has the power to win local legitimacy, because other factors such as aid and responsiveness also affect the credibility of the mission. If the force did not perform on the other three types, they would have no credibility whatsoever and may well have been unable to function in relative safety.

Security credibility includes human security as much as it does traditional deterrence. UNIFIL has earned credibility on some security issues, specifically local requests for assistance with issues relating to minefields, assistance with natural threats (such as wildfires), preventing military confrontations between the parties, and preventing the escalation of everyday incidents between the IDF and local civilians on the Blue Line. However, owing to the contested nature of what security goals UNIFIL should be focusing on, it has not been able to protect the local population from a succession of Israeli invasions, nor has it been able to prevent Hezbullah-related security incidents from taking place on the Blue Line.

The Benefits of Earning Credibility

Credibility wins UNIFIL cooperation and confidence. Why? It is because the local population has confidence that it will deliver on many of the types of credibility discussed in this chapter. The benefits delivered by UNIFIL that build credibility satisfy many of the material interests of the local population to the extent that many are, willing to cooperate with the mission and most do not actively seek to prevent it from functioning. As discussed earlier, at the international level, different types of credibility may be used in different contexts. In the case of a peace operation, all four may be used to help win local cooperation because the nature of peacekeeping itself involves deterrence and cooperation. Where there is contested legitimacy for the goals of a mission, the UNIFIL mission has focused on building credibility in areas that will produce cooperation and afford the mission maximum overall effectiveness.

The case of UNIFIL shows that by responding swiftly to local material and technical needs, and attending to security issues where it is able, the force has won sufficient cooperation on the ground to be able to patrol in relative security. By delivering on various types of credibility, UNIFIL is credible in the sense that the named parties and the local population have confidence in UNIFIL to deliver on various aspects of its mandate in a predictable manner.

An unpredictable military force can lead to unpredictable results, especially in the security space. While this situation means that "spoilers" such as Hezbullah can abuse the system by working around UNIFIL, it also means that UNIFIL avoids engaging head-on with Hezbullah in a competition for local legitimacy that Hezbullah would doubtless win. Hence, UNIFIL generates a predictable security environment: it is recognized as being a reliable and responsive partner to the LAF, a responsible and timely purveyor of information to the IDF, and a responsive provider of goods and services to the local population. UNIFIL then reduces the incidence of hostilities and creates the conditions conducive to everyday peace or the normalization of peace.

The Relationship between Credibility and Local Legitimacy

The final question to be asked, then, is if a force could deliver well on all four types of credibility, does it win legitimacy? This question is complex because it engenders the question of whether it is possible for an international interposition to win local legitimacy. What I have established in this chapter is that credibility is context dependent, satisfies material interests, and must be constantly sustained with evidence. Legitimacy, on the other hand, is based on ideas more than it is material factors. In the context of peace operations, I argue that winning legitimacy means that the norms of an organization have been internalized by the local population to the extent that material factors and evidence become less important than the belief that the aims of the mission are legitimate. Therefore, compliance is habitual and automatic, and it is noncompliance that causes psychological disequilibrium. In the case of UNIFIL, the practical benefits local legitimacy would afford the force would be explicit cooperation in the form of information about activities that subvert the goals of the mission, the ability to fulfill all of the mandate, the ability to make some mistakes without blowback, and perhaps a reduction in the provision of material goods and services.

If UNIFIL were able to deliver on all four goals, would it win legitimacy? Well, if the issue of Hezbullah's weapons were resolved at the national level, there might well be no need for UNIFIL at all, because one way or another, the situation with Israel would have been resolved. I argue that because of the varied demands of peacekeeping, credibility and legitimacy can work in tandem, or in the absence of each other, but they are underwritten by different things and should not be conflated.

Putting UNIFIL aside for a moment, the question still needs to be asked more broadly that if a force delivers well on all four types of credibility, does it then have legitimacy? The answer intuitively is no because, simply put, the values of the receiver are unlikely to uniformly match the values of an intervening force. A UN mission might be able to provide all the resources necessary to rebuild a state or bring peace, but not necessarily in a way that the local population would regard as legitimate or fair. And as I have already stated, legitimacy is based on shared ideas about the appropriateness of an institution and not just material interests.

The best way perhaps to illustrate this point is to look at the Lebanese Armed Forces, which, despite having poor resources, retain legitimacy at the local level in a way that UNIFIL does not. A great deal of this legitimacy has to do with the fact that UNIFIL is a foreign force, whereas the LAF is part of the Lebanese people and in consequence has their trust. Ultimately, then, we have to ask if in fact it is really possible for a peacekeeping mission to earn local legitimacy at all or whether in fact what most peacekeeping forces have won is credibility on various issues that affords them sufficient cooperation to function.

Ultimately, the main difference between credibility and legitimacy is perhaps best reflected in the key benefit that UNIFIL obtains from winning credibility, which is confidence. Confidence is largely built on experience and requires evidence. Trust, on the other hand, involves more emotion. As Mercer states, "Trust is an emotional belief. Emotional beliefs are generalizations about the internal, enduring properties of an object that involve certainty beyond evidence. Trust requires certainty beyond observable evidence and reliance instead on how one feels about someone."[92] As the UNIFIL officer acknowledged, they are "only as good as their last game," demonstrating that UNIFIL has won confidence but not trust. In the view of this author, even if the UNIFIL mission could win on all four types of credibility, it would not necessarily mean they are trusted to always do the right thing or to always work in the interests of the local community. Legitimacy, on the other hand, has been found to have a strong relationship with trust, although the precise relationship between the two has been insufficiently explored.[93] As such, I surmise that credibility wins confidence, but legitimacy has the capacity to win trust.

It is beyond the scope of this book to examine the relationship between trust and legitimacy in peace operations at the local level. But until now, the literature on the local legitimacy of peace operations has not fully examined this relationship.

In sum, the major difference between credibility and local legitimacy is that establishing credibility has earned UNIFIL confidence but not trust. Confidence, like credibility, requires constant evidence for it to be sustained. Trust, on the other hand, is an emotional response to an actor that does not require evidence to be generated. Like legitimacy, trust can be eroded by poor procedural behavior, but ultimately it is not based on an initial track record or constant maintenance to the extent that an actor is constantly being reevaluated. The literature on police legitimacy and political trust suggests that legitimacy has the potential to engender trust in a way that credibility does not. The limited literature on credibility has not yet made a distinction between trust and confidence.

Conclusion

Credibility is regarded by the UN as one of three second-order success factors in a UN peace operation along with legitimacy and local owner-ship, yet the concept has been ignored in the academic literature on peace operations or oftentimes conflated with legitimacy.

Credibility affords the UNIFIL mission cooperation, but this is moti-vated by self-interest, which is largely determined by the benefits that UNIFIL affords the local community. Cooperation and confidence are predicated on the idea that UNIFIL is a credible actor that performs well on certain tasks that benefit the local population, not necessarily because the mandate is considered legitimate. Credibility requires constant main-tenance in the form of evidence that the mission is delivering on what it says it will. What credibility does in a practical sense is that it enables the mission to move securely around the area of operation without fear of attack, but it does not extend to the idea that peacekeepers can—albeit accidentally—cause harm to the local population and be forgiven. Per-haps more helpful has been the generation of a predictable security envi-ronment that helps create the conditions conducive to the normalization of peace in the area of operations.

Local cooperation with the activities of the mission does not allow UNIFIL license to make mistakes or enact the mandate to its fullest extent. Should UNIFIL be suspected of working against the interests of the local population, or deliberately causing harm, its presence will be rejected. Furthermore, in the case of actors such as Hezbullah, the UNIFIL presence is currently deemed useful in light of the broader regional strategic environment. Were that to change, UNIFIL's situation could alter very quickly.

2 The UNIFIL Mission in Context

In this chapter I provide a brief history of the UNIFIL mission in Lebanon from 1978 to the present and show how the two mandates awarded to the UNIFIL mission since 1978 have been vague and unrealistic when compared to the conditions on the ground. This has made UNIFIL an easy target for those individuals wishing to either discredit the United Nations or discredit the actions of the international community in Lebanon.[1] I argue that the mission itself cannot be held responsible for a bad mandate, nor can it be held responsible for the complete absence of a political solution to the conflict.

The history of UNIFIL is important to understand because in many ways, it shaped how the mission runs today. The first UNIFIL mission (sometimes called UNIFIL I) was established when there was no peace to keep—something not recommended in peacekeeping practice.[2] As one former staff member remarked:

> First of all they were at a total loss. They didn't know why they were here—nobody was telling them. That was the Palestinian time. The whole of the South was under Palestinian control, and they were told by the UN that Yasser Arafat will be responsible for them. They were told, "Go and do your best." They were just thrown in here, without any clue. It was definitely not an environment conducive to peacekeeping. There's a war going on in Beirut, there's a war going on in the South, and any peacekeeping force will need some kind of local authority to back them up. There was no state. Well-meaning people here said, "Oh, yes, we love you, welcome" and all that, but basically you are on your own.[3]

Then, as today, there existed parties to the conflict on the ground capable of threatening the viability and survival of the mission. I describe the humanitarian work performed by the peacekeeping troops prior to 2006 that won UNIFIL support in the local community. Affection for the mission, under the new mandate, is in no small part owing to local historical memory of the humanitarian acts of peacekeepers in UNIFIL I while the area was under Israeli occupation.

This chapter also discusses the circumstances that gave rise to Resolution 1701. The new mandate brokered peace between Israel and Hezbullah but did not name Hezbullah as a party to the agreement, which has made UNIFIL's job more difficult, as it is unable to deal directly with Hezbullah's military wing in the post–Resolution 1701 era. I explain how the terms of Resolution 1701 have contributed to the local-international legitimacy gap.[4]

I conclude this chapter with a discussion of the current strategic environment in South Lebanon, the political position of relevant named and unnamed parties to the mandate, and how the Syrian crisis has affected the area of operations.

UNIFIL I

Despite inclusion of the word *interim* in its name, UNIFIL is one of the longest-running UN peacekeeping missions since the inception of peacekeeping missions in 1948. Like all UN operations, its mandate is reviewed and renewed periodically by the Security Council. The periods of renewal for UNIFIL have varied from one month to one year, demonstrating Security Council concerns about the effectiveness of the mission. However, currently, its renewal period comes up annually on August 31 each year. Like all older UN missions established prior to 1989, UNIFIL is labeled in the scholarship on peacekeeping as a "traditional" peacekeeping mission, in that it exists to act as a buffer between two states that remain at war.[5]

The UNIFIL I mandate began in 1978 in response to the Israeli invasion of South Lebanon up to the Litani River, which was called Operation Litani. The Israel Defense Forces invaded in response to continued attacks on Israel by pro-Palestinian groups operating in South Lebanon. These assaults had begun in the early 1970s, caused by the expulsion of the Palestine Liberation Organization (PLO) from Jordan[6] in 1971, which resulted in the Palestinian resistance movement moving its base to Lebanon.

UNSC Resolution 425 was issued on March 19, 1978, to address the deteriorating security situation in Lebanon. The resolution requested approval from the secretary-general for the establishment of an interim force composed of four thousand troops, drawn from member states, in the area south of the Litani River. The aims of the operation were stated as being "for the purpose of confirming the withdrawal of Israeli forces, restoring international peace and security, and assisting the Government of Lebanon in ensuring the return of its effective authority in the area."[7]

UNSC Resolution 426 approved the duration of the mission for six months,[8] and a third resolution (UNSC Resolution 427) approved an increase in troops from the original 4,000 to 6,000.[9] The initial troop composition of UNIFIL was regionally diverse and comprised troops from Canada, Fiji, France, Iran,[10] Ireland, Nepal, Nigeria, Norway, and Senegal.[11]

Israel unilaterally declared a cease-fire at the Litani River on March 21, 1978, and the first UNIFIL contingents arrived the following day. At the time, however, Israel made it clear that it had no intention of leaving South Lebanon until the PLO had been dispelled from the area and that they had zero confidence in UNIFIL being able to achieve this goal.[12] Israeli troops were therefore under their own orders from the Israeli government and had no intention of fulfilling the terms of the UN's instruction to leave until they had fulfilled their own objectives.

Other local militia were also predisposed to attack UNIFIL. These groups were initially Palestinian or Lebanese militia run by Palestinians who had other international objectives and to whom the domestic concerns of Lebanon were of little interest. Initial local doubts about UNIFIL's neutrality were not helped by the fact that the largest UNIFIL troop contingent was former colonial power France (which provided 1,244 troops).[13] The troops were seen by many on the ground as yet another foreign intervention aimed at consolidating the goals of Western powers, which supported and bankrolled the state of Israel, with whom they were at war.

Later UN peacekeeping missions have been established only when it was considered that peace prevailed. UNIFIL I was created and organized at a time when Lebanon was in the midst (and as it turned out at the beginning) of a protracted civil war and while the country remained victim to a hostile act by another state. Furthermore, the area of operation of UNIFIL, the region south of the Litani River in South Lebanon, was suffering from a power vacuum that had been filled by competing armed militia groups. The Lebanese Armed Forces had not been present in the area since 1968,[14] and the last local elections had been held in 1963.[15] The area was rural and underdeveloped, and it had largely been abandoned by central government. These circumstances meant that from the beginning, while operating under a mandate more consistent with Chapter VI of the UN Charter, peacekeepers were placed in an environment whereby their very survival and protection necessitated the use of force, which would be more consistent with a Chapter VII mission.[16]

The initial period after deployment was one of great danger owing to the security threats faced by UNIFIL as it was considered a foreign invader by many groups operating in the South. Its position was precarious, and it faced constant attacks on its personnel, bases, and equipment, as well as restrictions on freedom of movement and communication. In the first four years of the mission, 36 personnel died in direct attacks (shootings and mine explosions).[17] Of the three UNIFIL mandate objectives—reestablishing international peace and security, confirming the withdrawal of Israeli troops, and the reestablishment of the authority of the Lebanese government in the area—at least two had no credibility or legitimacy with the political organizations operating out of the South.

The 1978 Israeli withdrawal was planned to take place in four stages. In the first three stages the IDF handed over small pieces of territory under the auspices of UNIFIL.[18] However, in the fourth and final stage, the IDF ignored the UN resolution and refused to withdraw from the final sector in the South. Maintaining a skeleton of IDF troops, they initially handed over authority to a local militia—the South Lebanon Army, run by a former LAF officer, Major Saad Haddad—whom they continued to support.[19] The presence of the SLA prevented UNIFIL troops from conducting their operations up to the internationally recognized border with Israel. Literature on the UNIFIL mission between 1979 and 2000 reports that of all the factions operating in the South at this time, Israel and its proxy force the SLA were by far the biggest problem for UNIFIL.[20]

Ultimately, UNIFIL managed to gain a foothold in the area of operations, but in the course of their duties, they had to negotiate with up to thirty-seven different militias that coalesced around three main groups: the Palestinian militias, the Israeli-backed SLA, and the Shi'ite resistance groups—first Amal and later Hezbullah.[21]

Civilian Protection

While UNIFIL I was in many ways unable to fulfill the terms of its mandate, peacekeepers found other ways to make themselves useful during their time in South Lebanon in the form of providing civilian protection and assistance. Current affection for UNIFIL is often based on civilian memories of the Israeli occupation[22] at a time when life was very hard for southerners, owing to constant invasions and occupation: "The South was totally empty. People had escaped, and they were not going to come back. The Palestinians were holding the place and at war with the Israelis, so whoever was left behind was the typical Lebanese scene. Usually they leave behind their old people to take care of the property—all that sort of thing. And those people were absolutely dependent for everything; they had nothing. No medical care—nothing! Sometimes they didn't have food."[23] As such, UNIFIL was regarded by many civilians as saviors:

> I tell you during the occupation for the people they were the saviors. . . .
> UNIFIL were for the local people like a life raft for them. Because they felt they are protected. If in the occupied area they [Israelis] want to enter any house, UNIFIL tried to stop them.[24]

> So it was like a very warm and friendly relationship. Because they came here in a very critical situation, and they were the only refuge for the people. That's why the relations were very strong and memorable until now.[25]

UNIFIL troops also tried to protect local civilians from the worst effects of the occupying force:

> There was one scene I will never forget. In a village called Burj Ahal—it was raided by the Israelis—they were looking for some people. So they collected all the women and children in the school, and they took the men someplace else. It was a village in a French battalion area, and they [the Israelis] wanted to blow up a house. So immediately, the French commander, without asking, he ordered his guys to climb to the roof of the building and sit there. So fifteen French ran to the roof of the building and sat there. People saw those things, and it became legend.[26]

There was a strong sense that despite their limited resources, UNIFIL troops would go the extra mile to help the Lebanese. During the time of the Israeli occupation, UNIFIL battalions and resources were small. As such, UNIFIL gave much of what they could from their own supplies. The locals knew it and appreciated it deeply: "I can remember that we had no electricity—they provided the people with electricity. They used to have their own generators, and they used to give them to the people. And they used to provide them with water. . . . They started from the very beginning these humanitarian activities, providing people with services like medical, dental, even vet."[27]

UNIFIL also provided fuel for tractors and sometimes armed protection for local farmers trying to harvest their crops under challenging security circumstances. The local population speak of their sadness when UNIFIL soldiers paid the ultimate price for their tour of duty: "All the UNIFIL soldiers who died are martyrs. We have great appreciation for the soldiers who came from a foreign place and died for our land."[28]

The Pre–UNIFIL II Environment

UNIFIL's deployment coincided with the rise of Hezbullah in the 1980s as they surpassed the previous Shi'ite-led militia group Amal in terms of membership and organized resistance to Israel. UNIFIL's work with civilians during the Israeli invasions and in the subsequent recovery periods helped to ameliorate tensions with Hezbullah. Hezbullah appreciated that UNIFIL was genuinely caring toward the local population, and after a tense start, the relationship gradually improved.[29] This improvement paved the way later for UNIFIL to be able to engage with Hezbullah at the national level when it became officially involved in Lebanese politics.

In 2000 the Israelis withdrew from Lebanon very suddenly as a result of both domestic and international pressures.[30] The dismemberment of the "zone of security" meant that UNIFIL was for the first time since 1978 able to operate up to the internationally recognized boundaries and was no longer the target of attacks from the troublesome SLA, which had disbanded the instant Israel withdrew (with many of its members and their families going to live in Israel, fearing reprisals).

However, a number of factors conspired to prevent the long-dreamed-of peace for the region. Israel had failed to withdraw from two sections of internationally recognized Lebanese land: Shebaa Farms and the Kfar Shouba Hills. As Israel had failed to coordinate its withdrawal in advance with the Lebanese government, the vacuum that emerged in the area was quickly filled by Hezbullah, which was determined to reclaim the remaining pieces of Lebanese land as well as a significant number of Lebanese prisoners who had been abducted during the Israeli-SLA occupation and remained in Israeli jails. Extremely organized, Hezbullah swiftly established checkpoints, observation posts, and a visible military infrastructure across the area of operations and became the de facto politico-military authority in the area. Their presence prevented the deployment of joint patrols between UNIFIL and the LAF.[31]

Furthermore, the "line of withdrawal" (the Blue Line) remained contested in parts where the boundary was unmarked, leading to intentional and unintentional violations that led to confrontations between Lebanese and Israeli troops. Hezbullah justified its continued existence in South Lebanon by arguing, first, that Israel had not withdrawn from all Lebanese territory and, second, in the absence of the LAF, that it was acting as a deterrence to a future attack by Israel. This situation meant that UNIFIL required the continued cooperation of Hezbullah to carry out its duties. For the most part, this collaboration occurred, but there continued to be incidents, sometimes fatal, between Hezbullah and UNIFIL as well as between UNIFIL and the IDF.

Despite the constant insecurity during this period owing to clashes between the IDF and Hezbullah, some civilian respondents still argue that the presence of Hezbullah on the border made them feel more secure than they do currently while there is peace. It is UNIFIL's inability to deter or deflect Israeli invasions that contributes to UNIFIL's lack of local legitimacy with some sectors of the population. Experience has taught local civilians that when hostilities break out, UNIFIL will not be able to defend them, but Hezbullah will. As such, I found that many civilians maintain a plurality of consent: consent for the LAF and UNIFIL, on the one hand, and consent for the presence of Hezbullah, on the other. This plurality comes into conflict only when the LAF or UNIFIL are alerted to weaponry or explosive material near the border, or when UNIFIL (as occurred in the past) has attempted to monitor Hezbullah activities too closely. On these occasions, some locals will close ranks and prevent UNIFIL from entering certain areas.

The strategic environment between 2000 and 2006 was not conducive to UNIFIL doing much more than what it had done before, with one difference: they were able to now patrol the border areas. But they were not able to prevent altercations between Hezbullah and Israel. Thus, another major confrontation between Hezbullah and the IDF became inevitable. It occurred in July 2006 at the height of the summer tourist season.

The July War

Although Hezbullah maintains publicly that it never intended to start a war, it had been taunting the IDF in the years prior to the Harb Tamooz (the July War).[32] However, while there is no doubt that their actions on July 12 were highly provocative, Hezbullah had not counted on a shift in Israeli strategy. A small body of literature argues that Israel, tired of Hezbullah attacks on the IDF, was preparing for a war with Hezbullah with the aim of eradicating the organization and was therefore waiting for a legitimate justification to begin a new conflict.[33]

On July 12, 2006, it came. Hezbullah operatives ambushed an IDF patrol in the area of Zar'it-Shtula on the border with Israel. They kidnapped two Israeli soldiers and killed five more during an IDF attempt to rescue the first party. Hezbullah has always claimed it launched the attack to obtain a bargaining chip with Israel on the issue of the imprisoned Lebanese and Palestinians in Israeli jails.[34] Immediately after the kidnapping, Hezbullah demanded the release of Lebanese prisoners held by Israel in exchange for the release of the abducted soldiers. Israel, however, perceived these actions as an act of war and immediately launched a retaliatory response. It began with air strikes and artillery fire on targets in Lebanon aimed at Lebanese civilian infrastructure, including Beirut's Rafiq Hariri International Airport; an air and naval blockade; and a ground invasion of South Lebanon. Hezbullah then launched rockets into northern Israel and engaged the IDF in guerrilla warfare.

The war raged for thirty-three days and ended with the implementation of UNSC Resolution 1701 on August 14, 2006. During this time it is estimated that at least 1,191–1,300 Lebanese people and 61 Israelis were killed.[35] It severely damaged Lebanese civil infrastructure and displaced approximately 1 million Lebanese and 300,000 to 500,000 Israelis.[36]

The war caught UNIFIL by surprise, despite escalating tensions on the ground consisting of tit-for-tat incidents between Hezbullah and the IDF. Since the Israeli withdrawal in 2000, UNIFIL had been winding down the mission, and at the time of the July War, it comprised around 2,000 troops, with the objective of turning it into an observer mission. The resumption of hostilities, however, placed UNIFIL front and center of the peace process, and the mission received a new mandate, increased troops, and a significantly increased budget. This next phase of the mission was known as UNIFIL II.

UNIFIL II: Resolution 1701 and a Contested Mandate

Resolution 1701 was issued on August 11, 2006.[37] The named parties to the mandate are the governments of Lebanon and Israel. However, in the continued absence of a political dialogue between the two states, the representatives of the parties are the Israeli Defense Forces and the Lebanese

Armed Forces. As a result, in reality, on a daily basis, UNIFIL works with these two military organizations. This state of affairs is regularly clarified by both the IDF and the LAF and so there is no misunderstanding that they are authorized to operate in this way by their respective governments.[38]

In contrast with all other UNSC resolutions, the cease-fire brought about by Resolution 1701 did not come into effect until three days had passed on August 14.[39] Scholarly literature on the war has observed that this delay enabled Israel to intensify its bombing campaign of South Lebanon and so-called Hezbullah strongholds in the last three days of the war.[40] The effect of the last-minute Israeli efforts included the strewing of up to an estimated one million cluster bomblets (illegal under international law) across the width and breadth of South Lebanon that continue to kill, maim, and injure civilians in the area.[41] Richard Falk argues that the delay was engineered by the United States to afford the Israeli forces some political cover to "seize some vestiges of victory from the jaws of its defeat."[42]

There is speculation among those individuals who have studied the war that Resolution 1701 came into being in its current form only after it became apparent that Israel would not be able to achieve its objectives if it continued prosecuting the war.[43] Up until August 5, America was pushing Israel to continue the conflict in order to eliminate the problem of Hezbullah once and for all.[44] The first draft cease-fire agreement put forward by the United States and France on August 5 demanded a cessation of all attacks by Hezbullah and permitted Israel to continue acting in "self-defense." As the legality of what constitutes "self-defense" by a state is unclear, it could have allowed Israel to remain in Lebanon and to continue to conduct any military exercises it chose. As a result, the Lebanese government rejected the terms of the initial draft on August 6 and was accused by Condoleezza Rice of not being prepared to make peace.[45] The second draft of the resolution was finally agreed to on August 11 by all parties and passed on the same day.

There are a number of reasons Resolution 1701 has been critiqued for being fundamentally unfair.[46] First, an examination of the text reveals a lack of context when articulating blame for the start of the war, which is clearly laid at the feet of Hezbullah for conducting the kidnappings, which were illegal under international law: "Expressing its utmost concern at the continuing escalation of hostilities in Lebanon and in Israel since Hezbullah's attack on Israel on 12 July 2006, which has already caused hundreds of deaths and injuries on both sides, extensive damage to civilian infrastructure and hundreds of thousands of internally displaced persons."[47] The reference to injuries on "both sides" does not reflect the disproportionality of Israel's response to the kidnappings: a bombing campaign that has been recorded as resulting in more than one thousand civilian deaths on the Lebanese side (not counting further deaths as a result of unexploded ordinance) compared with sixty-one deaths (thirty-nine of which were civilians) on the Israeli side of the Blue Line.[48] It is argued that this disproportionality contravened the international laws of war, but it was not acknowledged in the resolution.[49]

Second, Israel had been illegally abducting and withholding Lebanese and Palestinian nationals over the course of many years during its occupation of South Lebanon. These acts were used by Hezbullah to justify the kidnappings, whereby they argued that they were not trying to start a war and were simply trying to effect an exchange of prisoners. Observers of the peace settlement argue that this point should have been relevant in this context.[50] The mandate alludes to the Israeli capture of civilians, but does not call directly for their release in the same unconditional terms: "Emphasizing the need for an end of violence, but at the same time emphasizing the need to address urgently the causes that have given rise to the current crisis, including the unconditional release of the abducted Israeli soldiers. . . . Mindful of the sensitivity of the issue of prisoners and encouraging the efforts aimed at urgently settling the issue of the Lebanese prisoners detained in Israel."[51]

Third, some scholars contend that by failing to call a cease-fire for thirty-four days, the UN was complicit in allowing an aggressor state to wage a military campaign that contravened the UN Charter and its prohibition on aggressive war.[52]

Fourth, there is no mention in the resolution of Israel's use of the illegal weapons of phosphorous and cluster bombs that are also widely regarded as being illegal under international law (although neither Israel nor the United States has signed the treaty banning their use).[53]

This imbalance in apportioning blame has led the local population in South Lebanon, who bore the brunt of the war, to regard Resolution 1701 as a fundamentally unfair and biased document. The lack of acknowledged Israeli culpability and the lack of proportionality have meant that Hezbullah continues to elicit support from a large segment of the population in the UNIFIL area of operation. As such, direct attempts by UNIFIL and the LAF to disarm and disband the organization, an implied aspect of their mandate, would trigger significant civilian resistance.[54]

In its mandate, UNIFIL is specifically charged with assisting the LAF to ensure that the area of operations is "an area free of any armed personnel, assets and weapons,"[55] that is, an area free of Hezbullah and other militias:

- security arrangements to prevent the resumption of hostilities, including the establishment between the Blue Line and the Litani river of an area free of any armed personnel, assets and weapons other than those of the Government of Lebanon and of UNIFIL as authorized in paragraph 11, deployed in this area;
- full implementation of the relevant provisions of the Ta'if Accords, and of resolutions 1559 (2004) and 1680 (2006), that require the disarmament of all armed groups in Lebanon, so that, pursuant to the Lebanese cabinet decision of 27 July 2006, there will be no weapons or authority in Lebanon other than that of the Lebanese State;
- no foreign forces in Lebanon without the consent of its Government;
- no sales or supply of arms and related materiel to Lebanon except as authorized by its Government.[56]

Falk has commented that by calling for the disarmament of military groups in the area, the main aggressor in the war, Israel was rewarded by an acknowledgment that intervention to disarm and attack Hezbullah was legitimate.[57] This "Chapter VII–like" aspect of Resolution 1701 has raised the question of how much force should be applied in the enforcement of the disarmament aspect of the current UN mandate.[58]

In addition to the above tasks, Resolution 1701 significantly increased the troop numbers patrolling the Blue Line to a recommended fifteen thousand. Bearing in mind the small size of the area of operation, these high troop numbers are rare in UN peacekeeping missions, demonstrating the force of political will involved in crafting the new resolution.[59] The resolution also called for UN troops:

> In addition to carrying out its mandate under resolutions 425 and 426 (1978):
>
> (a) Monitor the cessation of hostilities;
>
> (b) Accompany and support the Lebanese armed forces as they deploy throughout the South, including along the Blue Line, as Israel withdraws its armed forces from Lebanon as provided in paragraph 2;
>
> (c) Coordinate its activities related to paragraph 11 (b) with the Government of Lebanon and the Government of Israel;
>
> (d) Extend its assistance to help ensure humanitarian access to civilian populations and the voluntary and safe return of displaced persons;
>
> (e) Assist the Lebanese armed forces in taking steps towards the establishment of the area as referred to in paragraph 8;
>
> (f) Assist the Government of Lebanon, at its request, to implement paragraph 14.[60]

Since the implementation of Resolution 1701, the predominant concerns of the Security Council have been that UNIFIL prevent hostilities from breaking out along the Blue Line, increase cooperation and capacity building between UNIFIL and the LAF, ensure the removal of weapons from the area and prevent the transit of new weapons into the area, and maintain force protection.

Later resolutions have reflected the desire of the international community for an increase in cooperation between UNIFIL and the LAF with the stated purpose of establishing "a new strategic environment,"[61] which should probably be interpreted as meaning one without the presence of Hezbullah. The establishment of a LAF liaison office at Naqoura in 2006 was later enhanced by the addition of an extra LAF battalion in 2010 to assist UNIFIL, the commencement of a strategic dialogue between the

LAF and UNIFIL, and tripartite monthly discussions between the LAF and the IDF, mediated by UNIFIL.

To promote peace and security along the Blue Line, resolutions since 2006 have repeatedly referred to the need for a clear demarcation of the Blue Line by UNIFIL[62] to limit the scope for unintended violations by civilians and troops on both sides of the line. In the 2006 war the IDF reoccupied the northern Lebanese half of the town of Ghajar, which is divided by the Blue Line (owing to half of it residing in what is internationally recognized as the Golan region of Syria), and mandates since 2007 have repeatedly called on Israel to withdraw.[63] Perhaps in recognition of the difficulty that UNIFIL troops face in carrying out their mandate, and owing to popular support for the very organizations that they are being asked to help disarm, post–Resolution 1701 mandates have frequently "encouraged efforts aimed at urgently settling the issue of Lebanese prisoners in Israel."[64]

Problems along the Blue Line continue to concern the Security Council in terms of their effect on UNIFIL, the LAF, and civilians. These issues include roadside bombs, illegal incursions by Israel, and a brief outbreak of hostilities between the LAF and the IDF. However, since Resolution 1701, no major changes to the nature of the mandates have occurred, and the mission continues to host one of the larger UN peacekeeping forces.[65]

The Structure of the New UNIFIL

Once the new mandate was in place, UNIFIL II developed from a small mission in the process of drawing down into a large mission authorized to deploy up to 15,000 troops in the area of operations. In addition to the expanded military role, UNIFIL II also expanded its civilian component. Civilian staff at the base are a mixture of Lebanese and international staff, of which 257 are international and 591 are local.[66] Some international and Lebanese staff have been with the mission since 2006, as civilian staff are not forced to rotate, unlike military staff. The mission has a public information office, a political affairs office, and a civil affairs office at headquarters in Naqoura. It is important to note that over time, some staff have worked as civil affairs officers and as political affairs officers or both at the same time. The division of duties between the offices of public information, civil affairs, and political affairs tends to be fluid in that there is considerable interaction and engagement on local issues among the three offices.

The mission is run out of Naqoura, where the headquarters are situated. It is spread out across the area of operation and includes forty different troop nationalities.[67] They are housed under two main sectors: Sector West, which is headed by the Italian contingent, comprises five battalions, and is run out of the town of Shamaa, and Sector East, which is headed by the Spanish, comprises four battalions, and is run from the town of Marja'youn. The Force Commander Reserve is centrally located in the village of Burj Qallawiyah to support both sectors as needed. Unlike the civilian component of the mission, military staff rotate regularly, staying for periods as short as four months to up to a year. UNIFIL is also supported by about 56 military observers from the United Nations Truce Supervision Organization, based in Jerusalem, and they are organized by the Observer Group Lebanon (OGL). The mission also includes a maritime task force that patrols the sea between Israel and Lebanon.

The force commander is appointed for two years and is the head of the mission. Unlike many modern peacekeeping operations, the UNIFIL mission does not have a special representative of the secretary-general.[68] The military and civilian line of command in the UNIFIL mission goes from the force commander to the deputy head of mission, who is a civilian. The deputy head of mission is responsible for political and civil affairs, and under this position sits the deputy director of political and civil affairs. The military line of command goes from the force commander to the military heads of the two sectors and to various other units, such as the OGL and the Force Commander Reserve.

The force commander also directly heads three other chains of command: one that comprises six units, which includes the Liaison Branch; the deputy force commander, who commands four separate units, which include the capacity building project called the "Strategic Dialogue" with the LAF and troop contributing country management; and the director of mission support, who runs the logistics of the mission.

The Strategic Environment Post-2006

> There has been a strategic change subsequent to Resolution 1701.
> There have not been major military clashes across the Blue Line.
> There have been a couple of problems, a number of rockets, but
> nothing like before, an absolute sea change, as to what existed prior
> to the war in 2006.
> —Interview with UNIFIL political affairs officer,
> Beirut, Lebanon, 2013

The difference between the pre- and post-2006 environment in the area of operations has been commented upon by UNIFIL staff and local civilians alike. There is no doubt that the area is technically, although not officially, experiencing a period of peace longer than any other in the history of the UNIFIL mission. However, the political environment in which UNIFIL operates contributes to its weak legitimacy.

Unresolved Issues of Contention

The major issues of contention that exist between all the parties—both named (Israel and the Lebanese government) and unnamed (Hezbullah) in Resolution 1701—are recognized by the UN and the international community as being problematic to an official peace agreement. These problems are the continued Israeli occupation of the northern half of Ghajar, the Shebaa Farms area, and the Kfar Shouba Hills; a number of points on the Blue Line that relate to territorial disputes and unresolved markings;[69] Lebanese (and Palestinian) prisoners still being held in Israeli jails;[70] Israeli air and sea violations of Lebanese sovereignty; and rocket attacks into northern Israel by armed elements from South Lebanon.[71] Unofficially, however, there is another story as to why a political peace process is absent from the Lebanon-Israel conflict.

Preventing Peace? Hezbullah and the Palestinians

The major issue for the Israeli government is not minor points of contention over the marking of the Blue Line, but the presence of Hezbullah, which, they argue, remains on the Blue Line. The major issue for the Lebanese government and Hezbullah is the existence of Israel, but on this issue the two parties diverge in their views. First, there is no consensus at the national level about whether Hezbullah should continue to maintain its military wing. Second, some factions in the Lebanese government are less concerned with the existence of the state of Israel and more concerned with resettling between four hundred thousand and six hundred thousand Palestinians residing in camps in Lebanon.[72] The Lebanese government's official position on the Palestinian presence in Lebanon is that they cannot be naturalized, as doing so will irreparably alter the delicate sectarian balance between the religions in Lebanon that exists currently.[73] The majority of Palestinians in Lebanon are Sunni, and in a population of four and a half million people, it is feared the addition of so many Sunnis will give them an overwhelming demographic majority.[74] The Lebanese government's position is that the problem of displaced Palestinians is an international one that needs to be resolved internationally, and Lebanon is therefore not responsible for solving this problem alone. The view is that Lebanon has been a victim of circumstance and should not be made accountable for the policies of Israel, the United States, and the British since 1917.[75]

Hezbullah's position has, until recently, been that the state of Israel should not exist. Recent speeches have indicated the potential for a shift in this position, but it is unclear what this might mean in practice.[76] However, in relation to the Palestinian issue in South Lebanon, Hezbullah's position is that all Palestinians should be free to return to Palestine. The two-state solution is not something with which Hezbullah has ever explicitly stated that it agrees.[77]

One of the reasons, therefore, that the border dispute between Lebanon and Israel is so intractable is that it is linked to another intractable Middle East problem: the plight of the Palestinians. This issue ultimately prevents progress toward a peace agreement between Israel and Lebanon. One UNIFIL officer who had been present in the region for seven years felt that the actual issues between the governments of the two countries— small territorial disputes and the release of Lebanese prisoners—are not impossible to resolve:

I actually personally don't think it would take much to see some form of agreement: Lebanese government to Israeli government. Now the issue of the Palestinians and the presence of the Palestinians are something else, and in this sense, because of the weakness of the Lebanese state, I don't think you can possibly see an Israeli-Lebanese agreement coming out or happening before an agreement with the Palestinians that settles the issue of the Palestinian refugees on Lebanese territory. I don't think you can see that. It is linked; it is irrevocably linked. This government is not able to make an agreement like Egypt or like Jordan. . . . Before you deal with the issue of the Palestinian presence on Lebanese territory, I think it would be very, very hard for an agreement to be reached.[78]

This statement in part captures the issues that exist between Lebanon and Israel, because the Palestinian problem plays a big role. In addition, the Lebanese government is currently dominated by Hezbullah, which does not acknowledge Israel's right to exist and therefore does not wish to make peace with Israel. Despite Hezbullah's dominance, there is serious disagreement between various politicians in the Lebanese government over Hezbullah's right to maintain an armed wing and whether making peace with Israel is in Lebanon's best interests. Those individuals in government who oppose Hezbullah are not equipped to confront Hezbullah politically or militarily. Furthermore, the Israeli government is not prepared to allow around a half-million Palestinians to return in order to make peace with Lebanon, nor do they acknowledge Hezbullah's right to exist politically or militarily. There is an impasse that observers of the region argue will be resolved only by a large-scale, long, and vicious region-wide war.[79]

Israel

Israel is primarily interested in maintaining its security and its very existence. As such, along with its main ally, the United States, Israel maintains a policy of ensuring that it possesses a qualitative military edge over all its neighbors in the region (including nonneighboring Iran). This policy means that for Israel, the presence of any military force capable of compromising its security must be destroyed or disabled to the extent that it can no longer pose a significant threat.[80] This policy extends to the destruction of Hezbullah and the prevention of weapons transfers to Hezbullah. On a regional scale, it involves the prevention of any state, such as Syria or Iran, from obtaining nuclear weapons.[81] But this policy also means that Israel has lobbied extensively over the years to prevent the LAF from obtaining any serious weaponry: it does not allow the LAF to use tanks in the area of operation and has lobbied internationally against the LAF obtaining any kind of military hardware, particularly weapons such as surface-to-air missiles. However, at the same time, Israel argues that it wants to see the LAF's authority extended down to the border along with the removal of Hezbullah from the area.

The Israeli position is that peace could be made if Hezbullah no longer posed any kind of military threat to Israel. For that to happen, Hezbullah would need to disband its military wing, as it has a military presence close to Israel in the East of Lebanon in the Beqaa Valley.[82] However, as Hezbullah is currently a significant part of the Lebanese government and refuses to distinguish between its political and military wings, it is unlikely that this disbanding will occur, particularly as Hezbullah maintains significant support from the Shi'a across Lebanon and from some Lebanese Christian factions.

In terms of its support of Resolution 1701, Israel tolerates the presence of UNIFIL but does not regard it as a serious obstacle. One UNIFIL officer informed me that, according to an Israeli officer, Israel views UNIFIL as a "speed bump" should they choose to invade Lebanon again.[83]

In sum, the issues around marking the Blue Line, Israeli air violations, the occupation of Lebanese land, and Lebanese detainees in Israel would very likely be able to be resolved. But as long as Israel perceives Hezbullah to be an existential threat, peace with Lebanon is not possible. It is also highly unlikely at this time that Israel would be willing to take back the displaced Palestinians living in Lebanon for the sake of a peace agreement with Lebanon.

The Lebanese Government

The position of the Lebanese government regarding peace with Israel is harder to define, owing to the varying interests of the different political parties that constitute its whole, which means it rarely speaks with one voice.[84] The Lebanese government is divided on the issue of how to deal with Israel, mainly because of the issue of Hezbullah.

Broadly speaking, the main rival faction to Hezbullah that is also in government is termed locally "the March 14 movement."[85] It includes the three major political parties: the Lebanese Forces, the Kataeb Party, and the Future Movement.[86] At the international level, the March 14 group is aligned with the European Union, Saudi Arabia, the United Arab Emirates, and the United States. At the local and international levels, the March 14 group would like Hezbullah to disband and hand over its weapons to the LAF.[87] They argue that Hezbullah's weapons are the cause of trouble with Israel and assist in the projection of Iranian power into the region.

To some extent, this view is driven by a shift in local power politics. Hezbullah and the power of the Shi'a are a relatively new phenomenon in Lebanon. The reason is historical: for decades in Lebanon, the Christians dominated culture and education, and the Sunnis took care of trade and business, relegating the Shi'a to the lower socioeconomic strata of the population.[88] There is unquestionably some resentment around the rise of the Shi'a to prominence in Lebanese politics. However, it is also understood that the March 14 faction, aligned as it is with Western interests, is opposed to Hezbullah for reasons of compatibility with its international supporters.[89] Currently, Hezbullah is the most powerful political faction in Lebanon.

The March 14 faction is viewed by supporters of the resistance (Hezbullah) as being sympathetic to Israel, as this faction shares Israel's views on ridding the country of Hezbullah's weapons.[90] As such, the March 14 movement is largely supportive of Resolution 1701, but in particular the goal of disbanding and disarming nonstate militias, and through the LAF, extending the authority of the Lebanese government down to the internationally recognized "border."

That is not to say that the March 14 movement is pro-Israeli; the rhetoric of all political parties in Lebanon is strongly anti-Israel. But, other than Hezbullah, the impression obtained from UNIFIL is that for many of the parties in the Lebanese government, it is the Palestinian issue and small territorial disputes that prevent a peace agreement between the two states.

Hezbullah, Amal, and the March 8 Grouping

Hezbullah views Resolution 1701 as an agreement that favors Israel over Lebanon.[91] It argues that if UNIFIL is impartial, why are UN peacekeepers only on the Lebanese side of the Blue Line?[92] By the end of the 2006 war and after substantial civilian deaths, all sides were keen to end the hostilities, and so Hezbullah agreed to Resolution 1701.[93] While consent for Resolution 1701 was obtained, Hezbullah had no intention of assisting UNIFIL with its mandated objective of disarming and disbanding non-state militias (unless they were Palestinian militias). Hassan Nasrallah, the leader of Hezbullah, stated publicly that he did not believe that disarming Hezbullah was in the mandate of Resolution 1701.[94] Hezbullah supports the deployment of the LAF in the area of operations and continues to propagate the slogan "The Army, the People and the Resistance" as a way of aligning itself with a national institution.[95] Hezbullah's legitimacy within Lebanon depends on being seen as a national organization and as part of the national government.[96]

Hezbullah was created in part as a resistance movement against the state of Israel and, in their words, against Israeli aggression toward Lebanon.[97] This position became less tenable after the Israeli withdrawal from South Lebanon and especially after 2006, when calls from political factions for Hezbullah to hand over their weapons to the LAF became louder at national and international levels. Hezbullah has in part maintained its raison d'être with the argument that Israel has not fully withdrawn from "every inch of Lebanese land," which is one of their demands. In this respect, they refer to the occupation of northern Ghajar, Shebaa Farms, and the Kfar Shouba Hills.[98] The oft-used justification for their continued existence is that they are the only force that has thus far managed to "win" a war against Israel and eject them from Lebanese soil, and indeed they are right.[99] As yet, the LAF is not regarded as a credible deterrent. In contrast, Hezbullah has been trained, primarily by Iranian forces, in guerrilla tactics that make them extremely effective against conventional forces in a situation of asymmetric power. Hezbullah argues that the LAF has not reached this level of expertise and therefore does not present a credible deterrent against Israel. With regard to handing over their weapons to the LAF, Hezbullah is mistrustful that the March 14 movement will use those weapons against it to destroy the group entirely. This suspicion is not entirely unreasonable. WikiLeaks documents reveal that during the 2006 war, elements within the March 14 movement were discreetly advising the Israelis where to hit Hezbullah the hardest.[100] Furthermore, Hezbullah argues that the March 14 movement is soft on Israel and cannot be trusted to use the LAF against Israel to ensure that Lebanese sovereignty is respected in its entirety. In other words, Hezbullah feels it cannot sufficiently trust the state to put its weapons to good use if it were to hand them over.

Between 2006 and 2015, Hezbullah had not violated the Blue Line or had done so only in retaliation for an Israeli attack on their personnel. However, in 2015 and 2016 there were several flare-ups on the Blue Line between the IDF and Hezbullah.[101] None of these attacks triggered an escalation. The political effects of the Syrian war have put hostilities between Hezbullah and Israel largely on hold. From Israel's point of view, the threat posed by rogue militia operating inside Syria means that maintaining the status quo with Lebanon is the safest policy for now. Should a war break out with Hezbullah, the border area between Syria and Lebanon could become highly porous and lead to an influx of Islamic extremists who might be happy to take their fight to Israel.[102]

Hezbullah's position on the state of Israel itself has until recently been unequivocal: it should not exist.[103] However, the organization is unclear as to what this stance means in practice. Hezbullah's position on the Blue Line is theoretically that it should not exist in its current form unless it demarcates the legal border between Palestine and Lebanon (with Israel no longer a state). Hezbullah no longer holds visible military positions in the area of operations and has *officially* pulled back to north of the Litani River. Hezbullah tolerates the presence of UNIFIL as long as it does not interfere too closely with its military operations. As such, Hezbullah can be said to have given local consent to Resolution 1701 in the sense that it *largely* refrains from obstructing UNIFIL militarily and will engage with UNIFIL·politically.

Syria: Caution Is the Better Part of Valor

The Syrian crisis is briefly discussed here as it informs the strategic environment in Lebanon. The number of *registered* Syrian refugees in Lebanon was just over 1 million in 2016.[104] The area of operations has generally suffered less than the rest of the country, as access to it from northern Lebanon is restricted to Lebanese citizens; Palestinians and other foreigners require a pass from the military to enter the area. However, many Syrian refugees have managed to enter the area, presumably from the eastern side that borders Syria. Currently, they total an estimated 47,138,[105] are mainly located in rural areas, and often work for Lebanese farmers as agricultural workers or shepherds. UNIFIL has been allowing Syrians access to their free medical services for humanitarian reasons.

Aside from the issue of the refugees, the main issue for Lebanon in relation to the Syrian crisis is Hezbullah's involvement in it. Hezbullah is believed to have begun providing military support to President Bashar al-Assad from December 2012, but this suspicion cannot be confirmed. Hezbullah openly admitted it was providing support in April 2013.[106] Its actions have contributed to a number of political and security problems for Lebanon. In 2012 the Lebanese government signed the Baabda Declaration, which was a commitment to remain neutral and disassociated from the Syrian crisis.[107] As Hezbullah is now in contravention of that agreement, politicians from opposing sides have tried to block Hezbullah's inclusion in government, arguing that Hezbullah is prosecuting a war in another state without securing the agreement of the Lebanese people. This situation led to a political stalemate that began in April 2013 and ended only with the appointment in November 2016 of Hezbullah's preferred candidate, Michel Aoun, to the position of president.[108]

As Hezbullah is already involved in Syria, it stands to reason that it has fewer forces left on the ground in Lebanon, and with resources stretched, it would be challenging to manage a war on two fronts. As such, it is likely that it is unwilling to trigger a confrontation with Israel at the current time.[109] Furthermore, if Hezbullah were to initiate a new conflict with Israel at a time when the country is feeling the burden of the Syrian refugee influx, it is very likely this move would be highly unpopular within Lebanon. As a legitimate political actor within Lebanon, Hezbullah needs to be mindful of the need to retain domestic support.

The current strategic environment therefore means that both sides feel constrained because of the unknown variable of the effect of the Syrian crisis on them. In short, the region is currently highly unstable, and under such conditions maintaining the status quo would appear to be the safest course of action. Whether politicians in Israel or senior Hezbullah officials subscribe to this view is unclear, but the low number of incidents and their proportionality in the area of operations since 2013 would suggest that they might.

Conclusion

From the inception of the UNIFIL mission in 1978, there remains no national consensus on what the goals of UNIFIL should be. Political wranglings over the status of Hezbullah and the Palestinians remain key roadblocks to peace between Lebanon and Israel, not the other issues of contention such as minor land disputes, Lebanese prisoners in Israeli jails, and aerial violations of territory. However, these "minor" issues present significant risks to the region, as they are the sparks that can light the fire of a larger existential conflict.

3 Credibility in Interstate Conflict

This chapter is the first of three in which I discuss how UNIFIL wins credibility on the ground. In its international engagement, UNIFIL uses liaison, intervention, negotiation, and reporting to win technical and responsiveness credibility that affords it the benefits of confidence and cooperation from the named parties. Three short case studies at the end of this chapter illustrate the kinds of incidents that occur on the Blue Line and show how UNIFIL has responded to these violations using the strategies mentioned above.

By building credibility, UNIFIL helps to maintain peace on the line of withdrawal that divides the territories of Lebanon and Israel, known as the Blue Line. Management of the Blue Line is a key activity for UNIFIL, owing to the potential for violations to escalate into full-scale conflict, as was the case during the July War of 2006. As one officer noted, "Obviously, if any political decision is made, then the situation would change, but our role is to try to ensure that there are no accidental triggers. Something could happen, some small incident that could easily flare up into something much, much larger that both parties, all parties, end up regretting. As I think they did in 2006."[1]

As a Chapter VI mission, UNIFIL is not authorized to use peace enforcement measures, but more important, the contested legitimacy of the mandate over how and where force should be applied also constrains the mission. I show from UNIFIL's perspective how obtaining cooperation in this situation is more effective than deterrence to maintain international peace and security.

Two factors play a role in UNIFIL's management of the Blue Line: technocracy and time. Technocracy is used by UNIFIL to avoid entanglement with the political tensions that exist both between the parties and within Lebanese society. UNIFIL has made the Blue Line a social fact by marking it where possible, carrying electronic devices that show precisely where the Line lies, and managing each transgression on an individual basis. This bureaucratic behavior is typical of all international organizations that wish to be viewed as impartial. Time is the second critical variable. It affects how much credibility UNIFIL actors have with the parties and the extent of the influence they wield.

By detailing UNIFIL's response to violations on the Blue Line, I show how UNIFIL appears reliable and predictable to the named parties to the conflict. This technical and responsiveness credibility prevents the IDF from taking its own measures on the Blue Line that could antagonize the Lebanese and trigger an incident with the potential for a resumption of conflict. Equally, as the LAF manages transgressions on the Lebanese side, it relies on UNIFIL to inform them of every violation of the line and to negotiate on their behalf with the IDF.[2] UNIFIL's measures not only help prevent incursions but further reify the existence of the line in preparation for a formal cease-fire or eventual peace agreement.[3]

Maintaining Peace and Security on the Ground: Walking the Blue Line

UNIFIL's area of operation extends from the Litani River, which lies just south of Tyre (Sur in Arabic), down to the Blue Line, a UN-created line of withdrawal. Maintaining peace on the Blue Line is a priority for UNIFIL, owing to its importance to international security.[4] The political status of the line is simply a cessation of hostilities. A senior LAF officer described the situation, acknowledging the absence of a peace agreement with Israel: "And we worked hard in seven years in order not to go to war, without a decision to go to war. If there is no decision to go to war, we must not go to war over an incident."[5] The main aim of the mission is to prevent the occurrence of a violation that could trigger a resumption of hostilities and de-escalation if hostilities do break out: "Our words are to keep the place quiet. Keep the South of the country quiet to try to ensure that there are no outbreaks of hostilities as what happened in July 2006."[6] UNIFIL uses a mixture of regular reporting, liaison, intervention, and negotiation when managing security incidents on the Blue Line. The credibility won here is responsiveness credibility, which, as mentioned earlier, is a demonstrated ability to respond quickly to military and civilian concerns in a reliable manner. It helps UNIFIL establish effective relationships with the parties and builds confidence that UNIFIL can be relied upon to respond to incidents predictably and swiftly.

As noted in chapter 2, the risk of war breaking out on the Blue Line remains quite high, despite peace since 2006. In such an environment, it is important that no accidental violations of the Blue Line are misconstrued by either side as an act of aggression. UNIFIL conducts on average ten thousand activities, including some eleven hundred in close coordination with the LAF, every month.[7] UNIFIL ensures every type of violation is attended to immediately to reassure the parties that the line is being monitored.

Many Blue Line violations by civilians occur accidentally because demarcation of the Blue Line with blue barrels is ongoing and several sections of the line have yet to be clearly marked. But intentional violations still occur, either as a result of a deliberate incursion by one of the named parties to the conflict or as a result of the actions of another party—traditionally referred to as a "spoiler" in the peacekeeping literature.[8]

While UNIFIL monitors transgressions of the line and manages the outcome, the Israelis also monitor the area via surveillance towers that are manned twenty-four hours a day[9] and with regular military patrols, sensors on the ground, and a highly sophisticated electronic surveillance and communications network, which functions on both sides of the line.[10] The IDF's usual practice is to call in a violation to UNIFIL, to which UNIFIL then responds. Different types of violations call for different responses from UNIFIL depending on their seriousness, the least serious being wandering shepherds and livestock; slightly more serious are repeated violations by farmers, hunters, and resort visitors; and the most serious incidents are a deliberate violation with the intention to commit harm.[11]

Accidental Violations

Shepherd and Livestock Violations

Breaches of the Blue Line by shepherds occur regularly, usually because of roaming livestock and an absence of Blue Line markings in some areas. Once an animal has wandered, the shepherd tries to retrieve it and in the process violates the Blue Line. Because the shepherd's livelihood depends on maintaining his stock, he will still try to retrieve the animal, even if he knows that he is committing a violation.[12] In recent years, shepherd violations of the Blue Line because of poor markings have become more common owing to the increased use of Syrian refugees as stockmen who are less familiar with the lay of the land.

UNIFIL's strategy to prevent these accidental violations from the Lebanese side is to call out to the shepherd to advise him that he is crossing the Blue Line and that he needs to move back into Lebanese territory. UNIFIL is unable to detain or prevent the Lebanese from crossing the Blue Line should they wish to do so. Many of the shepherds now have mobile phones, and the patrolling peacekeepers can call the shepherds to advise them that they have crossed the line: "Our Indian battalion over there talk a lot to the local people on the ground. They have their cell phones; they try to call them to ensure they do not cross the Blue Line. A lot of violations I think are prevented by the close relations, but sometimes people do cross."[13]

Battalions also conduct regular seminars to educate local shepherds about the location of the Blue Line. For example, the Indian battalion holds bimonthly meetings to educate local shepherds about the location of the Blue Line in Sector East, which includes Shebaa Farms, where the line is unmarked:[14] "We call all the shepherds in the area. We sensitize them on the Blue Line. We tell them; we have a small tea party with them; we exchange our ideas. Then we tell them, 'See, this is the fact of the Blue Line. This is how you are supposed to be, you know, it's advisable.' So they do take it in good heart."[15]

On occasion, shepherds will cross the Blue Line intentionally because they disagree politically with its existence and because their families have lived in the area for generations before the line existed. They do so at substantial risk, not only owing to the threat of being apprehended by the Israelis, but also because many of the areas close to the Blue Line contain unexploded ordinance. Local farmers believe they are aware of the location of each and every mine, but it is not always the case. Thousands of unexploded cluster bomblets left over from the 2006 war remain in the area,[16] and from time to time deadly accidents occur. In the Shebaa region, preventing transgressions is difficult owing to political sensitivities: "We tell him, 'You are crossing the Blue Line.' We look to the Lebanese [LAF] to police their own people. We won't stop them. We can only advise. It's difficult for us, but it's even more difficult for the Lebanese, because if you go up to Shebaa Farms, the Lebanese see Shebaa as Lebanese. The Israelis and the UN consider Shebaa as Syrian. So if I ask a Lebanese soldier, 'Stop that shepherd from going in there,' he says, 'How can I stop him? He's going into his own country.' You know?"[17]

Peacekeepers are sympathetic to the local shepherds despite the fact that they cause them daily alerts and reporting duties: "Saying this to a guy who's concerned about his livelihood, who's been here all his life and will be here a lot longer than we'll be here. It's up to him, I suppose, but just on a given day, you try to lead him off it."[18] Whenever a shepherd is caught by the IDF entering Israeli territory, he will be captured and questioned for a period of between twenty-four and seventy-two hours before being released back to the Lebanese authorities. UNIFIL has appealed to Israel to liaise directly with UNIFIL when ground violations of this nature occur rather than arresting individuals, but thus far the practice of detention continues.[19] If a shepherd should resist arrest by the Israeli forces and run away, sometimes his animals are captured and detained for up to a week.[20] However, this punishment has on occasion turned out to be a blessing: "Once a flock of goats crossed—they were kidnapped, if you like—and they were vaccinated and sent back. The Israelis offered a free veterinary service for the goats!"[21]

Farmers, Hunters, and Resort Visitors

Violations by farmers in the region constitute a slightly more serious problem because of their repeated nature. The IDF perceives any repetitious behavior as potential intelligence gathering on the "border" area. Problems occur because the Blue Line crosses tobacco and olive farmland owned by Lebanese farmers that has existed for generations; in contrast, the Blue Line has been present only since 2000. Farmers working the land often disagree with the principle that they are not allowed to farm sections of their own land. The result is that even if farmers are aware that they are committing a violation, they continue to farm the land as they always have.

The other main cause of repeated violations lies in the existence of the Israeli technical fence (often confused with the Blue Line), a defensive installation that Israel constructed after its withdrawal from South Lebanon in 2000. Although the fence runs close to the Blue Line, it is set back farther south into Israeli territory, sometimes by a few hundred meters in most areas, to avoid conflict over unresolved territorial disputes on the exact location of the line. Some farmers who do not understand where the Blue Line is believe they are not in violation of it because they are not crossing over the fence. At harvest times this situation can lead to a high daily number of transgressions that always have the potential to generate more serious incidents. One peacekeeper noted, "One day we can report a violation of the Blue Line twenty times."[22]

UNIFIL's method of dealing with regular transgressions is to contact the LAF, and together with a UNIFIL patrol they will visit the farmer and try to prevent further transgressions by talking to him. Politics play a role in that while the LAF can physically prevent the transgressor, owing to the LAF's own concern with retaining a positive image in South Lebanon, LAF officers are highly reluctant to use force. As noted previously, UNIFIL can only advise the transgressor not to go any farther. To help resolve the problem of frequent violations by the same person, sometimes UNIFIL will bring in a local official to explain to the farmer why he is unable to farm a part of his land. If this visit fails, UNIFIL has, on occasion, brought in staff to demarcate the Blue Line on the farmer's land so that he is clear where he can and cannot go. If the violations continue, the matter is then passed up to the tripartite meetings between the parties and UNIFIL to try to reach an agreement on how the issue can be managed.

Repeated violations also occur with hunters; these situations are considered more serious because the hunters carry guns. In Lebanon the sport of hunting involves a group of men with shotguns trying to kill any bird that happens to be flying overhead. As such, it can take hunters anywhere, because in Lebanon there are no game reserves. Hunting is actually banned in the UNIFIL area of operations, but—as is the case with many laws in Lebanon—this fact is overlooked by the general population when it suits. In hunting season, up to one hundred instances can be reported within a four-month period.[23] UNIFIL is alerted to the presence of hunters whenever it hears the sound of gunfire or by the IDF calling:

> You hear the shots; the guys have a 24-7 watch on the post. And it will literally be two kilometers to your left. A patrol will be sent out, and it could very well be that the guy has done his business and gone, or if he's there he's just questioned. But he could be there with what they're after, shooting or whatever. That goes up to the reporting line, and the next day people are made aware. It's just obviously if there's shooting going on, it's of concern. We wouldn't be doing our job if we didn't report, because what's not to say it's the worst-case scenario. But that's how routine it is—I'd say the guys on the post would, 99 percent of the time, know that it's just an armed hunter, but it's just healthy paranoia that you have to go through the procedure, send out a patrol, and report.[24]

UNIFIL deals with these transgressions by attending to the scene with the LAF, which intervenes and negotiates with the hunters and persuades them to leave the area. As with all transgressions, the incident is reported and recorded by UNIFIL.

Repeated violations also come from people visiting holiday resorts that have sprung up along the Wazzani River, which runs through areas next to the Blue Line. One such resort caused particular problems for UNIFIL when it opened in 2010. The Israelis were concerned that it would be used as a launching pad for attacks by armed groups posing as tourists. As such, a great deal of liaison between the parties was required while the resort was being built. Water disputes between Lebanon and Israel are common,[25] and in this instance, the IDF argued that the resort would use more than its fair share of water from the Wazzani and should be denied planning permission.[26] These claims were not substantiated by the Lebanese authorities. As a precaution, the Israelis built a road down to the river and a helicopter pad opposite the resort, and UNIFIL and the LAF maintain a presence on the Lebanese side. Until now, no serious incidents from the resort have occurred, but for the occasional vacationer swimming in the river and inadvertently crossing the Blue Line.[27] Here the Blue Line lies down the middle of the stream and until recently was demarcated with a single line of blue rope. Tension remains over the access to the water, however, which can result in pettiness: "We asked permission to clean the river here, but the Israelis refused. Any work here, because we are on the Blue Line, you need the approval of the two sides. So the Israelis refused to allow us to do it, and UNIFIL did nothing so far to help us with cleaning it. Though the last two years the Israelis didn't object to us cleaning the river, and now they are. We don't know why."[28]

As a precaution UNIFIL needs to take every incident seriously, but the manner in which they are handled requires calmness and sensitivity. Peacekeepers understand that civilians feel they have the right to walk wherever they want on Lebanese land and simply are not aware of every twist and turn of the Blue Line. In addition, sensitivity to local political views about Israel means peacekeepers refrain from addressing transgressions in a forceful manner. Accidental violations ultimately cause a lot of work for UNIFIL, and in some cases repeated violations necessitate the need to come to a microsecurity agreement with Israel to manage the situation.

Deliberate Violations

Deliberate violations of the Blue Line occur by protesters, various armed groups, air violations, and rocket attacks. A serious category of violations involves confrontations between the LAF and the IDF, and in the view of the IDF, the most serious are violations involving Hezbullah (detailed in the final part of this chapter).

Stone Throwing

Protests against Israel usually (but not always) transpire at a very disorganized and local level and can consist simply of stone-throwing incidents

2. The Blue Line prior to the building of the security wall, Metulla. (Courtesy Vanessa Newby, January 2012)

by local Lebanese or, on occasion, by the IDF at Lebanese civilians if they are deemed to be undertaking suspicious activity.[29] They occur at points where Lebanese roads come close to the Israeli technical fence, when military patrols pass, or where IDF troops are standing in position. These events are dealt with by UNIFIL and the LAF, with the LAF taking the key role in dispersing Lebanese citizens.[30] UNIFIL does its best to prevent such incidents by increasing its presence in specific areas where tensions can develop, but liaison, intervention, and negotiation can and do fail. In the village of Metulla, where the Blue Line passes directly up against the village, a stronger defensive measure—a wall—was installed by the Israelis (see before and after in figures 2 and 3). The Israelis justified the building of the wall as being necessary to deter other types of attacks.

> So the Israelis went ahead building the wall. This was done in extremely close coordination with us, and through us, with the LAF to ensure that

3. The Blue Line after the construction of the security wall, Metulla. (Courtesy Vanessa Newby, August 2012)

no part of that wall, the wall itself, its foundations belowground, barbed wire on the top, protruded into Lebanese territory. And it's right there— it is on the Blue Line. . . . All the parties felt they didn't want to do that. But the Israelis decided that operationally that was the decision they were going to take. Which has obviously helped to decrease incidents a lot in that area.[31]

Organized Protests

Organized protests occur on the Blue Line on significant days on the calendar of the Palestinian resistance movement. These days include Land Day, March 30 (which commemorates resistance by the Palestinians in 1976 in response to forced Israeli land appropriations), Nakba Day (the tragedy), May 15 (which marks the Israeli announcement of the independent state of Israel), and al-Naksah (the setback) on June 5 (which commemorates Palestinian dismay at the Israelis winning the Six-Day War). On these occasions a gathering of Palestinians and supporters of the Palestinian cause can lead to confrontation with Israeli troops. The worst case was reported on May 15, 2011, when protesters attempted to scale the technical fence and enter Israel. These events led to intense discussions between Israel, Lebanon, and UNIFIL in the tripartite meetings about how operations could be mitigated to prevent death, injury, and escalation (discussed later).

Air Violations

Another major source of tension is the daily Israeli air violations conducted in the form of drone and fixed-wing aircraft surveillance. At times the Israelis will increase aerial activity, generating sonic booms that sound like bomb explosions and occur across the length and breadth of Lebanon. Alternatively, from time to time, particularly after an incident with Hezbullah, they will conduct mock air raids over local towns in the South.[32] UNIFIL can only record and protest these violations at the tripartite meetings and in their reports to the secretary-general, who unfailingly mentions them in every report on Resolution 1701.[33] UNIFIL recognizes that the air violations are a major source of irritation to the local population, who view UNIFIL's inability to prevent them as an indication of UNIFIL's weak position vis-à-vis Israel or as a sign that UNIFIL is biased toward Israel.

Weapons Pointing

Incidents involving weapons pointing have the potential to swiftly escalate tensions between the LAF and the IDF. In these instances, UNIFIL peacekeepers often try to intervene by walking unarmed between the two parties: "And take last month, the IDF were doing work on the Blue Line; we sent our teams to both sides. The LAF eventually came down; suddenly, they started pointing rifles at each other. It could have escalated very quickly, but our liaison team was on the ground and just told everyone to calm down and put their rifles down. They didn't want to lose face, so we had to organize that both sides put their rifles down at the same time."[34] At other times, the parties have pointed their weapons at UNI-FIL.[35] This type of confrontation occurs sporadically and differs in the level of seriousness attributed to it.[36]

Rocket Attacks

Rocket attacks from Lebanon into Israel constitute a serious violation of the Blue Line. These incidents usually cause insignificant damage, owing to the inaccuracy of the rockets, which rarely pierce the "Iron Dome" created by Israel.[37]

After a rocket attack, UNIFIL is quick to respond and conducts an investigation in order to reassure the Israelis that it was not launched by Hezbullah, as Israel perceives a Hezbullah rocket attack as a much more serious threat relative to an attack by other less organized groups. The most common sources of random rocket attacks in recent years have been al-Qaeda-affiliated groups and pro-Palestinian groups that operate in the area. A random rocket attack from other groups may not receive a response in kind from Israel, as UNIFIL works hard to liaise with the IDF to reassure them that this event is in fact a one-off and not the resumption of hostilities by Hezbullah. As one UNIFIL officer noted, "You see, for example, you have, from time to time, firing of rockets. This is not the main players who are doing it. Let's say Hezbullah and Israel. And immediately we tell Israel it is not Hezbullah, [and] things cool down."[38]

The parties on both sides of the Blue Line do not always cooperate with UNIFIL in these instances. For example, after a rocket-launching incident on August 22, 2013, UNIFIL was denied permission to investigate the site of the rocket landings in Israel until the Israelis had investigated the site and removed the remnants of the rockets. UNIFIL officers were then taken to a laboratory in Israel and shown the remains of the rockets but could not verify whether they were the actual rockets that had been fired, as they had not been allowed to access the site before it was tampered with: "At the impact sites in Israel, remnants of the rockets had been removed by the Israeli authorities prior to the visit of the UNIFIL investigation team. On 27 August, UNIFIL investigators inspected the purported remnants of the rockets at a laboratory in Israel and found them to be 122-mm caliber rockets. The 'Brigades of Abdullah Azzam, Ziad Jar-rah Battalions' claimed responsibility for the rocket attacks, but UNIFIL is not in a position to determine the veracity of this claim."[39]

Equally, a secretary-general's report of June 26, 2013, noted that UNI-FIL requested permission from the LAF to excavate a rocket-launching site after it had been denied access to the site by local civilians shortly after the launch had occurred. The LAF also refused permission:[40]

> With regard to the explosion in Tayr Harfa (Sector West) on 17 Decem-ber, UNIFIL found that eyewitness accounts, the material damage caused and the metallic ordnance fragments collected at the site all pointed to the detonation of a large quantity of explosives. UNIFIL was unable to determine the cause of the explosion definitively, however, as the site had been disturbed before UNIFIL and Lebanese Armed Forces investigation teams could access it, leaving the possibility that evidence had been lost. The UNIFIL request to excavate the explosion site was not accepted by the Lebanese Armed Forces.[41]

At the international and national levels, accurate reporting is part of how UNIFIL wins technical and responsiveness credibility. Hence, these situa-tions leave UNIFIL frustrated that it is unable to fully and effectively play its role as an impartial observer if it cannot be relied upon to provide a clear and full explanation of these attacks when they occur.

Random rocket attacks also erode confidence between the parties, most particularly on the Israeli side, who use these incidents to justify intrusive security measures on the Blue Line, such as building defensive walls, conducting ground incursions, and installing electronic surveil-lance equipment along the technical fence capable of eavesdropping on the entire population of Lebanon.[42] The attacks also weaken the LAF's standing with the IDF, as they demonstrate that they are unable to guar-antee Israel's security against such attacks. This situation is frustrating for UNIFIL, as part of UNIFIL's exit strategy is to ensure that the LAF is viewed by Israel as a capable defense force.

Rapid response, investigation, and the provision of information are the strategies used by UNIFIL to earn responsiveness credibility from the parties while monitoring the Blue Line. Having recorded everything, the information is sent to the secretary-general's office in New York to inform the triannual reports on Resolution 1701. These reports act as a constraint on the parties by shining an international spotlight on them, neither of whom wish to receive negative international attention. As noted by Mac-Queen, "Providing a certain element of political theatre has always been a significant part of the peacekeeping role."[43]

How Technical Credibility Assists with Prevention

Technical credibility refers to a demonstrated commitment to good governance. In a peacekeeping environment, it can include helping to build institutions, managing negotiations between the parties in a transparent manner, providing training, providing accurate information, and capacity building. UNIFIL's technical credibility at the international level has been earned by generating several transparent processes that facilitate good governance of the Blue Line. To conduct this work, UNIFIL is highly engaged with the military forces of the parties at the strategic level to try to prevent confrontations. This work is conducted largely by UNIFIL liaison officers, political affairs officers, and the force commander. The governance mechanisms used by UNIFIL are the tripartite meetings, microsecurity agreements, and marking the Blue Line. The pursuit of these activities involves extensive liaison between UNIFIL, the IDF, and the LAF.

The Tripartite Meetings

The tripartite meetings are a security institution established on August 14, 2006, the day that Resolution 1701 was implemented, and are unique to UN peacekeeping. The meetings are extremely unusual because they involve the coming together of the militaries of two states that remain technically at war, with UNIFIL acting as intermediary. While at the international political level there is a complete absence of a peace process, in a small room on the Blue Line in Ras Naqoura (in Arabic) or Rosh Haniqa (in Hebrew), security issues on the Blue Line are debated between the IDF and the LAF. At these meetings, the parties do not speak directly to one another, despite being seated across the table. Instead, each side addresses the UNIFIL force commander, who relays the information to the other side.

The tripartite meetings are held on average once every four to six weeks. Present at the meeting are the force commander of UNIFIL, fourteen senior UNIFIL staff, and six or seven representatives each from the LAF and the IDF. The schedule, which includes a script and the order of the discussion, is agreed upon several days beforehand, which helps make events at the meeting predictable. The tripartite meetings are regarded by UN headquarters in New York as an extremely positive aspect of UNIFIL's work in maintaining international peace and security, as evidenced by their frequent mention in the secretary-general reports: "[The meetings are] the most significant stabilizing factor within the framework of resolution 1701 (2006), serving to build confidence between the parties and defuse tension in potential flashpoints, as well as providing a platform through which UNIFIL can facilitate practical arrangements on the ground between the Lebanese Armed Forces and the Israel Defense Forces."[44]

The benefits of the tripartite meetings are multiple and important as a confidence-building mechanism. In emergencies they ensure that UNIFIL can keep the parties in communication to avoid a deterioration of relations. For example, on December 15, 2014, a LAF soldier shot and killed an IDF soldier patrolling on the Israeli side of the Blue Line. UNIFIL convened an extraordinary tripartite meeting the following day to preserve confidence and establish the facts and circumstances of what had occurred. On this occasion the LAF was able to directly express its regret over the incident to the IDF and reiterate that it had been an isolated incident.[45]

The meetings also provide an opportunity for liaison on key security issues that enable both sides to plan and prepare for upcoming political protests near the Blue Line, conduct maintenance work on the Israeli technical fence, mark a point on the Blue Line, or arrive at a microsecurity agreement on a specific issue that has the potential to spark incidents.

Another important result of the tripartite meetings has been the development of a liaison protocol between the parties to better manage security incidents. The liaison protocol ensures that UNIFIL liaison officers are able to contact a counterpart in the IDF and the LAF immediately when a problem arises on the Blue Line. The sheer number of UNIFIL liaison officers (twenty-seven from fifteen countries) indicates the important role that they play in managing tensions that arise from incidents. Like the tripartite meetings, the liaison protocol is not a written document but a verbal agreement to which the parties and UNIFIL adhere. One LAF officer described it thus: "There is a system, but we can put it as goodwill; it's not a document. . . . And so this worked very well [since 2006]."[46]

Additional benefits of the tripartite meetings are that they not only provide a forum for UNIFIL to report the findings of its investigations into incidents on the Blue Line, but also allow UNIFIL to protest to one or both of the parties simultaneously. The meeting enables UNIFIL to discuss how similar issues can be resolved in the future. "And so it's a forum for liaison and coordination. . . . Once we've written these reports we give them to the parties and we discuss them. And the parties protest or say they like this or they don't like this, etc. But generally we have a basic agreement on what needs to be done to ensure these incidents don't happen again."[47]

The meetings also provide an environment whereby both sides can air their grievances, vent their feelings, and protest an incident: "The tripartite meetings allow them to let off steam. If both sides want to shout and yell about each other, they can do so. They can let off steam, they can put their points of view—they have very different points of view—they have very forceful arguments, but it is an effective forum in that sense. Both sides get a lot out of it."[48]

In creating the tripartite meetings, UNIFIL has won technical credibility, and the resultant governance that has emerged from this informal institution has been helpful in negotiating the politics between the parties and building some stability and predictability into the everyday security practices of UNIFIL on the Blue Line.

Brokering Microsecurity Agreements

As noted above, the tripartite meetings have also enabled both sides to agree on microsecurity arrangements that are preventative. For example, on May 15, 2011, pro-Palestinian protesters attacked the Blue Line, triggering a violent response from the IDF, leading to the death of 6 civilians and 111 injured. After an investigation, an agreement was reached between the parties on what measures could be employed to prevent incidents of a similar nature from recurring:

> We conducted a very thorough investigation, and we recommended that the LAF do more to ensure, well, firstly, do not allow such demonstrations so close to the Blue Line. And secondly, make proper assurances that they will be policed to ensure that people do not move to the Blue Line. And on the other side, we said to the Israelis that they should use rubber bullets and various antiriot gear, tear gas, etc., along the Blue Line. . . . [W]e very clearly laid out our recommendations; we very strongly implored the parties to fulfill those recommendations. . . . [A]nd both parties have implemented those. We haven't had another problem on the Blue Line, on this side, since then, and the Israelis, as I understand it, have implemented quite a few changes to the way that their soldiers comport themselves along the Blue Line.[49]

Many of these agreements are proactive, designed to reduce tensions before they occur. For example, there are agreements designed to enable Lebanese farmers to harvest land that now lies south of the Blue Line: "Like, for example, we have olive fields at Rueda, where we have fields that cross the Blue Line. In 2010 we were able to persuade the Israelis to allow certain farmers to cultivate their olives south of the Blue Line—we had to fence them in. This was on the understanding that we would mark the Blue Line, but because of lack of agreement between the two parties, we weren't able to finalize that marking. But it was an effective way, at least for that year, for farmers to cultivate their olives."[50]

These agreements are not easy to achieve and require patience and transparency. One officer described how these deals are struck:

> You know, it's so difficult to even get the smallest little step because there is such mistrust between the two sides. We've had successes; we've had a lot of failures. And then we've had successes that last for a little while and then evaporate. You just, you know, there's no mystery to it

either. You just use your common sense; you try to get them to agree to a small, little agreement. Something at the local level. You can look at the local level, not at the political level. I can arbitrate between this guy and this guy, "Okay, you do this, and you do that," that way I can do it. And that can work, and then you get a little bit of confidence in that and then you try . . . it's like going up the stairs, one step at a time. But you can sometimes go one up and two back.[51]

The liaison and communication channels that UNIFIL has established since 2006 appear to make a strong contribution to the prevention of war. That UNIFIL has managed to establish the tripartite meetings and sustain them is no small achievement. However, as noted previously, the strategic environment is currently conducive to both sides not wishing to engage militarily. Should the environment change significantly, there is every chance that these important mechanisms for conflict prevention could be discarded. But while the named parties remain in agreement to the terms of Resolution 1701, these agreements help to prevent needless security incidents on the Blue Line that always have the potential to escalate into a bigger conflict.

Marking the Blue Line

Marking the Blue Line is another example of how UNIFIL earns technical credibility. The concept of the Blue Line came into being in 2000 as Israeli troops were preparing to leave the "security zone" they had occupied since 1982. The need to agree on a line became imperative in order for the UN to be able to declare that Israel had fully agreed to the terms of UNSC Resolution 425 that called for Israel to withdraw from Lebanon within its "internationally recognized boundaries."[52] The politics of agreeing to the Blue Line, while myriad,[53] were in principle not difficult because the UN already had two existing lines to work with: the Paulet-Newcomb of 1923, named after the two diplomats from France and Britain, respectively, who had drawn it up,[54] and the 1949 Armistice Line (sometimes known as the Armistice Demarcation Line), agreed upon between the states of Israel and Lebanon in March of that year.[55] Both states in principle agree with many parts of the Blue Line, with some exceptions, such as Shebaa Farms.

The Blue Line was so named because it was originally drawn on a map in blue ink.[56] Once the line was agreed upon, on July 24, 2000, UNIFIL was able to certify Israeli compliance with Resolution 425.[57] In 2000 the Blue Line became a "fact," consisting of three elements, according to Meier: "the map, a list of selected points entitled 'electronic line' and the markers on the ground." After the war of 2006 and subsequent revisions to the mandate, part of UNIFIL's new remit is to assist in delineating the Blue Line as much as possible because the potential for conflicts is higher in the unmarked areas. Although this task was not clearly defined in Resolution 1701, it appeared in a later mandate (UNSC Resolution 1884 in 2009) referring to Lebanon.[58]

Marking the Blue Line is an arduous technocratic task that involves extensive liaison and negotiation. UNIFIL's Joint Geographic Information Service provided a digital version of the Blue Line, and the marking of 470 coordinates (of an originally volunteered 741) has begun. As of June 2016, 249 markers had been placed on the Blue Line, of which 237 have been verified by the parties.[59] The LAF currently contests 13 areas of the Blue Line, known as "reservation areas."

Despite the time-consuming nature of marking the Blue Line, doing so reduces violations because it creates facts on the ground. Potential flare-ups usually occur in unmarked areas or LAF reservation areas. When work on the Blue Line takes place, such as repairing the Israeli technical fence, liaison officers have to negotiate extensively between the parties: "We have to control all of that and get the approval from the LAF and also notify the IDF because work cannot take place on the Blue Line until we have IDF and LAF approval. And then when work occurs on the Blue Line, I have to send a team down there to witness what's going on as the impartial referee."[60]

An unexpected challenge occurred when UNIFIL received a complaint from Israel that plainclothes men, who could have been Hezbullah or LAF Intelligence, had started standing on the blue barrels to take photographs of Israel. This situation peaked in January 2016 when the IDF threw smoke grenades to deter what turned out to be LAF Intelligence taking photos, and soon after a weapons-pointing incident occurred between the LAF and the IDF. The solution has been to put concertina wire on the Blue Line barrels to prevent people from standing on them, which requires a great deal of administrative effort: "To put a concertina wire on one Blue Line barrel means you have to cut through a minefield, and then they are doing up the Blue Line barrels because that then won't be done for another five years. And then they put concertina wire on it. . . . You can only get approval for four barrels at a time. And that takes two letters, a letter for the recce and a letter for the approval."[61]

By marking the Blue Line and making it a social fact, UNIFIL has achieved technical credibility that affords it some compliance in managing transgressions by employing a technocratic approach that utilizes "objective" knowledge and enables it to appear impartial. In light of the strong political tensions between the parties, this approach enables UNIFIL to navigate politics at the international level and put in place preventative security measures on the ground.

The Nature of Liaison between the Parties

> The Liaison Branch to me is the purest form of peacekeeping because we are not armed. We are standing there in our blue berets, and we are relying on the trust of both sides.
> —Interview with UNIFIL liaison officer, Naqoura, South Lebanon, 2016

The Liaison Office is responsible for the bulk of communication with the IDF, along with some senior staff in the Political Affairs Office and in the force commander's office. The growth and development of the Liaison Office is proving to be an effective mechanism for helping UNIFIL to quickly reassure both parties:

> We have built a very good relationship with the Israelis in that they are constantly requesting that we put a liaison team there. They don't really know the sectors, and the different units in the sectors, they might have different levels of trust with. But they're always asking us, "Can you get a liaison team there?" And the LAF normally will approve work on the

Blue Line quicker if we put in the letter that a liaison team will be there. Because they know that we will talk to them and explain what the situation is and that we will explain to both sides.[62]

The fractured nature of UN missions, whereby each battalion tends to work relatively autonomously, is caused in part by the constant rotations of peacekeeping battalions. The parties, therefore, usually prefer to speak with the Liaison Office not only because it is more efficient, but also because they will have established a relationship with a liaison officer.[63]

The liaison work of political affairs officers and liaison officers at the international level involves building strong relationships with personnel within the LAF and also the IDF. UNIFIL staff perceive trust to be crucial: "My major concern, as I said, is the level of trust. That we never lose that level of trust. That's my major concern. That is paramount to me being successful and being able to do my job."[64]

At this point it is worth briefly returning to the point made in chapter 1, where I discuss the difference between trust and confidence. I argue here that UNIFIL has built credibility, and that delivers UNIFIL the confidence of the parties that it has ability to deliver on what it says it will deliver. Confidence is built on experiences and requires evidence. Trust, on the other hand, relates to an emotional belief about the intentions and behavior of another and does not require evidence.[65] As such, while UNIFIL officers spoke about the need to build trust between the parties, I argue what they are actually speaking about is confidence, because, like credibility, confidence needs to be sustained by evidence; it cannot be won on a feeling, unlike trust.

Maintaining this confidence is a key concern of new UNIFIL staff who rely on it when navigating specific issues and have to build confidence as quickly as possible. New staff who are usually on a one-year rotation can find this challenging and sometimes do have to act in good faith: "You have to build up a relationship with the guy, the interlocutor you're talking to. Because when you need him—sometimes you have a general's foot on your neck looking for information very quickly—we have to make a request like 'Look, I need this information now.' But you have to rely on goodwill that the stuff that he's giving you isn't like—you know?"[66]

Some key members of staff in the Political Affairs Office have been working for UNIFIL for ten years or longer. These staff members are invaluable in terms of enabling UNIFIL to maintain important relationships over time, educate newcomers, and retain institutional memory. Having been involved with UNIFIL for this length of time affords these staff members a great deal of leverage with the parties: "And I have my own credibility. I've been working with them a long time, you know? So they know my, the cut of my jib. . . . This job that I do is all personal. If I get a degree from somewhere, that won't stand with me—it's purely personal. It's a personal relationship you have with the two sides, simple as that. It's how you do business with them. Just try to be honest with them, and hopefully they will see you for the honest broker that you are."[67]

The qualitative difference between long-term and short-term staff is partly a solid working knowledge of history or institutional memory. This knowledge can be particularly useful when negotiating with the parties over the location of Blue Line markings, microsecurity arrangements, or farmer compensation. Recalling what concessions either side has made in the past is useful in persuading the parties of a particular course of action:

> The advantage of corporate knowledge (not attainable over a twelve-month period) is a major help, to know to what was agreed in the past, what arrangements succeeded or failed. Sometimes one party or the other will try to bluff you. . . . Sometimes the parties can play with you. Maybe they tried for something in the past that was unsuccessful, and then they will try again with the new or less experienced person. It's nice to know also what are the red lines and not to fall into the same hole or mistake. One problem with UNIFIL is the turnover of military staff and this is something we have suffered from very badly.[68]

However, credibility is not just built from historical knowledge; it is also generated by long-term relationships between specific individuals. In the Middle East, as in many parts of the world, relationships are key. Track record and reputation can only be acquired over time. As one senior staff member noted, "Only after you have been involved in a number of incidents or events do you get the 'added value' with the parties. When they deem that you are objective and understand or empathize with their position while also respecting the other side—so being an honest broker—you get the recognition. It's also about having influence within your own organization and with the other party and your ability to get a deal and deliver."[69]

Another difference in the nature of the relationship between a rotating staff member and a long-serving staff member was described as being tactical versus preventative. The tactical benefits of the liaison officer are that he can deconflict soldier-on-soldier or civilian incidents along the Blue Line efficiently, a task one UNIFIL staff member described as the "first line of peacekeeping defense."[70] The work of the Liaison Office therefore is regarded as critically important as an on-the-spot de-escalation mechanism. It can be achieved with very little mission knowledge of the big picture, and the main attributes of a good liaison officer are common sense and an ability to communicate.

Ultimately, in this relationship there is only so much that can be achieved in the short term because the parties know that the rotating staff member is not in it for the long haul. As such, it is unlikely that a short-term staff member will obtain exposure to the decision makers further up the chain. The more experienced and long-term staff, on the other hand, are responsible for finding longer-term solutions or arrangements. As one long-term staffer remarked, "It's about your ability to influence over time, and this is predicated on your knowledge of the mission, its history, and agenda."[71]

While long-term relationships are important and helpful, UNIFIL's self-professed need to constantly maintain the confidence of both sides again illustrates how it has built credibility and not legitimacy. Time plays a role in helping staff to exercise influence at higher levels, but UNIFIL staff are acutely aware that one mistake can easily erode that confidence.

Another key issue for staff in political affairs and liaison is the need to maintain impartiality at both the professional and the personal levels. Just as the troops on the ground have to maintain the same posture irrespective of whom they are dealing with, so do officers at headquarters, irrespective of their personal perspective on the security policies of either of the named parties.

In the Liaison Office a key task is to make sure that liaison staff who work on the Israeli side are not co-opted and are able to remain impartial at all times: "We have one team on their side—sometimes two teams—and they would go to functions with the Israelis just to build up relationships with the Israelis, but we have to be careful then that they aren't overly built up and that suddenly these guys aren't being plugged for information the whole time."[72]

UNIFIL's approach to ensuring that the parties view UNIFIL as impartial is to maintain transparency and honesty in all aspects of its dealings with both sides. As part of this effort, key staff members must ensure that they are not credited by either side for having been the decision maker on any given issue. It is crucial that the parties understand that liaison officers are passing on the message; they represent the UN and have not made the decision personally. It means sometimes passing on information that is unpopular and that it is essential to be clear about: "Transparency is easy. But honesty, because sometimes you don't want to tell it. Because sometimes you have to deliver information that they don't want to hear and that they don't accept. And they don't like it. You know the story 'Don't shoot the messenger'? You know, we are often the messenger and the go-between. Sometimes I've said, 'I'm trying to do the exchange, but it's not me. . . . I am not negotiating for myself.' And that's where you have to be careful in that respect."[73]

Personal sentiments also need to be managed. UNIFIL mission staff live on the Lebanese side of the Blue Line, and they have to be careful not to let their local environment influence their impartiality. Time plays a role here too in that some staff witnessed the events of 2006 or even earlier Israeli occupations of the area. As a result, one long-term staff member commented that it was crucial "not to allow your own sentiments to get involved. Basically on a day-to-day basis, you can't afford that luxury, you just can't. Because then you are one-sided, you know?"[74]

The challenge for UNIFIL politically is that the mission is unable to patrol on the Israeli side of the Blue Line and thus far has not been given permission by the Israeli government to establish an office in Tel Aviv.[75] However, the fact that key senior UNIFIL staff reside on the Lebanese side of the Blue Line means that the IDF has the perception that UNIFIL staff may be biased. In addition, the highly politicized environment in which UNIFIL operates means that both parties resent certain nationalities. The Lebanese are more suspicious of states that have diplomatic relations with Israel, and Israel is more suspicious of states that they view as pro-Palestinian.

Daily Life on the Blue Line

In the final part of this chapter I discuss the everyday security practices of UNIFIL and provide very different examples of how UNIFIL has managed three different types of incidents on the Blue Line: livestock hostages and natural disasters, a confrontation between the parties, and incidents between the IDF and an unofficial party to the conflict, Hezbullah. These examples illustrate how the smallest of incidents can escalate into conflict, how the political environment constrains UNIFIL, and how UNIFIL navigates these challenges.

Livestock Hostages and Natural Disasters

As mentioned previously, one of the most common complaints the UNIFIL Liaison Office receives is from local farmers communicating through the LAF that their livestock have been captured and detained by the IDF. These hostage situations can last for up to thirty-six hours, but not indefinitely, because the Israeli Ministry of Agriculture and Rural Development does not want livestock to remain in Israel that may not be vaccinated.

The Liaison Office responds to these complaints by calling their contacts on the Israeli side and organizing for a release. The situation becomes more challenging when one of the parties is not aware of or denies the incident, because it can damage the confidence that UNIFIL has in the parties. An example of this type of incident occurred between the parties in July 2016 with the rumored kidnapping of 450 goats that the Israelis denied having captured. A liaison officer explained the situation: "We have to have a trust that we're getting the right information, that we're not telling lies. I mean, yesterday with the goats; I have my doubts, but they said to me four times 'We didn't take them,' so I believe the liaison officer didn't know that they had taken them."[76]

On this occasion the liaison officer had to believe that the Israeli liaison officer had not received communication from staff in the area where the incident occurred. Similarly, UNIFIL can be just as ignorant of events:

> A month ago the Israelis rang me and said they had sheep and goats. The LAF and Sector East said no one took any goats! And they [the Israelis] said, "But we have them! We want to give them back." I said, "Well, no one here is missing them." And then he said, "The Israeli Department of Agriculture is getting on to me, and I have to give them back immediately," and I said, "But no one is missing any," you know? So we had to ring around, "Anyone missing sheep?" and nobody said yes.[77]

On this occasion, the livestock were returned to Lebanon by the IDF under cover of darkness and unfortunately were deposited into a minefield. This move necessitated UNIFIL clearing a path by which to herd the livestock back to safe ground, despite not knowing to whom they belonged. Eventually, the livestock were claimed by a local farmer.

Other issues of tension can arise from natural events such as a tree growing into the technical fence or forest fires, which are common in summer. On the same day as the alleged goat kidnapping, a forest fire on the Lebanese side raged close to the Blue Line, setting off land mines and threatening to spread into Israel, damaging the technical fence in the process. The Liaison Office was drawn into this situation because of a dispute arising on the ground as to who should douse the fire. A standoff occurred because the Israeli fire engine arrived first on the scene and wanted to extinguish the fire by spraying water over the technical fence. The LAF opposed this idea, stating that the Lebanese would put out Lebanese fires and the Israelis could put out their own fires. The liaison officer had to decide on the spot whether to allow the IDF to direct their hoses over the technical fence to extinguish the fire, risk upsetting the LAF, and possibly triggering a security incident. On this occasion, before events degenerated further, the Lebanese fire engine arrived and dealt with the fire.

Both these cases show that regular communication between the liaison teams and the parties prevents these minor incidents from escalating. In this way, UNIFIL wins responsiveness credibility, in that the parties rely on the liaison team to be present and impartial.

Shoot-Out at al-Addaisseh

At the international level, one of the more serious violations of Resolution 1701 occurs when the armies of Lebanon and Israel engage. One of the major fears of UNIFIL is the risk that one actor on the ground, termed the strategic corporal,[78] will take an action that is not supported at higher levels, triggering an incident neither side wants: "So the strategic corporal is the guy on the ground—some soldier, some officer—who can make a stupid mistake, or make a stupid decision, that brings his country to war. And that's the chap you have to watch out for."[79]

An example of how the most minor of events can trigger a serious confrontation can be seen in the last serious engagement that occurred between the LAF and the IDF in 2010 on the Blue Line near the village of al-Addaisseh. The incident revolved around the trimming of a cherry tree whose branches were overhanging the technical fence and triggering the sensors on a regular basis. Unfortunately, the tree was located in an LAF reservation area.[80] On this occasion, the IDF had called UNIFIL only two hours before they started to cut the tree. UNIFIL requested that the work be delayed by a day so that UNIFIL could conduct the trimming of the tree. Both parties declined this offer, the LAF on the grounds that they would not accept any attempt to alter the tree as it resided on contested land. As a result, both militaries faced off on either side of the line, while the IDF attempted to trim the tree from the Israeli side. The moment the LAF felt that the IDF had stepped into Lebanese territory, shots were fired, and the incident spiraled into a three-hour gunfight involving machine guns, rocket-propelled grenades, tank rounds, artillery rounds, and missiles fired from helicopters.[81] In the course of the skirmish, three LAF soldiers and one journalist were killed.

Present at the time was an Indonesian UNIFIL battalion on the Lebanese side, but as a peacekeeping force they were unable to do more than observe and advise the LAF not to escalate the situation. When the battle broke out, the Indonesian troops ran for cover into a nearby building.

UNIFIL's response was to contact the headquarters of the parties, through a series of telephone calls, to stop the battle: "We get on to Tel Aviv, to IDF headquarters, and then from there on to Northern Command of the IDF, and we say, 'Listen, tell your guys to back off, cool down.' Same with the other side: 'Pull back, pull back, stop the firing, you know, relax.' No mystery, other than talking."[82]

Often at the senior levels the escalation on the ground is not supported. Timing and repeated communication are essential to allow both sides to cool down at the same time. The liaison officer has to work as quickly as possible, with the aid of other senior colleagues, to ensure that at the senior level the parties are able to contact their troops on the ground to cool them down: "[We need to] get a cease-fire in place. Because with a cease-fire, one guy [will say], 'They're still firing.' [We say,] 'Where are they still firing?' [and then they say,] 'Well, we stopped firing, but they started firing. We stopped, but they didn't, so we returned the fire because they didn't.' So we've got to go through all this kind of stuff, so eventually you've got to, kinda, put the fire out."[83]

Once the incident had been de-escalated, the process of investigation took place, and UNIFIL liaised with both sides to establish what occurred. The incident was reported back to UN headquarters in New York and received mention in the secretary-general reports. In Lebanon, UNIFIL convened an emergency tripartite meeting to discuss the incident and its repercussions. UNIFIL sought agreement between the parties on putting measures in place to prevent a similar incident from occurring. UNIFIL now ensures that an unarmed liaison team is present when maintenance work needs to be conducted on the Blue Line and that plenty of advance notice is provided.

The shoot-out at al-Addaisseh has not been repeated, but the immediate and long-term effects were damaging. One UNIFIL official told me that the incident had destroyed about "two years' worth of trust" between the parties that UNIFIL then had to try to rebuild.[84] The event also illustrates the political challenges that UNIFIL faces within the operation itself. UNIFIL is currently composed of troops from forty countries, and different nationality contingents deal with situations very differently. The Indonesian battalion at al-Addaisseh that day did not attempt to walk between the parties to prevent an escalation of a tense weapons-pointing situation. Another battalion may have chosen to do so or managed the situation in another way.

Present at the scene were also a number of Lebanese journalists and television crews observing the action, which meant that the incident received a lot of attention, not least because one journalist was killed in the crossfire.[85] The local civilian interpretation of the event was that UNIFIL was doing nothing, whereas behind the scenes it was doing everything to stop the fight. This event, however, damaged UNIFIL's reputation with the local population because it illustrated to civilians that UNIFIL did not have security credibility; in the local view, UNIFIL could not prevent the IDF from attacking Lebanon.

Despite the poor performance, or perceptions of poor performance, on the ground that day, UNIFIL was able to contribute to the prevention of another war through their liaison with both sides at the time of the incident:

> Yes, we are a stabilizing force, because of al-Addaisseh and lots of other incidents. We are the water on the fire; we can put out the wars. . . . UNIFIL can intervene and stop it at that critical time. So yes, we are that force that can stop the fighting, we do stop the fighting, and we have stopped the fighting. We have stopped a war breaking out on a few occasions. For sure we have stopped it. But if they decide to go at it, they'll do it; they'll do it. Like at al-Addaisseh, somebody decided they wanted to fire.[86]

The LAF and the IDF have not resumed any battles since the incident at al-Addaisseh, and UNIFIL has been able to prevent the escalation of tensions between the parties when incidents occur on the Blue Line. However, the conflict that UNIFIL faces between its mandate and the politics of both inter- and intrastate struggles is particularly acute when faced with the challenge of controlling a nonstate actor that is not an official party to the terms of Resolution 1701.

Hezbullah versus the IDF

While UNIFIL engages with Hezbullah at the political level within the municipalities, it does not have a mandate to liaise directly with Hezbullah's military wing. This political problem (detailed in chapter 2) causes UNIFIL the most damage to its security credibility with Israel and is the hardest to manage, as Hezbullah is not a named party to Resolution 1701.

Hezbullah's local and national supporters argue that a Hezbullah presence close to the border is justified because the LAF is currently insufficiently equipped to defend Lebanese soil in the event of another Israeli invasion. When asked, Lebanese civilians in the area of operations argued that they want the LAF to be the only source of security, but not until they present as a stronger force capable of deterring Israel.[87] Local support for Hezbullah in the area of operations is high, which makes it impossible for UNIFIL to place too much emphasis on proactive weapons searching without risking the loss of local consent.

Officially, UNIFIL argues that because Hezbullah was part of the Lebanese government when the resolution was agreed upon, it should be subject to the terms and conditions of the resolution: "Look, when 1701 was signed, Hezbullah were part of the government, right? So they knew what they were signing themselves up to. So they removed themselves from the South. They weren't kicked out. They removed themselves."[88]

Prior to 2006, border clashes between the IDF and Hezbullah were frequent owing to Hezbullah's presence on the line in UNIFIL's area of operation. Since 2006 Hezbullah has withdrawn north of the Litani River, and it is generally acknowledged by the LAF and UNIFIL staff that Hezbullah's physical armed presence in the area of operations has been greatly reduced: "You know, we didn't push them out—they left. Because you can never push these guys out—you can't. These guys left because they wanted to leave. And they signed up to something, and they left. They only left across the river. They're just on the other side, fine, but they left. So we don't see Hezbullah. I was here before the war, and during the war, you don't see Hezbullah day to day anymore."[89]

Hezbullah, however, is perceived by the IDF to be the only real threat to Israeli security. Israel believes UNIFIL's security credibility lies in eradicating Hezbullah's presence, not monitoring the border. As such, any activity that Israel deems to be the work of Hezbullah receives a much stronger reaction.[90] Oftentimes, when Hezbullah is active on the border, it is in response to IDF breaches, such as in the village of Labouneh near the Blue Line in August 2013 when four Israeli soldiers crossed over into Lebanon and were injured by booby traps laid by Hezbullah, for which the organization publicly took credit.[91] However, in 2015 and 2016, Hezbullah and the IDF engaged in brief military skirmishes, which again damages UNIFIL's security credibility and its claim to be maintaining international peace and security.

Hezbullah's violations of Resolution 1701 cannot be dealt with in the same way as violations between the parties for three reasons. First, Hezbullah is not considered to be an official party; second, UNIFIL would have to speak with Hezbullah's military wing, which is not permitted; and third, UNIFIL must be very careful not to inflame local sentiment by going hard after Hezbullah. Therefore, in terms of dealing with a deliberate violation of the Blue Line by Hezbullah, there is little that UNIFIL can do other than conduct an investigation after the fact. UNIFIL staff admit that there may be some weapons in the area of operation, but they are constrained in their ability to locate them: "We do what we can under our mandate. Some people say it isn't enough and we should do more, but then, you know, if you want to do more, you have to have a Chapter VII peace-enforcement mandate; you'd be acting without the authority of the government, and you would come across widespread opposition from the local people, and you'd probably end up similar to what happened to the MNF [Multinational Force in Lebanon] in 1983."[92]

The current strategic environment currently precludes overly aggressive action by Hezbullah against Israel and vice versa. The Syrian crisis has taken precedence, and neither side is keen to relaunch a full-scale war. Hence, the skirmishes of both 2015 and 2016 were proportionate and non-escalatory. UNIFIL officers are pragmatic about the current strategic environment: "But I don't think the situation is calm because Hezbullah left [the area of operations]. I think it's calm because until now, the parties are living up to 1701 like they said they would. That's why it's calm. Because there is no intention to start shooting, no side wants to start shooting."[93]

Hezbullah and Israeli confrontations render UNIFIL's security credibility at the international, national, and local levels very low. But as a peacekeeping force, UNIFIL can keep the peace only when there is a peace to keep. UNIFIL cannot be blamed for the mandate or the highly politicized conditions under which it functions. UNIFIL therefore concentrates on building other types of credibility such as responsiveness and technical credibility to reassure the parties that it is doing everything in its power to neutralize tensions. On a day-to-day basis it does so by effectively preventing small incidents from escalating into the resumption of conflict.

Conclusion

Between two states at war, there is always the potential for small localized incidents to develop into a conflict that precipitates war. While UNIFIL cannot change the larger strategic environment within which it operates, it can make a significant contribution to the local security environment by supporting the normalization of peace. Much depends on the provision of accurate and timely information and constant liaison that maintains the confidence necessary to de-escalate incidents at critical moments. Irrespective of the international legitimacy of the United Nations, on the ground it is credibility with the named parties that affords the mission cooperation.

4 Credibility with National Institutions

At the national level UNIFIL works with national and local institutions in Lebanon. The techniques UNIFIL employs—liaison, negotiation, pragmatism, collaboration, and technocracy—win technical and material credibility and obtain the mission the benefits of cooperation and confidence with local government and the LAF.[1] Documented largely through the eyes of UNIFIL, I show how the mission not only engages in a traditional "peacekeeping" role, but has also proactively engaged in peacebuilding activities to assist the national government of Lebanon by working to consolidate the authority of the Lebanese Armed Forces and local government in the South of the country. UNIFIL's work at the national level is designed to "bring the state back in" to the area of operations, which for decades was severely neglected by central government. This task is not always easy: "Sometimes we find ourselves to be a bit of a political football, kicked around. But our primary focus is to stay out of Lebanese politics as far as possible. And I think we are quite successful at staying out. . . . Our key central message is that we are here to support the LAF and Resolution 1701 in our area of operations in the South of Lebanon. And it will remain like that unless the Security Council were to change it."[2]

Despite UNIFIL's long-term presence in the region, the mission has an exit strategy, albeit perhaps a distant goal. In the absence of a peace agreement between the Lebanese and Israeli governments, UNIFIL's objectives at the national level are twofold. In supporting local government and capacity building the LAF, UNIFIL works to ensure that South Lebanon possesses a functioning local government in the region (to avoid the reemergence of an administrative vacuum) and a national security presence in South Lebanon up to the Blue Line. The corollary is that a secure environment coupled with a national government presence in the South will facilitate the necessary stability to stimulate economic growth and help to create conditions for peace.

At UNIFIL headquarters in Naqoura, staff involved in national institution building are the political affairs officers and civil affairs officers. Political affairs officers ensure that the force commander is informed of political developments, produce reports for the UN headquarters and the secretary-general, manage tripartite and bilateral liaison with Israel, liaise with the United Nations Special Coordinator for Lebanon (UNS-COL), and capacity build the LAF.[3] Civil affairs officers work at the local level and liaise with the local population, manage civilian funding projects (quick impact projects), and work with local government "municipalities."[4]

Despite their subnational remit, UNIFIL political affairs officers occasionally engage with the national government, mainly through the office of UNSCOL. UNSCOL coordinates the work of the UN in Lebanon with the Lebanese government, and its key focus is the implementation of United Nations Security Council Resolution 1701. This work includes liaising with Lebanon's political parties and neighbors to obtain full adherence to Resolution 1701, advocating for coordinated donor assistance to Lebanon in consultation with the UN country team and the Lebanese government, and coordinating that donor assistance from the core group of donor countries. Most of UNIFIL's work, however, is conducted directly with the LAF and the local government in South Lebanon.

UNIFIL's Support of Local Government

In its work with local municipalities, UNIFIL wins technical and material credibility through negotiation and liaison, collaboration, and a technocratic approach. As with the international engagement of UNIFIL, these techniques are designed to navigate the political environment in which UNIFIL operates to retain the appearance of impartiality. UNIFIL also works to engage national government in the South in the hope that it will establish regional offices, further strengthening local governance and fill-ing the administrative vacuum.

Resolution 1701 calls for the restoration of government authority in the area of operations. Earlier resolutions supported "the extension of the control of the Government of Lebanon over all Lebanese territory,"[5] and Resolution 1701 reiterated the need for "the Government of Lebanon . . . to extend its authority over its territory."[6] Although not specifically spelled out, it would appear that the UN Security Council would like the Leba-nese government to have a visible presence in South Lebanon.

It is unclear what it might mean for UN actors on the ground, but one Lebanese civil affairs officer interpreted the mandate thus: "Ah, it means for me on the ground . . . we help the local authority understand their role, their job. And help them against their shoulder to go ahead in doing their job. This is the way we are fulfilling our mandate."[7] As such, UNIFIL civil affairs officers work closely with the municipalities to raise their profile in the community. As some are Lebanese nationals, their local knowledge means that they understand local political dynamics and are able to dis-cuss with civilians and politicians alike the issues faced by the villages in the area of operations.

Until 2004, there was no functioning local government in South Lebanon. Prior to that date, the 1963 elections were the last to be held before the start of the civil war.[8] "So the state institutions were absent from 1963 until 2004. So you can imagine this big area of the country—which represents more than 15 percent of the area of the country—without any government representation for three decades. So UNIFIL's main task is not only to maintain peace and stability, but also to help the state take over its role in this area of the country. And we do this through various ways."[9]

The municipalities' main challenge has been securing funding to pro-vide the necessary services to their constituents. After decades of govern-ment neglect, the local population is not used to paying taxes for services provided by the municipality: "This area of Lebanon was out of any kind of state control. Simply, this was under occupation, and the government cannot cut the water supply or the electricity supply for the area because it is under occupation. But it cannot collect the revenue of the supply because there was occupation, you see? So people are used to not paying taxes to the municipalities. During occupation, twenty-two years of occupation here, you didn't have municipalities."[10]

Municipalities also face regular funding shortfalls caused by constant political crises at the national level. The national government is often unable to agree on or assign budgets to the regional municipalities, so most municipalities receive minimal funding from the national government, which is often two or three years in arrears. A local municipality may have money if the mayor is personally wealthy: "In Marja'youn the head of the municipality . . . he is a rich man. And all the projects he is making are from his own pocket. You know, it is not the municipality that is working; he is working to improve the town. When he will go, I don't know if we will repeat it again. Because not many people pay their taxes. Collecting money is impossible."[11] This type of situation does not contribute to the long-term strategy of having a functional local government in place. Once a wealthy mayor has left his post, there are no guarantees that an equally wealthy or generous mayor will replace him.

The region also suffers from mayoral absenteeism. Many elected officials live and work in Beirut during the week and visit their village only on weekends. One Lebanese civil affairs officer explained the situation thus: "Let me tell you something. Here with elections, it's typical Lebanese way of elections. The post of the mayor is not a place to serve. It's a place to show off. Why? Because his family is big, he is affiliated to a strong party, and his party decided to make him a mayor because his father was very important person, for so many reasons. You see? So they elect him, and the next day he disappears—for six years."[12] If the mayor is rarely present in the village, decisions cannot be made quickly, sometimes taking up to more than a month. This kind of inefficiency undermines civil affairs officer efforts to promote municipalities as committed local authorities and causes logistical problems, as the mayor is not available for meetings in the area of operation during the working week.

The positions of mayor, deputy mayor, and other members of the municipal council are regarded more as prestigious appointments than as democratically elected offices. Influential families nominate a candidate for the municipality who is expected to "win" by virtue of his family name: "Okay, it's like this. First of all, the municipality is a mix between politics and families. So our municipality is a mix between Hezbullah and Amal, but through families. So some families will say this is the name of our candidate, and we are just going to say that he is neutral, for example. And he's not Amal or Hezbullah. So some families do this. But some families don't. Some families, maybe they have two representatives, one Amal, one Hezbullah."[13] Members of the municipality do not like to be unpopular, as losing the election might prove to be an embarrassment to their families. This concern affects their ability to do their job effectively. For example, some mayors do not like to pressure the villages to collect taxes because it will make them unpopular.[14]

Technical and Material Credibility to Support Municipalities

There are 162 municipalities in UNIFIL's area of operation.[15] Each municipality consists of a mayor, a deputy mayor, and some councilors. Depending on the size of the town or village, the number of members in a municipality varies from nine to fifteen.[16] UNIFIL educates municipality members, communicates the importance of the municipality to the local population, and provides quick impact projects to local municipalities, usually costing around $25,000 per project, the majority of which involve improvements to road, water, and power facilities.[17]

UNIFIL civil affairs officers provide local municipalities with workshops on bureaucracy: "Members of the municipal councils, they come and take part in a workshop for three days, in which we bring academic professors to explain to them how to prepare their plan, how to prepare the budget for the municipality, how to do it, in a very technical way. You see, this is also capability building for the local authorities, to strengthen the local authority, regardless of what political affiliation for this municipality or that."[18]

By educating the municipalities about bureaucracy, civil affairs officers encourage responsible governance. UNIFIL hopes that this preparation might reduce corruption and inefficiency and improve the local standing of the municipalities. UNIFIL's training might not be useful in less developed states, but Lebanon is a modern democratic state (albeit with a confessional system), and this model of the state is accepted by the local population.[19] It is unclear the extent to which this assistance substantively reduces corruption or inefficiency, but municipalities do take up the offer of training. The real benefit of UNIFIL's technical expertise in this area is that it helps build communication between the mission and municipalities, which is another way of obtaining local cooperation.

UNIFIL civil affairs officers also communicate to the local population about the need to pay taxes and not to steal resources. This interaction is often done on an informal basis by traversing the area of operations and passing the time of day with local civilians. This approach is very much in tune with Lebanese village culture, which is very social and where dropping in to chat is regarded as very normal. During the course of their conversations with the local population where they inquire about local needs, civil affairs officers also explain that paying taxes is a civic duty. In regard to resource theft, they also try to educate people about the need to think of the larger community as opposed to just one's own family by explaining the importance of not stealing electricity and water from the main supply.

The key focus for civil affairs officers is to raise the profile of the municipalities among the population to convince locals to pay their taxes and become responsible citizens. This work to change local perceptions of the local municipality is important to build trust in national institutions. Civil affairs officers encourage local civilians to approach the municipalities first when they are seeking project funding to encourage them to view the municipality as the first port of call rather than UNIFIL.

Local perceptions of municipalities are affected by both the amount of resources provided and sectarianism. Some local civilians view their municipality as useless because they do not have money: "This area follows the municipality of Wazzani, which is a very, very poor municipality. It cannot help with anything."[20] Others acknowledge that many of the problems faced by the local municipalities originate from the national problems that besiege Lebanon: "We know that when they do projects, they do according to what capabilities . . . they have. They cannot spend more than what they have, and we can understand this."[21]

Sectarianism influences local perceptions of efficacy and trustworthiness of the local municipality, particularly in towns and villages where the population is divided between different religions: "It's about 40 percent confidence [in the municipality], because . . . here also the prejudice of the sectarian problem. . . . For example, when they have a festival in Marja'youn—you see, this is an annual festival. And they know that I have all the facilities, light and sound facilities, for the festival. They don't bring me, even though I give a lower price than the Christian guy. So they bring the Christians. I make a big festival in Qatar and Kuwait, but they don't want to work with me because I am Shi'a."[22]

The bulk of civil affairs officers' work with the municipalities involves the mayors in the implementation of quick impact projects to raise the profile of the municipalities among the local population. In this way they are trying to demonstrate to the local population that the municipalities are the source of local authority in the area and not UNIFIL, as one officer noted: "Whatever information or project you make through your contact with normal people, we have to go back to the municipality; we have to go back to the mayor, the deputy mayor, or the municipality."[23] UNIFIL civil affairs officers ensure that they work on every quick impact project together with the municipalities from inception to conclusion, ensuring that the municipality is involved in the end in project ceremonies.

Funding for municipalities also comes from local charities and nongovernmental organizations that approach UNIFIL for suggestions about where to donate money in the area of operations. Civil affairs officers often connect charitable organizations with the municipalities: "But we are not involved directly. We just connect them and coordinate their work with the municipality to play its role. And here we are under our mandate: to support the local authority maintain its power over the area."[24]

Being credible means demonstrating impartiality consistently over time. UNIFIL depoliticizes its assistance to the municipalities by taking a technocratic approach and builds technical credibility in three main ways: by dealing only with the municipality, by dealing with all political parties in the same manner, and by respecting the hierarchy within municipal government.

First, civil affairs officers do not approach any other community leader (such as the *mukhtar*[25] or religious leaders) when they first make contact with a village, unless the village is too small to have its own municipality and it sits under the umbrella of the municipality of another town. While civil affairs officers talk to civilians at any level of society in the course of their duties, the municipality, particularly the mayor, is always the first point of contact when seeking to establish ties with a village.

Second, UNIFIL civil affairs officers do not differentiate between political parties in the region. They operate using the hierarchy of the system as it exists on the ground. They are as happy to contact a mayor from Hezbullah as they are to contact a mayor from any other party. It is crucial that UNIFIL does business with everyone, because to refuse to do so would lead to marginalization: "We deal with them not as political parties; we deal with them as local authorities, and here we start to teach them how to be an authority. Because the municipality is the highest authority of this village or this town."[26]

Third, civil affairs officers are careful to work according to the established hierarchy within the municipalities. They therefore deal with the mayor first and foremost and then the deputy mayor. UNIFIL avoids becoming embroiled in local divisions within the municipality: "If the deputy mayor and the mayor are not on good terms, it's not our business. We deal with the mayor. He is the authority, and we explain it for the deputy mayor, because according to the law of municipalities, the mayor is the real leader of the municipality."[27]

The biggest challenge for civil affairs officers is negotiating the political gap between the international and local legitimacy of the mission. Officially, Hezbullah municipalities are given a free rein by the party to liaise with UNIFIL as they see fit. However, despite Hezbullah's consent to Resolution 1701, many Hezbullah supporters view it as a one-sided agreement that favors Israel, and therefore some Hezbullah-dominated municipalities view UNIFIL as a pro-Israeli organization that may be spying for the state of Israel.

For many municipalities, UNIFIL's assistance is appreciated, not just because of political affiliation but rather on the basis of personal relationships. Just as one mayor can refuse to do business with UNIFIL because he is affiliated with Hezbullah, another Hezbullah mayor is very happy to work with them: "This is human beings, and they are not the same everywhere, even though they are from the same party. I know people. A mayor of Hezbullah in this village is different from a mayor in that village. Completely different. One of them, you cannot say hello to him. He is all the time not friendly with you. And the other guy welcomes you, 'Hi, how are you? How's the family?' He takes fifteen minutes just asking about them before you discuss anything, just asking about your health and your family. You see?"[28] Friendly Hezbullah-run municipalities are in a better position to take advantage of UNIFIL resources, to take credit for projects, and to ensure that they are not being spied upon by making sure that cameras are not placed in buildings, infrastructure fixtures, or other equipment provided by the mission.[29]

Managing relations with the municipalities is a balancing act. UNIFIL must maintain the same attitude to all municipalities in order to remain impartial, even when some municipalities are friendlier than others. Equally, the municipalities must be seen by the local population to be independent of UNIFIL and not codependent. As such, civil affairs officers walk a fine line in terms of how much contact they maintain with each municipality while simultaneously retaining the confidence of the municipalities. Time plays an important role in building stable and predictable relationships. Furthermore, as noted previously, sustaining that confidence requires regular contact. In this way, UNIFIL obtains cooperation from the municipalities that will assist when any friction occurs between the local population and UNIFIL.

Bringing the National State Back In

One of UNIFIL's main aims in South Lebanon is to bring the national government back into the area by encouraging the establishment of regional offices to prevent a political vacuum from emerging when UNIFIL eventually leaves. If these offices are not established, nonstate groups may fill the void, creating an ungovernable area and heightening Israeli security concerns:

So the government wasn't in the South. So we try to engage these other ministries and say, "Look, guys, you need to get your people, get your offices down to the South, to support the people. Because if you don't, you have a vacuum. If you have a vacuum, somebody else is going to fill it." And somebody else like lightning will fill it. And they did after the war, because after the war was a real example of that. After the war Hezbullah were down overnight, around to the people. "Your house is damaged." Next week, guy comes along, does an inspection of the house, "Here's $1,000, maybe $10,000. Okay, look after your family, and we'll give you more later when you build a house." You know, this kind of stuff. You know, so they were very quick to get in there.[30]

Although politicians from other political parties have been hesitant to even visit the area because of the presence of the large Shi'a population that supports Hezbullah, political affairs officers have been able to persuade some of them from across the political spectrum to visit: "Now we are in a phase for the first time in history, since 1978, ministers are visiting UNIFIL. We had the minister of social affairs come here. We are bringing the government back, you see? The minister of information came, minister of social affairs came, minister of environment came, you know? So this is also part to assist the Lebanese government to restore law and order, which brings the police bringing the law, bringing the administration, and all this."[31]

Working with the municipalities earns UNIFIL both technical and material credibility. As the community sees the benefits of its municipality working with UNIFIL, it is less likely to engage in unfriendly or hostile behavior toward the patrolling contingents. When friction arises, which it does from time to time, UNIFIL can draw on the credibility it has established with a municipality to help smooth things over. By bringing the state back down to the South, UNIFIL can be said to be working toward an exit strategy and reducing the space for other substate actors to provide material benefits and further consolidate local support for their presence. While these relationships may, for all intents and purposes, be instrumental, this situation is the nature of credibility, as it is based on material interests and requires constant maintenance.

The second part of UNIFIL's national engagement is with its strategic partner, the LAF, to which I will now turn.

Cooperation between the LAF and UNIFIL

Building technical and responsiveness credibility with the Lebanese Armed Forces is an important activity for UNIFIL. Political affairs officers are engaged at the national level in peacebuilding activities with the LAF to fulfill three main objectives of the mandate: first, to assist with the reintroduction of the LAF into the area of operations; second, to work with the LAF to improve its operational capabilities; and third, to seek international funding for the LAF to improve its technical capabilities. The overall objective for UNIFIL in this respect is part of its stated exit strategy: to ensure the LAF has full authority in South Lebanon to the extent that it can control security in the area. In theory, this authority would mean the elimination of the presence of Hezbullah's military wing and other armed groups in the area.[32]

The reintroduction of the LAF throughout Lebanon is a major goal of Resolution 1701:

> Welcoming the unanimous decision by the Government of Lebanon on 7 August 2006 to deploy a Lebanese armed force of 15,000 troops in South Lebanon as the Israeli army withdraws behind the Blue Line and to request the assistance of additional forces from the United Nations Interim Force in Lebanon (UNIFIL) as needed, to facilitate the entry of the Lebanese armed forces into the region and to restate its intention to strengthen the Lebanese armed forces with material as needed to enable it to perform its duties . . . (Preamble, para. 8).[33]

The resolution also states that one of UNIFIL's duties is to provide assistance to the LAF:

> 11. Decides, in order to supplement and enhance the force in numbers, equipment, mandate and scope of operations, to authorize an increase in the force strength of UNIFIL to a maximum of 15,000 troops, and

that the force shall, in addition to carrying out its mandate under resolutions 425 and 426 (1978): . . .

(b) Accompany and support the Lebanese armed forces as they
deploy throughout the South, including along the Blue Line, as
Israel withdraws its armed forces from Lebanon as provided in
paragraph 2; . . .

(e) Assist the Lebanese armed forces in taking steps towards the establishment of the area as referred to in paragraph 8.[34]

Despite initial reservations from the local population about the reintroduction of the LAF, since 2006 UNIFIL's work with the LAF has contributed to a sense of stability in South Lebanon, particularly as the political environment remains highly unstable: "Even in times when the country didn't have a prime minister, a president, government, the South was always okay. We were always able to conduct our activities. Because the Lebanese Army has always been there. Even in times when no one was around, the Lebanese Army was there. Which is a big plus, I have to say."[35]

Prior to the outbreak of civil war in 1975, the LAF was not present in South Lebanon because the area was sparsely populated and was not regarded as strategically important.[36] After civil war broke out, a poorly resourced Lebanese military and defections to sectarian militia made any presence in the South impossible.[37] During the war, the Palestine Liberation Organization operated extensively in the area (after moving from Jordan in 1970), as did up to thirty-six militia groups, which reduced the political and operational space for the national army.[38]

The occupation of South Lebanon in 1982 by Israel also meant that there remained no space for an LAF presence. When the Israeli occupation finally ended in 2000, the LAF was not sufficiently equipped to retake the area and, having been absent for so long, no longer had the confidence of people in the South to do so.[39] While the southern Lebanese population was supportive of the idea of their national army, prior to 2006 some were more comfortable with the presence of sectarian militia groups or UNIFIL. Since 2006 UNIFIL has facilitated the return of the national army by including LAF officers on patrols, providing them with equipment and resources, and placing the LAF at the front line to deal with local and international incidents: "Everything we do, the patrolling, everything is done in coordination with the LAF."[40]

The LAF is composed of 61,400 active personnel comprising eleven mechanized brigades, four land-border regiments, six intervention regiments, three elite special operations units, and a very small army and air force.[41] In 2006 the LAF estimated it would cost about US$1 billion to equip its combined infantry, naval, and air force.[42] In 2016 the LAF maintained two brigades in South Lebanon.[43] As part of the objective of reintroducing the LAF to the area of operations, the LAF and UNIFIL conduct daily joint patrols (an estimated one thousand each month) to prevent violations of the Blue Line and to search for unexploded ordinance and unauthorized weapons.

Naturally maintaining confidence requires constant communication, coordination, and extensive liaison. At every level of the LAF and UNIFIL command structures, coordination takes place through liaison officers on both sides. These officers communicate on a daily basis to ensure that both parties are aware of the day's events, planned or otherwise. To ensure that communication is clear, liaison points have been established at different levels: the LAF officer who is designated head of the South of the Litani branch of the LAF liaises directly with the force commander of UNIFIL, and below that level the commanders of UNIFIL's two sectors, Sector East and Sector West, liaise with LAF brigade commanders.

Every morning in the UNIFIL Liaison Office a summary is produced of the events of the past twenty-four hours and discussed, usually at the most senior levels between the liaison officers of both organizations at UNIFIL headquarters. If necessary, the issue is raised to the level of the head of the South of the Litani branch of the LAF and the force commander. In addition, the headquarters of every UNIFIL battalion has a LAF officer living in the compound to ensure that there is full communication between UNIFIL and the LAF at every level.[44] When a serious incident occurs, communication between the two organizations is immediate and conducted at the top level. In this way, the two forces aim to monitor the situation on the ground as closely as possible.

When patrolling alongside the LAF, UNIFIL is careful to play the role of observer as much as possible. The LAF is deliberately placed at the forefront of any Blue Line violations involving locals to empower the LAF to deal with any situation in its own way and to help build the LAF's credibility. Furthermore, as UNIFIL is not allowed to physically restrain anyone who is violating the Blue Line, the LAF plays a key role in deciding what measures (physical or verbal) they wish to take in regard to Lebanese citizens on Lebanese territory. Intentional violations of the Blue Line occur in some areas that are close to Israeli patrol paths. Often these violations are minor, such as civilian stone throwing at IDF troops. In these situations the LAF are called in to disperse the local population, but UNIFIL maintains a presence to ensure that the LAF and the Israel Defense Forces do not engage directly.

Despite its broad popularity in the area, UNIFIL is sometimes involved in incidents with local civilians.[45] Usually, these are minor and relate to UNIFIL patrols taking the wrong road or patrolling at night and making noise. Occasionally, criminals will hold up the convoys and steal equipment. On such occasions, UNIFIL's strategy is always to stand back, take a passive posture, and call in the LAF to defuse the situation. This strategy works because the local population will not attack its own army, and it reinforces the idea that the LAF are primarily responsible for security in the area. It also reinforces UNIFIL's image as a peaceful force, which has been identified as important if peacekeepers are to retain local support.[46]

The relationship between the LAF and UNIFIL is not without its challenges, owing to national political tensions that UNIFIL and the LAF must navigate and that work to constrain them at times. These challenges revolve around retaining local consent, local support for Hezbullah, and Lebanese legal and political constraints.

Local Consent and the Role of Hezbullah

As mentioned earlier, one of the main tasks of Resolution 1701 is to ensure that the area south of the Litani River is free and clear from armed personnel, weapons, or assets other than those items belonging to the Lebanese government.[47] For many Lebanese citizens, particularly the Shi'a in South Lebanon, the continued presence of Hezbullah's armed faction—who use a combination of traditional and guerrilla warfare techniques—is considered a necessary deterrent to Israeli aggression. The LAF is currently not considered strong enough by locals to deter any Israeli actions—they too suffer from an absence of security credibility. However, after years of living under foreign occupation, local residents across the political spectrum are happy to see the LAF patrolling the area with UNIFIL: "This was our demand, long ago, to have our army spread or deployed on the borders. When you have money to invest in this area, you would like to see your national army protecting this area, not another organization. But as far as we don't have peace in this part of the world, it's very difficult to see the LAF taking over from UNIFIL."[48]

Civilians also understand that the LAF is underfunded and underrequipped and therefore not able to be fully in control of the security situation. One civilian summed up the situation: "We would prefer that the international community made a decision to allow the military to be armed properly, and then we don't need the resistance."[49]

It is not possible for either UNIFIL or the LAF to aggressively hunt for weapons stored in the area without risking the loss of local support. In the early years of Resolution 1701, French and Spanish troops conducted raids on private property to find and destroy illegal weapon caches. However, this approach quickly proved unacceptable to the local population, which could make operating conditions impossible for UNIFIL. A great deal of diplomacy was required from UNIFIL civil affairs officers to smooth over relations between UNIFIL, the LAF, and the local population as a result of these raids. It very quickly became clear that the raids could not continue, as one LAF officer put it: "We told them, 'Look, it's not an area of operation. It's like your villages in your countries—there are people living here. You cannot work with them as an area of operation. You cannot move in your tanks; you cannot move as if you are in the field. It's not a field; its villages, people living in villages. If you want to drive your tanks, you will destroy the roads, and you will have problems.'"[50]

UNIFIL is pragmatic when negotiating the tension between its mandate and local perceptions of its role in relation to local security. When unauthorized weapons are found, UNIFIL interprets the mandate on this issue by asking the LAF to retrieve the weapons. They report the find to the LAF and then wait for the LAF to arrive and deal with recovery.[51] This approach means that UNIFIL does not have to deal directly with the removal of illegal weapons, which may or may not belong to Hezbullah but which can be a contentious issue with the local population: "If we find UXO [unexploded ordinance] or an IED [improvised explosive device] of some sort, they are called initially. Practically on the ground, it would be a case of securing the area until they arrive, and they come in and deal with the situation. . . . We try to provide them with as much professional aid as we can and experience, but it's definitely their country and their place to carry out that side of things."[52]

The LAF also has to walk a fine line in this regard, because as one UNIFIL officer noted, when UNIFIL leaves, the LAF will remain with the people: "So the LAF came back, a state institution. They had to first of all have a presence—to assert themselves. And also they had to work out how they were going to dovetail with the resistance on certain issues. They have to live with these guys. You know, how do you, on a day-to-day [basis], at a working level, how do you do business, you know?"[53]

One civilian referred to this issue and acknowledged that the army often knows where arms caches are stored but deliberately turns a blind eye: "The army, they know about the activities of Hezbullah. They know where they are, where their positions are, and what is their role. But at the same time . . . some of them are covering their activities. . . . Because also the LAF know that, after all, UNIFIL troops will withdraw, and those people will remain here. And tomorrow if we come to certain agreement that UNIFIL should go, that means the people of the area should protect the area no matter what."[54]

One LAF officer attributed the situation with Hezbullah not just to the LAF's weak technical capabilities, but also to global politics in that many Lebanese in the South view the international community as biased toward Israel and are suspicious that Israel will reinvade. His assessment reflected the psychological comfort that Lebanese civilians draw from having the resistance as a deterrent. On balance, however, LAF offi-cers appeared pragmatic about the presence of Hezbullah in the area of operations, arguing that although Hezbullah is still present, it is no longer out in the open, which has been one of the effects of Resolution 1701: "There is Hezbullah and other groups south of the Litani—we know that—but it's invisible. You can tell us there are weapons in a house, and we are okay, but it's a house and we cannot go there—you must have a judge to give an order to search it. It's not important to have the weapon. It's most important not to use them."[55]

Lebanese Legal and Political Issues

Although UNIFIL and the LAF are criticized as being ineffectual for not searching and seizing illegal weapons on private property, for both legal and political reasons it is not possible for UNIFIL or the LAF to do so. In regard to the legal issue of entering private property, the LAF is very sensitive to the risks it faces to its reputation if it employs a more forceful approach to weapon requisition: "They are very concerned about their own image, their own standing in the South. . . . In the civil war years, the LAF was quite active in confiscating property, and they faced a number of court cases, since the war ended, about their confiscations of property and their actions toward private property during the civil war years. And they are very, very cautious about ensuring that they have the right legal documentation and the right grounds to search private property."[56]

In regard to the political issue, Hezbullah's political wing constitutes a powerful and legitimate faction in Lebanese politics. It is not in the LAF's interests to compromise Hezbullah's operations in the South: "The LAF is on a political tightrope—they walk a very, very taut, narrow tightrope— often, for them, political cover from the government in Beirut is extremely important. Often it's very difficult for them to have that full cover when there is only a caretaker government in charge."[57]

This national conflict of interest at times creates tension between the LAF and UNIFIL. However, UNIFIL senior staff argue that despite the difficulties the LAF face, they have demonstrated a commitment to showing their authority: "I won't lie to you and say that life is very easy in our dealings with the Lebanese Armed Forces all the time, but on the whole, we found the LAF to be dedicated to be fulfilling Resolution

1701. . . . But, you know, it's clear that they are in a very, very tricky political situation."[58]

UNIFIL officers' perceptions of how they work with the LAF were that the relationship is good. The relationship on the ground between UNIFIL soldiers and the LAF appears to be very congenial, apart from language barriers. UNIFIL peacekeepers spoke highly of the LAF's manner and professionalism. They also commented that they found the LAF very responsive to their requests for assistance and that LAF personnel were willing to search areas that had been identified as potentially containing illegal weapons.[59]

UNIFIL staff also commented positively about the LAF's determination to prove that it is just as tough as Hezbullah in terms of confronting Israel, with one officer commenting: "I think the LAF want to be the people who are in charge of security. It's clear in their minds: they don't see a role for Hezbullah. They want to take ownership of this. . . . I think they are very highly motivated as a force."[60] While the LAF is keen to take over local security, and wishes to be seen as the only defense force in Lebanon, Hezbullah's raison d'être is similar. Both parties must work together for reasons of legitimacy, as both require local support to survive politically. UNIFIL takes its lead from the LAF in terms of how the army deals with Hezbullah, which remains an important unnamed party to the conflict and constrains UNIFIL's agency, particularly in terms of searching for illegal weapons. Both the LAF and UNIFIL demonstrate pragmatism on the issue in the face of local sensitivities that at times favor Hezbullah.

A further political challenge for UNIFIL in its dealings with the LAF is the different posture adopted by different troop contingents in terms of how they patrol and search for weapons. One LAF officer suggested that non-NATO (North Atlantic Treaty Organization) troops tended not to look actively for weapons, describing the Indians as not serious and only there for the money, noting, "If there is something wrong, they don't try to stop it."[61] Conversely, another LAF officer complained that the French and the Spanish were treating the Lebanese like a foreign enemy and that only the non-NATO troops were good.[62] While these differences do not severely impact UNIFIL's relationship with the LAF, they are an additional political concern that the mission has to navigate.

UNIFIL uses a combined approach of pragmatism, technocracy, and flexibility in its relationship with the LAF. As with the municipalities, UNIFIL avoids embroiling itself in the politics of LAF-versus-Hezbullah weapon storage, and it is on this issue that UNIFIL receives the most criticism nationally and internationally. The March 14 political alliance, consisting mainly of Sunni and Christian parties and its supporters, and the international community dislike UNIFIL's refusal to go after Hezbullah's weapons and rebuke UNIFIL for not engaging with them. Conversely, Hezbullah supporters rebuke UNIFIL for not standing up to Israel, which, therefore, they argue, cements the need for a Hezbullah presence on the Blue Line. UNIFIL is thus in a no-win situation, torn by the demands of sectarian politics and vilified by all sides of the conflict. In addition, the IDF criticize UNIFIL for not doing enough to prevent Hezbullah's attacks on Israel.

The Role of Time and Flexibility in Building Relations between the LAF and UNIFIL

UNIFIL operates a close liaison system with the LAF that has developed into a positive relationship. In this regard, the factors of time (in particular) and flexibility have played key roles. The retention of some long-term staff who have developed strong relationships with LAF officers has in turn allowed for the development of good local cultural knowledge that LAF officers value. UNIFIL has demonstrated flexibility in terms of being on call and available when needed without imposing a schedule or hierarchy.

The importance of time is demonstrated in several ways. First, UNIFIL has helped to reintroduce the LAF into the region, and long-serving senior staff at UNIFIL headquarters have been positive in their assessments of the growth of the LAF's popularity. They have witnessed the development of the relationship between the LAF and the locals over time, and they have seen changes in local perceptions. This improvement benefits both organizations that require local legitimacy to operate in the area: "From the moment the Lebanese Army came to the South of Lebanon, you can see that people's perceptions—their initial understanding— of the LAF were very poor. State authority was not something that has ever been present in the South of Lebanon. Little by little, we have seen that actually trust for the Lebanese Army has been increasing since 2006. . . . Increasing their credibility means increasing our own credibility, because the long-term goal of the mission is to hand over the responsibilities to the Lebanese Army."[63]

Second, time has allowed good UNIFIL-LAF relations to develop. Long-term staff members who understand the local political and social culture in the region are valued highly. The most frustrating aspect of working with UNIFIL for the LAF has been the constant military staff rotations: "Everyone has to discover how to deal with this culture, how to deal with these people, something not easy. So the people who are spending more time in Lebanon, they know our culture, they know how to be with the issue, they know how to deal with people."[64]

Flexibility has also helped UNIFIL build strong relationships with key LAF personnel. Senior LAF officers gave very positive reports of their relationship with UNIFIL staff and in particular their commitment to resolving problems when they arose: "Yes. They always do their best. If you ask for an appointment—they say it's up to you. Afternoon, morning, whenever—they are ready to come. They try their best not to disturb us and not to put us under tension—they want us to work in a good mood. Many incidents happened, and they really, they help us a lot."[65]

The Syrian crisis was stretching the LAF's capabilities across Lebanon. For the past few years, this issue led to a reduction in patrol numbers in the South, but UNIFIL was careful not to push the LAF for more brigades. It recognizes the pressure that the LAF is under and the importance of being flexible.[66]

The key to building responsiveness credibility with the LAF has been, of course, responding to every request and maintaining regular and frequent contact. But in addition, the presence of long-term staff affords UNIFIL access to senior staff, extending their influence over the course of events when problems on the Blue Line arise. Interestingly, UNIFIL has helped to build the credibility of the LAF by reintroducing them to the South of Lebanon. While patrolling with the LAF does not afford UNIFIL legitimacy, it does provide evidence to the local population that it has credibility with a legitimate institution, which in turn helps improve perceptions of UNIFIL and at the local level reduces hostility to patrolling troops.

Technical and Material Credibility in Capacity Building

UNIFIL also builds material and technical credibility with the LAF through its capacity building activities. UNIFIL works to help build the LAF's capabilities in two main ways: by supporting financial donations among the troop contributing countries and other states to provide the LAF with the necessary equipment required of a modern-day force, and by helping make improvements at the operational level. The staff members overseeing this process are from EU contingents whose national interests do not conflict with UNIFIL's objective of building up the LAF. Since the Syrian withdrawal from Lebanon in 2005, the European Union has increasingly been supportive of UNIFIL's efforts to capacity build the LAF.[67] Furthermore, since the emergence of ISIS in 2014, Lebanon is viewed as a key buffer state, so international interest in providing assistance to the LAF has increased.[68]

The LAF suffers from an acute lack of resources because there is no set budget from the national government, which means that it sometimes does not possess basic equipment: "And I don't only mean the weapons. I am not talking about antiaircraft missiles; I am not talking about sophisticated stuff. I am talking about the soldier on the ground needs a uniform, he needs a rifle, he needs a place to stay, he needs food. Basic things!"[69]

The LAF is often not able to procure modern weaponry from external donors for political reasons. The Israeli government campaigns internationally against any of its border states obtaining weapons deemed to pose a threat to Israeli security. This strategy, termed the "qualitative military edge," refers to the idea that Israel, with the support of the United States, will prevent any state in Israel's neighborhood (described as "numerically superior adversaries") from obtaining weapons that provide technological, tactical, and other advantages over Israel.[70]

UNIFIL's mandate objective of removing all illegal weaponry from the area of operations is designed to reassure Israel that Hezbullah will not have the capability to launch a military attack. UNIFIL's objective is to increase the LAF's capabilities so that the LAF can fully take on the role as national security provider. It is hoped that a fully equipped LAF will erode and eventually eliminate the perceived need for (and therefore legitimacy of) Hezbullah's military wing in Lebanon, which, in theory, should alleviate Israeli security concerns. Aside from constituting intrusive interference in the domestic affairs of another state, blocking the LAF's requests for modern weaponry would appear to be a self-defeating strategy on the part of Israel. The result has been that it serves to consolidate Hezbullah's stated rationale for retaining its presence and thus preserving the conditions that prevent peace: "The LAF has suffered greatly because Israel has always had very strong lobbying *not* to support the LAF. Don't give them weapons; don't give them the technology. But at the same time, the IDF berates the LAF for not doing the job. But at the same time, they won't give them the means to do it. So you say, 'What do you want, guys? . . . You can't expect them to do the job if they haven't got the weapons.'"[71] UNIFIL therefore lobbies the international community independently to gain support and donations for the LAF, often working in conjunction with UNSCOL and going beyond the mandate of Resolution 1701. However, as one political affairs officer admitted, "UNIFIL will be here forever if we don't build up the LAF!"[72]

UNIFIL also seeks funding for LAF battalions that are based throughout Lebanon, not just south of the Litani River; thus, they offer donor countries a choice of donating to a particular area of operations, which not only prevents those countries from being deterred from investing, but also ensures that an increase in the LAF's resources does not make the Israelis nervous: "We make this distinction, because, for example, if the Germans wanted to give the LAF some main battle tanks, we would say, 'The LAF doesn't need any tanks down south,' you know? . . . So this is trying to watch the line between what the IDF will complain about. But they can have the main battle tanks everywhere north of the Litani, but not south of it."[73] UNIFIL has also assisted by securing around $500,000 from the UN General Assembly for the specific purpose of assisting the LAF to purchase essential supplies.

UNIFIL's flexible approach to interpreting its mandate has also led to a joint project entitled the "Strategic Dialogue." In recent years, political affairs officers and the LAF engaged in a full analysis of the LAF's structure and capabilities and produced an internal joint report that identified gaps in the LAF's structure. The political affairs officers organized a coordinating mechanism with UNSCOL and now work jointly to seek contributions from the United States and European states to specifically fill these gaps.[74]

UNIFIL has also helped the LAF develop civil military cooperation capacity. Locating civil military cooperation offices in key areas of tension (such as Palestinian camps) helps improve relations between the LAF and the civilian population, and UNIFIL has sought funding for this project from the European Union Peacebuilding Fund. These organizations do not usually provide military forces with money, but UNIFIL has successfully argued that civil military cooperation activities are important to help the LAF preserve peace in Lebanon.

UNIFIL also regularly supports the LAF materially with its own donations. For example, UNIFIL vehicles at the end of their life cycle are donated to the LAF, as are compounds that have been vacated by battalions. In addition, UNIFIL runs joint exercises between the forces of troop contributing countries and the LAF that can include shooting, artillery, computer exercises, and administrative training.

Conclusion

Despite being a "traditional mission," UNIFIL is engaged in peacebuilding activities in the form of supporting local government and capacity building the LAF. In both these activities, UNIFIL has to deal with sectarian political issues. As with its international engagement, UNIFIL depoliticizes its work by taking a technocratic approach. Pragmatism in dealing with local government involves respecting the structure of local government and ensuring all political parties are dealt with equitably to preserve the perception of UNIFIL as an honest broker. For the same reason, UNIFIL places the LAF at the forefront of all incidents when weapons are found or altercations occur on the ground with civilians.

Time also assists UNIFIL in its relationships with key individuals in local government and with the LAF when confidence in UNIFIL is under threat. Flexibility in interpreting the mandate has enabled UNIFIL to find creative ways to capacity build the LAF and assist with local governance that helps UNIFIL work toward its exit strategy of building national institutions at the national and subnational levels.

5 Credibility through Aid

Thus far, I have examined how UNIFIL wins credibility in its dealings at the international and national levels. Here I examine UNIFIL's local engagement and show how material assistance and responsiveness win UNIFIL credibility with the local population that affords the mission cooperation. In this context, material credibility refers to the provision of funding for local projects and other benefits such as health care, services, infrastructure, and equipment. Responsiveness credibility refers to a demonstrated ability to respond quickly to military and civilian concerns.

Maintaining local consent for UNIFIL's operations is crucial, as without it UNIFIL would not be able to carry out its patrols, as one civilian noted: "UNIFIL doesn't want problems with towns, you know. They respect the mentality or habits of the town. And for security reasons, you know, they don't want problems. In 2007 there was a bomb, and soldiers were killed from UNIFIL, from the Spanish. And from that time there were some restrictions to go into the towns, and there were some alerts . . . or security measures. For this reason they cannot go into towns and talk to everybody without the interference of the *mukhtars* or municipalities or the LAF."[1]

UNIFIL's security credibility is low, among many audiences, owing to the contested nature of its mandate. However, providing a visible presence in the form of patrols does help to render a symbolic sense of security. This presence does not award it legitimacy, but it helps to act as a restraint on all parties to the conflict. Both MacQueen and Rubinstein have noted the symbolic importance of a peacekeeping mission, and patrolling is a large part of that purpose, irrespective of its deterrence capabilities.[2] That

UNIFIL is able to patrol is in large part due to its engagement with local civilians.

In this chapter I discuss the work of civil affairs officers and civil military cooperation officers and show how they win local cooperation. CIMIC and civil affairs officers work creatively to navigate the politics of peacekeeping to prevent and resolve problems at the local level. Local consent and cooperation are born of credibility and not legitimacy, and therefore UNIFIL has to constantly sustain relationships and provide material evidence that it is working in the best interests of the local population. But all peacekeeping missions require local consent. Why is consent for UNIFIL so important?

The Importance of Maintaining Consent

Attacks have been launched on UNIFIL patrols since the implementation of Resolution 1701. However, the most serious occurred on June 24, 2007, when a Spanish battalion was bombed on the road to al-Khiam, a town near the Blue Line, in the area of operations. The attack, triggered by an improvised explosive device, killed six peacekeepers.[3] Although not officially confirmed, the perpetrators were believed to be Hezbullah, and the incident was seen as a warning to UNIFIL not to interfere with Hezbullah's operations north of the Litani River.[4] Prior to the attack, the Spanish had been seen monitoring Hezbullah activity north of the Litani River, which is outside the area of operations.[5] Subsequently, security measures for UNIFIL troops were greatly enhanced, including supplying mobile phone jammers to armored personnel carriers (APCs) on patrol. The incident was a painful reminder to UNIFIL that despite its best efforts to obtain local consent, security cannot be guaranteed.[6]

Other less deadly reminders of the need to maintain local consent are incidents involving the local population, such as confrontations with hostile groups of locals, stone-throwing incidents, crimes against UNIFIL troops (including armed theft), and even a brief kidnapping incident. Not all of these incidents take place in the area of operations. Often they occur when UNIFIL troops are north of the Litani River because civilians in that area do not benefit from UNIFIL's goods and services. The route from Beirut to South Lebanon is via a single road that is relatively easy to ambush. In 2013, for example, a UNIFIL logistics convoy and its occupants were held for several hours outside the area of operations by armed civilians before the LAF was able to secure their release.[7]

Within the area of operation, CIMIC officers attribute the cause of confrontations to new battalions losing their way and taking a wrong turn in the middle of the night.[8] In these situations, the role of the strategic corporal acting on behalf of UNIFIL is highly important: "The worst-case scenario for us is that we have to defend ourselves by the maximum, if you know what I mean. So we would always try to err on the side of common sense, you know. There are different degrees of use of force, but there's an awful lot to be said for the guy who's in charge on the ground at the time showing a bit of restraint and common sense . . . and having a bit of manners goes an awful long way when it comes to things like that."[9]

While these incidents are not regarded as serious, they reflect the very real concerns that UNIFIL holds about the potential to lose consent on the ground, which would very quickly make the mission impossible to execute. Of crucial importance is that these incidents do not descend into fighting, which would tarnish UNIFIL's reputation. Blowback from such an event has the potential to threaten the viability of the entire mission. The area of operation is simply too small to allow UNIFIL the physical space to avoid direct attacks on a regular basis, as the Israelis discovered to their cost when they were occupiers. If an occupying force cannot withstand the guerrilla-warfare tactics that would undoubtedly be used, a lightly armed peacekeeping force certainly could not, especially one with a large number of European contingents.

When incidents have occurred, CIMIC officers work with the municipalities in the vicinity of the incident to further reduce tensions:

> Maybe through CIMIC [we] go out and meet with the local village leader and then just try to say that it was human error, you know? So it's that kind of . . . they appreciate it, a lot of the locals. If you can give them as much of a heads-up as possible without infringing on your own security measures as to what your plans are, or what you are trying to achieve,

you know, I think that's a big deal with them, which is understandable. You know, it's their country at the end of the day.[10]

These types of incidents do not necessarily reflect the sentiment of everyone who lives in the area of operation. Some local civilians comment that UNIFIL's patrols make them feel safer.[11] Hospitality is such an entrenched aspect of Lebanese village culture that many local people express dislike for these kinds of confrontations because they regard UNIFIL as guests in their country. However, UNIFIL officers are very aware of the disruption that constant patrolling causes to the daily lives of villagers. As one civil affairs officer noted, "Sometimes even getting your child to school can be a challenge if you're stuck in a convoy of UNIFIL trucks going here and there."[12] But in areas where UNIFIL has little or no legitimacy, it has to be cautious to avoid friction between the troops and local civilians. CIMIC and civil affairs officers are therefore extremely active in the area of operation to prevent problems between UNIFIL and the local community. Building material and responsiveness credibility is essential for UNIFIL to maintain good local relations and therefore the security to operate.

CIMIC Activities and Services

CIMIC officers are employed by UNIFIL to ensure the security of peacekeepers on the ground.[13] In contrast to civil affairs officers who concentrate on helping the municipalities and building long-term relationships, CIMIC officers are time-bound in that they need to perform their duties in a short space of time before the next battalion rotation. As such, their approach is more instrumental in that they strictly focus on providing material support for the purpose of maintaining a secure environment for the peacekeeping troops. Local civilians understand this relationship. One former public official explained how as mayor of a village he responded to the Korean contingent when they arrived. "So there was a mutual need for both of us to have this kind of relation. They needed to have stability, security, and peace. We needed so many things for the needs of the village."[14]

CIMIC officers deliver an extensive range of goods and services that earn UNIFIL material credibility from the local population. Each battalion is assigned a specific area (within the larger UNIFIL area of operation) with a specific number of towns and villages in which to conduct their CIMIC activities and a budget for these activities (as well as delivering on centrally funded projects paid for by the UNIFIL mission as a whole). Most UNIFIL battalions provide some form of medical and dental care for the local population living in their area. Some have a hospital that local residents can visit twenty-four hours a day, and all medical services and medication provided by battalions are free. In addition, many battalions also operate an outreach service whereby they visit the villages in their area on a rolling basis and set up a medical center to provide care locally. The frequency of these services varies greatly, as they are dependent on the resources of each battalion. The Indian battalion, for example, visits all the villages in its area on a biweekly basis, whereas the Ghanaian contingent rolls out its service on a biyearly basis.

UNIFIL headquarters in Naqoura also possess advanced medical facilities that include a physiotherapy unit and specialized medical care. Headquarters take the cases that the battalions are unable to treat, and in cases of severe emergency, UNIFIL will dispatch a helicopter to collect patients. It is estimated that UNIFIL treats around forty-seven thousand people a month across its area of operation.[15] These medical services make UNIFIL extremely popular, owing to the dearth of existing medical services in the region and because those services that are available are often unaffordable for many locals. Of late, UNIFIL has also been treating Syrian refugees who continue to enter Lebanon and are often very poor and have pressing medical and dental needs.[16] UNIFIL is aware that it is not part of its mandate to assist the Syrian population, but for humanitarian reasons they allow Syrians to access medical care. However, Lebanese civilian concerns about resource shortages have grown as the Syrian crisis endures.[17]

UNIFIL battalions have identified and filled important gaps in other local services. One unique service that the Spanish and the Indian contingents offer is veterinary care in Sector East. Among the farming community, this aid is even more popular than the medical services. Civilians described it as an incredible advantage in a country where there are few veterinarians, who charge high fees for their services. One farmer informed me that without this help, he would be unable to operate his farm.[18]

Assisting civilians with their veterinary needs is one way that UNIFIL helps to improve the economic environment of the region, as it enables farmers to continue to function and therefore produce goods for sale on the market. But it also enables UNIFIL to exert some influence over the local population when it comes to maintaining peace and security:

> If you look at a veterinarian here in Lebanon, firstly, he is not available, and secondly, if you do get him from outside, then, ah, you end up paying quite a hefty sum. I think it's about fifty dollars, which is too much for a shepherd. . . . So when a shepherd gets a doctor who comes to his flock and then treats them, it goes a long way in establishing a relationship. Then it's easier for us to tell the shepherd, because we do have a point of contact. Because the vet has met him earlier, the men have also met him, so it's easier for us to tell him, you know, "Okay, this is the Blue Line. Respect it."[19]

The scheme also affords the battalions access to local intelligence from civilians: "We do get a lot of intelligence. For instance, the veterinarian, when he went on a normal veterinarian rounds. A guy, a farmer who was there, after he was treating his goat or something, so after that he told us, 'There is something happening three kilometers from here. So there is likely something happening.' . . . So the veterinarian approached the operational branch here, and we sent a patrol there and we found some rockets and something. This helps in our operational activity to a greater extent."[20]

Other schemes that CIMIC officers have run include training in organic agriculture, manufacturing agricultural products for farmers, agricultural cooperatives, training for medical staff, donating computers and sewing machines, and providing training in sewing.[21]

The CIMIC teams in the battalions first meet with the municipalities to assess village needs. This activity serves two purposes. First, it enables members of the battalion to engage with public officials in the villages within their area. This interaction is important for maintaining good relations to enable the battalions to conduct their patrols without fear of security incidents:

Obviously, the locals here—and you wouldn't like it wherever you lived, if there was a foreign army running up and down your village at nighttime, maybe keeping you awake, of course you are not going to like it. But we can maybe iron out these issues. We can meet key leaders with the company commanders and say, "Listen, they have an issue with this, and the issue is because . . . Is there some way we can maybe change the patrolling time table, or maybe we won't go through the village at nighttime or we won't go down this narrow street?" And all these things can be sorted out at these key leader engagement meetings. CIMIC has to be central to that.[22]

Second, it enables the battalion to conduct a needs assessment in each village that informs their decisions to fund projects. CIMIC and civil affairs officers are responsible for assisting villages across the region with quick impact projects. These types of projects include building underground sewage systems, roads, water pumps, street lighting, public parks, and school playgrounds as well as repairing important civic buildings and support walls on the roads. These services are invaluable to locals, who greatly appreciate that without UNIFIL's assistance, their lives would have been much harder because of a lack of funding or interest from the central government. The improvements to local infrastructure also help to attract more business and commerce into the area. Two former mayors commented on the contribution UNIFIL has made to local infrastructure:

Simply we can say that the Korean contingent gave us more than what the central government gave us. . . . And now they are working on the pavement of the main road of the village. Since four years the Ministry of Public Works promised us, and they didn't do it. Now the Koreans are doing it.[23]

After the 2006 war UNIFIL contributed a lot. Our infrastructure was destroyed—our roads, water system, telecommunications, electric, everything. They helped us rebuild our water and electric system and cleared the roads.[24]

Quick impact projects are a recent innovation. Prior to 2006, battalions donated goods and services to the local population that were paid for by their nation-states.[25] The quick impact projects were designed in recognition of the need to win local consent: "This policy was not [there] before 2006 . . . and then they started to go out in the villages and ask them, 'How can we assist? How can we assist?' And this is how they started these quick impact projects, so this is now very famous and very popular in the area after 2006."[26]

Quick impact projects are funded by UNIFIL headquarters, and the projects are assigned a total annual budget of US$500,000. Funds are provided to each battalion to spend on local projects according to local needs. CIMIC officers submit proposals for funding based on their village assessments that are subject to committee approval. Awards are based on three conditions that are designed to afford the current rotation of troops the maximum benefits of civilian goodwill. First, the cost of the project must not exceed US$25,000; second, it must be completed in three months or less; and third, the project should benefit the maximum number of people possible in any village. The local mayor is involved in the project from inception to conclusion, and the project completions are always inaugurated in a ceremony with a commemorative plaque to promote UNIFIL's involvement with the project to the local population.[27]

Battalions from poor countries run two or three projects a year, whereas battalions from wealthier troop contributing countries can access funding from their home countries (up to US$40,000) and run projects more frequently. Wealthier battalions tend to be European—mainly the French, Spanish, and Italians—and South Koreans: "If you go to most of the villages here [in the Spanish area] they are having the solar-system lights. Why? Because these projects are funded by the Spanish Kingdom."[28]

South Koreans are perceived to be the most generous of all the battalions. They have a small area to cover that comprises five to six villages, and once they had saturated the area with infrastructure projects, they began to take Lebanese civilians on cultural trips to South Korea. Villages that lie in areas with poorer battalions tend to envy the ones that sit close to the wealthy ones, as one civilian commented: "The other villages say,

'We envy you—you have the Koreans in your area.'"[29] However, the relatively high level of global awareness among the local population means they understand that poorer nation-states are unable to provide a lot of services, and these battalions are not resented for their fiscal poverty.[30] Poorer battalions demonstrate creativity by undertaking other projects for the community that do not require a big spend. The Indians were especially motivated to engage with the community in this way:

> There are activities that we carry out that doesn't involve the financial part, that is within our capabilities, like classes, yoga classes, computer classes, English classes. So that empowers them in a way. So these are the things that we are doing. In addition to that, we do participate in community activities, if in villages they are having a party or some function. We go and help them out, and any arrangements that they want to do, you know, we participate in those. So, for example, last year during the summer vacation there were a lot of village festivals that were there. Every village had a festival. So we did go. We did establish a stall for us; we made a stall for Indian snacks. So we distributed Indian snacks to them. So we gave them some decorations, some carpets and stuff. With any assistance they needed, we helped them with that.[31]

Sometimes the smallest of gestures can go a long way to improving local relations, winning responsiveness credibility: "There was a fire in the church at Ayn Ibli—smoke damage, the crib caught fire. It was bad smoke damage. No structural damage, but they wanted us to do something. So we went down there, sent our fire brigade, and we cleaned the place and they were delighted with that."[32] These kinds of activities are not restricted to the less wealthy battalions. For example, the Spanish and French run language courses, the Italians teach pizza making, and the South Koreans run tae kwon do classes. These activities are again an important vehicle through which battalions can engage with the local population and show their nonmilitary, human face.

Some battalions also run public information sessions about the Blue Line. The Blue Line is still a relatively new concept for the Lebanese, and in the unmarked areas it is easily crossed. As noted previously, the Indian battalion runs evening briefing sessions for shepherds and farmers on a bimonthly basis to educate them about the Blue Line. But the meeting is also another opportunity for civilian engagement: "What happens is also . . . this meeting is not just for passing one-way information. It's for two-way information. They give their point of view, and they tell us their problems. So whatever is within our capacity, we help them out with it."[33]

The Limits of Material Credibility

CIMIC activities afford UNIFIL battalions an opportunity to build relationships, which helps generate local cooperation for mission patrols. Additional benefits can be obtaining local intelligence and effecting some influence over local observance of the Blue Line. However, both CIMIC and civil affairs officers face challenges in the course of their work that include high local expectations, local frustration over rotating battalions, corruption, wastage, and a need to demonstrate impartiality and transparency. The more serious challenge for CIMIC officers lies in forging relationships with villages that are unfriendly toward UNIFIL.

The instrumental and short-term nature of CIMIC engagement has led to municipalities and civilians having high expectations of what UNIFIL can do for them. Civilians are all too aware that UNIFIL has money to spend, and many municipalities will not hesitate to ask for it or try to play off one battalion against another.[34] The local population has become very savvy about knowing what they can get from UNIFIL battalions: "There's an element to it—your checkbook—of course, I mean, I've gone to meetings where they can be very dour toward my battalion commander. When they find out I am CIMIC, they start smiling—and really. So you have to be careful of that."[35]

There is a perception among the less wealthy battalions that European battalions have raised expectations to a high level: "It has become a sort of competition now. If you look at the sort of projects being undertaken in the European areas, okay, with all their money, yes. And so sometimes they feel we are not doing enough."[36]

CIMIC officers must ensure that they do not create more tension in the local communities by making promises they cannot keep, so there is a need for transparency. This approach again relates to the overall credibility of the mission, being sure that it is always seen to be delivering on what it says it will. The approach to this type of problem differs among contingents. The Irish battalion had a strict policy of not making the local municipalities wait around for an answer because they felt their relations with the locals would be more damaged than by saying no in the first place.[37] The Ghanaians, however, felt that asking the municipalities to wait for an answer was unproblematic as long as they were clear with the local municipality about what was happening. Their policy was to explain to a municipality that they have limited resources and that they have had to forward the village's request to the headquarters at Naqoura and are waiting for a response from UNIFIL headquarters.[38] It is possible that the local population has different expectations of the Irish, as a European battalion, as compared to the Ghanaians. As noted previously, the local population understand the limitations of the non-EU battalions, and, as such, the Ghanaian strategy works, because they are Ghanaian. If the Spanish or another wealthier battalion employed this approach, it might not work because locals might assume the battalion simply did not wish to spend the money.

Time plays an important role in determining the quality of the relations between CIMIC and local civilians. Maintaining relationships is an ongoing concern. One CIMIC officer noted that building an initial relationship is one thing, but maintaining it takes a great deal of work.[39] Constant troop rotations are frustrating to local civilians, particularly the ones who want to maintain good relations with UNIFIL peacekeepers. One local hotel owner complained that he had built strong relations with members of the Spanish contingent, only to have them leave and be replaced by a very different set of individuals: "This frequent rotation hurts the relations a lot. Because as soon as you make relations with someone, they disappear and you have to start from zero."[40]

CIMIC and civil affairs officers also have to be very careful to avoid corruption and ensure that all projects funded are sustainable. The Irish contingent noted that several years earlier, they had provided a garbage truck to a village, only to have the municipality sell it and use the funds.[41] Staff need to exercise caution and at times risk unpopularity to ensure that projects benefit the maximum number of people in the municipality.[42]

UNIFIL has received project proposals that benefit members of the municipal council only: "In one village the mayor asked for a public park, and he told us, 'We want it here.' And it ended up that this 'here' was near his own house, and it ended up this public park was a garden for him!"[43]

Officers also need to avoid wastage and duplication. For example, solar lights have been installed in a number of villages in South Lebanon (as previously there was no lighting at night). One local municipality that had not yet received solar lights asked for them when UNIFIL came to assess the village needs. However, the village already had streetlamps, just not solar-powered lamps.[44] Understanding the needs of the local environment is key to avoiding wastage. In the early days of the new mandate there was a tendency to build public parks at the request of the village mayors, but as many mayors don't spend time in their municipality, they don't always understand the needs of their village. As a result, when CIMIC or civil affairs officers asked what the village needed, the mayors often requested a public park. Driving around the area of operation, it is possible to see quite a number of public parks that are rarely, if ever, used. UNIFIL now avoids spending money in this way.[45]

The politics of allocating money is a constant concern that needs to be managed. At the local level in South Lebanon, just as at the international level, demonstrating impartiality is crucial to avoid offending specific groups. CIMIC officers deal with this issue by tracking the projects completed in each village to ensure that each village receives an equal number—for example, the Indian battalion keeps a spreadsheet.[46] Some villages do, however, require more money because have been more damaged than others, so UNIFIL must evaluate each case, and some villages will receive more projects than others, which can lead to resentment toward UNIFIL. However, the aim is to ensure that all the villages in the assigned area of a battalion receive a similar level of attention.

Another challenge is when a village mayor refuses to meet with CIMIC officers to discuss projects for his village. Some municipalities will simply not present at meetings or cancel at the last minute to avoid speaking with UNIFIL.[47] When this situation happens, the lack of communication between UNIFIL and the village can evolve into a security problem for the battalion: "But other villages, if they don't engage with you, then you can't do anything. So I think they know that. One of the villages just wouldn't engage with us. They just wouldn't, and as a result the CIMIC projects are very low. . . . It's just something I need to be aware of as a CIMIC officer, constantly trying to engage, and if they say, 'No, no, no,' then you can't do anything for them. . . . And that then sometimes causes a problem operationally in that it's a no-go area—incidents happening there with local people."[48]

This issue is at the heart of UNIFIL's civilian engagement work. If UNIFIL is unable to conduct patrols in a secure environment, then it cannot function. UNIFIL's presence tends to be more politicized in Hezbullah villages, although, as previously noted, it is not a hard-and-fast rule and depends on the personality of the mayor and how he chooses to deal with UNIFIL, because ultimately Hezbullah does not try to prevent its political representatives from contacting UNIFIL. However, a story, related here in full, demonstrates how a local municipality can act as a gatekeeper to prevent contact between UNIFIL and the local population:

Not all the villages have the opportunity to have contact with people because there are restrictions, unfortunately. Some people, some towns, prohibit, if we can say this, UNIFIL from making contact directly with the people without the intervention of the municipality. I had a bad experience with this, because one time, once, a woman came to me from a town nearby, and she told me that she has sick cats. And she wanted me to talk to the Spanish veterinarian to go and consult to see them and give them the medicine. And I have a good relation with the medical staff. I contacted the veterinarian who was here, and I sent him to her. When the municipality knew, they make a big problem with me and the veterinarian. They said to me, "Who told you to send this guy directly to this woman? You are making a big problem because there will be a danger for them if they go to the town without our company," and something like that, blah, blah, blah. Then I got embarrassed in front of the veterinarian, because I did not know all these complications. You know, and this town is Shi'a and unfortunately I am saying this, because they said, "If someone will make harm to the veterinarian, who will be responsible? You must go through us, to accompany them to go to the house of this woman and to protect them." Yes. This was my bad experience, and from that time I did not interfere with anybody. They forbid to me have the sense of helping people. I was shocked. Really. This is embarrassing.[49]

The same civilian noted that when UNIFIL is not welcome in certain villages, it is owing to politics that can be imposed on the population of the village:

> It's political, unfortunately, yes, because in the towns of the Muslim area, there are political parties, Hezbullah and Amal, you know. And these laws are from this, I think. In contrast in the Christian area, there is no political parties that are governing the mentality of the people. Everybody can do what he wants, without restrictions, with some limits, of course, that he will not violate the general security of the town. But I don't need to go to the municipality to get the permission to get the Spanish people in my house, for example. But a woman from Tibnin needs that. You know? And it puts a barrier. Even when they are going to make the medical visit, every week? They need the permission of the municipality of the towns. The people have the confidence in UNIFIL. They like to have contact with UNIFIL, but they don't dare. To say it loudly. You understand me?[50]

As noted previously, opinion in South Lebanon is not uniform. The above civilian enjoyed close relations with the Spanish battalion and was very supportive of the mission. Equally, many others interviewed for this research were not. But of note is that support for UNIFIL was not dictated purely by religion. Experience with the battalions played a role in determining personal attitudes along with political preferences.

UNIFIL staff are extremely conscious of the fact that they are guests in Lebanon, and therefore it is impossible to impose themselves on a local community. There is little that can be done when it has not been possible to make contact with a village and the area remains off-limits for informal visits. For CIMIC and civil affairs officers, the challenge is always to keep trying to get through to a village where the municipality is not in favor of UNIFIL to try to turn the relationship around. Sometimes battalions have been successful, based on the length of time that the battalion has been in the area. The Ghanaian contingent found in some cases that sheer persistence paid off, and after several years they were able to build relationships with villages that had previously refused to engage with them.[51]

While UNIFIL has succeeded in building positive relationships with many in the local community, this fact alone does not afford them legitimacy. Perhaps one of the best examples of how UNIFIL has won credibility and not legitimacy is the observation made by one civilian about the nature of the relationships UNIFIL has built in the South. Owing to the importance of this issue to the argument of this book, this story is also related in full:

> They accept them, within like . . . "I am a civilian. I am happy with UNIFIL as long they are doing humanitarian services, they are socializing, they are visiting me for tea or coffee. But if they are seeking information, or going to places where they are not supposed to go, I turn against them." I'll give you an example, like in Blat village. The village is under the Spanish. We have the Litani river nearby; it's outside the UNIFIL border [area of operation]. The Litani is a known place for the Hezbullah, or the armed elements, whatever you want to say. So people, they know that the Spanish, if they want to carry out patrols, they should go to the border, yes? So the moment they feel that they are coming, they try to give signals to the people that say, "Don't encourage them. Don't let them go. Try to stop them." You feel that if there is a movement for the Hezbullah, they try to make sure that the UNIFIL vehicles are not there. If they know that they are monitoring from one place, they make sure that as long as the patrol is there, no one moves. So people cooperate with UNIFIL to a certain extent and protect their own people in the other way. So they are playing a smart role, I can say.[52]

UNIFIL navigates the politics of its mandate and troop contingents by endeavoring to engage with actors from all political sides. Material credibility can be beneficial in breaking down barriers and building relationships with local government that can smooth UNIFIL's patrolling path in a particular village. The difference between legitimacy and credibility is particularly noticeable in UNIFIL's local relationships. Material credibility wins cooperation that enables the mission to patrol, but it does not win trust or legitimacy. Furthermore, UNIFIL has to work hard to maintain confidence on an ongoing basis by maintaining relationships and by continuing to provide material benefits.

Responsiveness Credibility

Civil affairs officers are differentiated from CIMIC officers in two ways. First, while both liaise with the local population about service provision and problem resolution, civil affairs' approach is more social. Civil affairs officers spend a great deal of time simply talking to members of the local population, sometimes about their issues, but sometimes just passing the time of day. They regularly attend local ceremonies that celebrate local achievements or the completion of a quick impact project that UNIFIL has sponsored.[53] Second, civil affairs officers are civilians (as opposed to military), and some are Lebanese citizens. This status affords them local cultural knowledge that can be essential when problems arise, and the long-term nature of their posts means they are able to develop long-term relationships with members of the local population:

> We have this daily contact with the local people. It starts from building friendly relations. I just go to a shopkeeper and sit with him, to take a cup of coffee. And through this friendship he starts to talk about the needs of the village or whatever. This shopkeeper might tell you that, you know, we have a problem with the sewage system. . . . So we go to the municipality and say, "How we can help in solving this problem?" In some cases we cannot help, but even when we cannot help, at least we show them the path how to do this. And this makes us have good relations with these people.[54]

The course of civilian relations does not always run smoothly, and locally employed staff in the form of civil affairs officers try to prevent and then manage problems when they arise between the local population and battalions. As mentioned earlier, civil affairs officers liaise between the local population and UNIFIL to ensure that the message of UNIFIL's mandate is clearly conveyed to the population at every level. They prevent

or resolve problems or misunderstandings on the ground as quickly as possible and convey public concerns about UNIFIL back to UNIFIL staff and
battalions to avoid future misunderstandings. Civil affairs officers' responsiveness and the time they spend getting to know the local community are
crucially important in helping to build credibility for UNIFIL.

The Civil Affairs Office exists in part to support the CIMIC services
offered by the individual battalions. It is important to afford battalions
credit for quick impact projects to provide them the greatest opportunity
to build local relationships with the municipalities. This credit is particularly helpful for the poorer battalions that may not be able to fund
large-scale projects. When a charity has donated funds toward a particular
project, Civil Affairs will try to involve a local battalion with that project.
For example, Civil Affairs asked the Ghanaians to give a dancing performance during the handover of new school computers.[55] Battalions looking
to fund projects from their own national funds will often ask Civil Affairs
for their advice on project proposals from a village. The battalions do not
have to listen to the advice of the Civil Affairs Office, but CIMIC officers
within the battalions recognize that they have local knowledge and experience that they lack, owing to the constant troop rotations.

Political Perceptions

International politics affects local perceptions of UNIFIL and UNIFIL
officers. I found both international and Lebanese officers understand very
well local sentiment and are pragmatic about it: "You know, people can
be sympathizers; they don't have to be activists. . . . It doesn't mean they
have a weapon in their hands. I know where their loyalties are. They don't
have to explain to me, and it's not a problem for me. It doesn't mean they
are a raving Hezbullah guy who wants to go running over the hill, like. It
doesn't mean that."[56] A local civilian described it thus: "[Support for Hez-
bullah] is in their blood. . . . I don't see that these people will give them
up, because in every single house you have someone who was killed. It is
not easy to inhale the wound."[57]

In my research I found that suspicion of UNIFIL tended to be higher
among Shi'a civilians, and there was more skepticism about their "true"

intentions. These doubts reflected the political position of Hezbullah, whose argument is that Resolution 1701 has been constructed to benefit Israel more than it does Lebanon. But as noted above, differences in attitudes toward UNIFIL do not totally depend on the sectarian allegiances of civilians. To be sure, the political allegiances of some in the Shi'ite community can lead to a perceived conflict of interest for civilians in terms of their relationship with UNIFIL. But these differences are not as simple as a Shia-Christian split. Within the Shi'ite population, views differ depending on which of the main parties that civilians support (Amal or Hezbullah). Equally within Hezbullah's supporters, levels of support vary: some are committed followers, others less so.

The extent of true and unflinching support among locals for Hezbullah is impossible to gauge because of the overriding desire for peace among the people of the South. At times respondents spoke the discourse of resistance, but they were more concerned that peace be maintained. While local civilians know UNIFIL is not able to protect them from another war, unlike Hezbullah, they also know that ultimately it will not be UNIFIL that starts another war, whereas Hezbullah can provide no such guarantees. As such, it is possible that respondents speak the language of resistance, but unless Israel launched an unprovoked attack, they would prefer that Hezbullah not engage in provocative maneuvers that could trigger another invasion. One civilian described it thus: "This is the mentality of the people. Like, okay, they don't encourage Hezbullah to provoke, or to create the troubles or clashes, because this will have a bad effect on them. But at the same time, they will never encourage that you will tell where are they, where they gather, where are their positions. They just give a blank about any information they ask in this regard."[58]

Regular Challenges

As mentioned earlier, civil affairs officers act as the liaison point or interface between the local community and the peacekeeping operation. The use of local civilian staff presents a more informal interface to a population weary of militia and the military. To illustrate the nature of how UNIFIL retains the confidence of the local population and therefore cooperation, it is useful to discuss the problems that occur regularly that civil affairs officers need to manage and the techniques they use to do so. Problems most commonly faced are local political views about the foreign policy of troop contingents, a lack of cultural and religious awareness, troops taking photographs, and speeding vehicles. These issues are for the most part caused by the frequent and constant troop rotations. Some battalions (such as the Indians) rotate once a year, some (like the Irish and Ghanaians) every six months, and some (such as the Spanish) every four months. This heavy rotation schedule renders local battalion knowledge of the area extremely poor at times.

New UNIFIL troops often lack awareness of religious customs. Simply knowing these small details can prevent many unintentional mistakes: "Misunderstandings . . . you know, here they occur mostly at Ramadan times and all these people who drink these things. . . . And I don't blame them because they don't know, and we keep teaching them, you know?"[59]

Civil affairs officers work hard to educate battalions about local religious norms:

> I am Lebanese, so I know exactly what the tradition is, and we transfer this cultural awareness to the military contingents from different countries. You know, UNIFIL has forty different countries' troops in this country. So imagine you have forty cultures. So it's not an easy job, and, every six months or four months or one year this contingent is changed, so new soldiers come. Old soldiers go and new soldiers come, so we have to begin this process again. Because even those soldiers have some training about cultural awareness in their countries before coming here, but having the training is something, and living the reality is something else, you see, so this is kind of our work.[60]

The population of South Lebanon is extremely sensitive about foreigners taking photographs of the area. This issue is connected to the mandate's local-international legitimacy gap and the perceived political preferences of European troops that have diplomatic relations with Israel. The Hezbullah perspective is that foreigners (including tourists) taking photographs in the area of operation pose a security risk, because if the photographs were to pass into the hands of Israel, they would provide important strategic geographical information. Despite UNIFIL's long-term presence, when foreign troops take photos of the region, some locals view this activity as spying. Civilians expressed their belief that troops from these countries can and do pass security information on to Israel:[61] "They are always afraid of UNIFIL because they think that maybe they will take photographs and information and give it to Israel. This is the only thing that they are scared of. . . . As long as they don't touch their own people, their own roots, they have no problem. But the moment they feel that, 'Okay, they are, like, looking for something,' they turn against."[62]

UNIFIL officers demonstrate sensitivity toward complaints from local municipalities and civilians on the issue of photo taking, and civil affairs officers consistently remind battalions not to do it. In every battalion compound I visited, there was a sign at the main gate instructing soldiers not to take photographs. Despite all the warnings, it still happens, often because many troops have never been to the region and want to take mementos; they just do not comprehend the depth of local sensitivities.[63]

Civil affairs officers are also concerned about speeding vehicles on local roads. Heavy APCs damage local roads, which upsets local civilians, and speeding vehicles raise safety concerns, as children play on the roads. This issue concerns UNIFIL[64] and illustrates UNIFIL's awareness of its constant need to prove itself in the sense that it is unable to make mistakes and be forgiven for them. When asked about his biggest fear, one Lebanese UNIFIL officer said, "Oh, yes, I will tell you. My main worry is a car accident. Our APCs are very heavy. If we smash a family in a car, kill them all, this is one of the things I am afraid of."[65]

Cultural Sensitivities

Another political problem that UNIFIL navigates locally is troop contingents' behavior on the ground. Aside from religious misunderstandings and local suspicions of European troops, communication style and posture are also very important. Face-to-face contact in the Middle East is regarded as extremely important, and some civilians found certain battalions easier to deal with than others: "Because face-to-face, especially here in the Middle East, I think, it's very important. When they trust you as a person, they will trust the whole mission. You know, it's important—the individual relationship that you may have with someone is paramount."[66]

In general, the personal characteristics of Asian battalions were more popular than the Europeans'. Many civilians spoke of the respectful nature of Asian battalions, their friendliness, and their shared values, such as family ties and hospitality toward guests. Civilians commented that Indians, South Koreans, and Indonesians had manners and a communication style that were more compatible with their local culture:[67] "Usually, the Asian approach is a very respectful one. You know the Asian system, so they are different from the Europeans."[68] Sometimes, battalions are liked more for their personal style that other nationalities cannot mimic: "You know what the difference is? The Indonesian battalion, for example, smile and wave at the people as they go past! They smile and wave."[69]

The Europeans face a far harder time for a number of reasons. As noted above, the foreign policy of EU troop contingents means some civilians view them as spies for Israel. Locals always complained that European troops took photos but the non-European troops did not. In addition, European mannerisms have often given offense. An Italian CIMIC officer raised this issue: "The military operations can reflect the cultural differences. . . . Northern Europeans are more direct, you know, are more serious when they approach someone, even though they are the best, warm, and simple person. Southern people like me—I am from the South of Italy—we do move our hands a lot when we talk, we smile a lot, and we are more friendly, but it doesn't mean we are easy people."[70]

Europeans in particular are perceived as arrogant. Their behavior on patrol was regarded as a particular problem: "Yeah, for example, passing by in the patrol and throwing chocolate for the kids. This is very bad. If you to give [it] to them, stop your patrol and give it by hand. And shake hands with the kid. This is the way to give help. Even if it's charity. If you want to give them a bottle of water, don't throw it from the window or off the top of the vehicle. This is arrogant."[71]

For Asian peacekeepers, local sympathy is a distinct advantage. The Indian contingent was able to connect more easily with the local population because of similar customs,[72] and the Ghanaian contingent was aware that they suffered lower threats to their security: "Well, to be very frank, I will say that the threats especially to our battalion are very low, very low, as compared to those of the Europeans."[73]

The Spanish in particular have experienced more problems than other European battalions. Their posture can come across as quite aggressive, perhaps because they have been affected specifically in South Lebanon and by past experience of other peacekeeping missions.[74] Many civilians interviewed felt that the Spanish adopted an aggressive and unfriendly attitude at the beginning of their time in the mission and have remained that way.[75] Civil affairs officers are frank with these battalions when they think they have behaved insensitively toward the local population. For example, when the Spanish arrived at a school for special needs to put on a show, they were armed with pistols, which the civil affairs officer felt was highly inappropriate.[76] The civil affairs officer reprimanded the battalion for their actions after the event.

UNIFIL navigates the politics of the different troop nationalities by constantly reminding locals that all troops represent the United Nations and not their nation-states, but this point largely appears to fall on deaf ears and battalions are often judged by the foreign policies of their state and their posture.[77] The issue of cultural compatibility may seem a frivolous factor on which to focus in terms of its power to inform local perceptions of peacekeepers. However, it is not trivial, given the importance attributed to face-to-face contact in the region and its potential to turn a bad situation into a serious security incident, as the following section shows.

Earning Responsiveness Credibility

Communication and negotiation have earned UNIFIL responsiveness credibility, and creativity and spontaneity also play an important role. Some concrete examples of UNIFIL's successful local engagement can be seen in the experiences of one civil affairs officer who has worked with UNIFIL for ten years.

One winter's morning, the UNIFIL civil affairs officer was instructed to go to Marja'youn, a town in Sector East of the area of operation. There had been an accident in the center of Marja'youn between a Spanish armored personnel carrier [APC] and a bus full of schoolchildren. When the civil affairs officer arrived on the scene, he found an angry mob, including members of Hezbullah, surrounding the Spanish APC. Senior LAF officers were present, but they had been unable to control the crowd or prevent them from encircling the APC. The crowd had blocked off the APC through the use of parked cars in order to prevent it from leaving the area. The Spanish troops were outside the APC with their weapons cocked. Making the situation far worse than it already was were the cultural misunderstandings between the locals and the Spanish:

> I reached there, [and] there were two APCs, and local people put a civilian car in front and behind each vehicle to prevent them from moving, and they wanted the driver of the APC. Why? Now you see the difference in culture. Here in Lebanon, if a car accident occurs and there are wounded people, what do people do usually? They do not wait for the ambulance; they just take the wounded people to the hospital. The Spanish culture is that you are not allowed to touch the wounded people. You wait for the ambulance until it comes, and then the ambulance will take you. And the accident occurred with a school bus. Ten wounded children, shouting in the bus, blood coming in their faces . . . and the soldiers not allowing anybody to approach the bus.[78]

The situation was also aggravated by Spanish security precautions, which meant they were using technology that jams all the cell phones around the APC—a precaution most European troops use to avoid remote detonation of improvised explosive devices when patrolling. Locals who had tried to call ambulances had been unable to get through. The situation was turning nasty. As noted by the respondent, "I reached there, [and] everybody was shouting. The LAF can't prevent people from approaching the APCs. Soldiers on the APCs, their fingers on the trigger, they are afraid because any wrong move might lead to a massacre out there."[79]

The outcome of this incident was positive and well handled by the civil affairs officer, demonstrating how invaluable the presence of local staff is to a UN mission:

I reached there, and I know the people of the area and I know who is leading them—it's Hezbullah. "We want the driver who wounded our children." I told them, "I am the UNIFIL civil affairs officer. My name is . . . You know me. . . . I am UNIFIL, and those kids are my kids. You trust me or you don't trust me?" They said, "We trust you." I said, "Okay. I will be with you until we solve the problem. What we need now is to provide medical help for the kids, isn't it?" They said yes. I said, "Okay, I will remain with you until you receive confirmation from UNIFIL that your kids will be treated on our account. Regardless of who is responsible for the accident, those are our kids." Here I have to take the initiative, first of all to prevent contact between soldiers of UNIFIL and the local people, because any contact might lead to a massacre. I told them, "The first thing now is to see the military here go from here. Let them leave, and if you trust me, I will stay with you." And they allowed the Spanish troops to leave. So I defused the tension. Now also I am a UN officer, so I can be a hostage in this case. So how to solve it? LAF Intelligence was there. I told them, "Is it possible to stay here in the winter on the street?" It started to rain. "Let's go to the LAF office. It's our partner." As if I brought them to my office. So in the LAF office I know I won't be taken hostage.[80]

The Spanish Embassy in Beirut covered all the costs for the wounded children in the hospital, but the civil affairs officer had no way of knowing it at the time. He simply knew he had to take the initiative in order to prevent what would have been a disaster for UNIFIL in terms of retaining local consent to operate in the area: "So regardless of who is responsible for the accident, we should help because this is very important to us. And the accident did not happen with a small car. It's an APC; it's like a tank, so they must drive more carefully. And the tank hit the bus in the middle. You see, this is confidence building. To take a courageous decision at a crucial time, in a crucial situation, you have to take the initiative."[81]

Personal experience with UNIFIL troops plays a big part in civilian views of UNIFIL, highlighting again the importance of making contact with as many people as possible. Those individuals who had good experiences with UNIFIL tended to be more positive than the ones who had not. It also suggests that those municipalities who forbade their villagers from making contact with UNIFIL are all too aware of this fact.

Another example of the creativity and spontaneity of the civil affairs officer relates to the influx of Syrian refugees into the area of operations. As mentioned earlier, UNIFIL is unable to directly provide assistance to the refugees, other than allowing them to use the free medical and dental services that the battalions offer. When refugees began to flood into Shebaa, the mayor of the town contacted UNIFIL for help. The UNIFIL civil affairs officer then contacted the Lebanese government and the UN High Commission for Refugees, both of which provided material assistance on the very same day.[82]

Even when problems do not exist, the civil affairs officer works to assist the population in any way possible, irrespective of the constraints of the mandate. Every positive connection or incident contributes to the success of the mission as a whole and helps in building positive relationships with the local population. The civil affairs officer can relate to the concerns of the local population because he is Lebanese and demonstrates creativity by assisting local people without having to use UNIFIL resources. One local school benefited from the media attention that the civil affairs officer generated when the headmaster had a problem accommodating all his students in the class. The headmaster had tried to fix the problem by using shipping containers to provide extra space:

He bought three containers and put them on top of the roof of the building and made them into classrooms. So I went to the principal, and I asked him, "What are you doing with these containers?" He said, "I have an extra number of students, and, you know, we are a very far village and people are very poor. Those who send their kids to a public school are poor people. I am not going to say no for them; there is no place. So I use my budget. I cannot build a new building, but I bought these containers and I made them a classroom." I told him, "Are you crazy? In winter you are there, seventeen hundred meters above the seashore, and it snows in winter up there. You are putting them in a refrigerator! And unless the student is very close to the stove, the others will feel cold!" He said, "Yeah, better them feeling cold than being illiterate." I told him, "And even during the sunny days, it will be very hot, putting them in an oven." He said, "What to do? Do you have any other proposal?" I told him, "No, we cannot build this school."[83]

The result on this occasion was that the media attention embarrassed the government in Beirut, and it responded by building extra classrooms for the school immediately. Media has consistently been a useful tool for civil affairs officers in cases where UNIFIL does not have the budget or the mandate to help. Traveling around the area of operation regularly and talking to local people means civil affairs officers are able to identify the issues that bother local civilians and try to help them find solutions. This kind of assistance goes above and beyond the mandate of UNIFIL staff, and the autonomous conditions under which civil affairs officers operate enable them to be spontaneous and use informal networks in order to respond as quickly as possible to changing circumstances.

As noted previously, it can be difficult for UNIFIL to engage with municipalities that hold political prejudices against the mission. While this is often more of a personality issue than a political one, civil affairs officers have to work to convince the local mayor that UNIFIL is impartial and wants to help. In some cases, the confidence of local government has been won by the battalions themselves—for instance, by the Ghanaian contingent, where sheer persistence paid off.[84] In situations where municipalities are unfriendly, the civil affairs officer can sometimes find a way through that CIMIC officers cannot by using local connections and knowledge of local sensibilities:

I can give you a fine example of a village. The mayor is Hezbullah, and I know that he is Hezbullah but I don't know him personally, but I know that he is. I went to meet him, and I told him that there is an NGO [nongovernmental organization] in Beirut that wants to help, giving some trees. "Are you interested to have trees? Because I heard that you have a project of planting trees in the outskirts of the village." He said, "What is this organization?" I was joking with him! I said, "This is a Zionist organization. Why do you care what is this? Take the trees. . . . I don't mind what is the political affiliation of this organization. They want to help. You want the help or you don't want it?" And he said, "Let me think about it." . . . The next day the mayor called me and said, "Yes, we want this thing."[85]

In facilitating this project by talking to elected officials, the civil affairs officer managed to build a relationship with a mayor of a village who otherwise would have rejected contact with UNIFIL. Now, thanks to this project, UNIFIL is able to visit the municipality and maintain cordial relations with the community there.

Ultimately, my time in the area revealed to me that while UNIFIL works hard to build relationships with the local population and perceives these relationships as being trustful, they have in fact won confidence. This fact is demonstrated by local willingness to receive goods and services yet be largely unwilling to assist UNIFIL in allowing them to patrol wherever they like. Furthermore, when crises like the Spanish bus crash happen, the local response was negative and swift, which also does not suggest trust. UNIFIL staff appeared to conflate confidence with trust, but at the same time they were aware they can't afford to make mistakes. Understanding by UNIFIL of the material nature of their relationship with the local population appeared to be limited.

Conclusion

The local civilian engagement of UNIFIL provides a clear picture of the material interests underlying the credibility of the mission. While UNIFIL has earned local cooperation and confidence, this relationship does not extend to trust. It is clear that the local population will tolerate patrols and engage with the mission, but should the mission try to intercept activities related to Hezbullah, local communities who support them will close ranks. Furthermore, UNIFIL itself is well aware that it does not have license to make mistakes in the area of operation. The relationship, therefore, between UNIFIL and the local population appears to be largely positive, but is underwritten by instrumentality, often contingent on the regular provision of material resources and a high level of responsiveness to local needs.

Conclusion

Despite being listed as an important second-order success factor in UN peacekeeping operations, the concept of credibility has received minimal attention in the scholarship on peacekeeping. In this book I have unpacked credibility and revealed a number of its attributes. I conclude that it is underwritten by material interests and has three main features: it needs to be constantly sustained with evidence, it is context dependent and can be won in specific areas but not across the board, and it cannot be obtained up front but must be earned over time. The benefits of winning credibility are cooperation and confidence.

In the process of describing credibility, I have shown in detail how the UNIFIL peacekeeping operation in South Lebanon navigates the political tensions that surround its mandate. I have shown how an international institution can be constrained by weak local legitimacy born of a complex political situation that comprises both inter- and intrastate war and that by winning different types of credibility, the UNIFIL mission has been able to exercise a large part of its mandate.

By the end of my research, I realized that some UNIFIL staff were aware they did not have legitimacy, but many still appeared to believe that with sufficient effort, trust and legitimacy could be won. In light of the conflicted nature of the mandate, and the fact that the local population is composed of around 74 percent Shi'a, many of whom harbor support for Hezbullah, it is unlikely these two elements can be won. This issue serves as a reminder that institutions can develop their own cultures that at times can be remote from the communities they are working within. In my view, many UN staff need to believe they have the capacity to win trust as part of their passionate belief in the legitimacy of the United Nations itself.

Legitimacy and Credibility

Five themes emerge in this book, and they are worth clarifying here. First, is the difference between legitimacy and credibility. In my search to understand credibility, I have shown that credibility and legitimacy have often been conflated in discussions of peacekeeping, and I show how legitimacy is underwritten by ideas, whereas credibility is underwritten by material interests. As such, I suggest here credibility has the capacity to win confidence and legitimacy has the capacity to win trust.

Trust, as an emotional belief, can be won upfront but can be eroded over time by untrustworthy behavior on the part of the trusted. Legitimacy shares many of the same attributes. It can be won up front but eroded by poor peacekeeper behavior in the field. Credibility, on the other hand, takes time to be built and requires not only evidence to build it in the first place, but also a continuous supply of evidence to maintain it. I also argue that as separate concepts, credibility and legitimacy can coexist, but that credibility can function where there is weak or minimal local legitimacy.

I examine in this book the relationship between local legitimacy and local credibility. What remains in question is the relationship between source legitimacy and credibility. The United Nations assumes that in peace operations, legitimacy translates from the international source to the local level. We can see in the UNIFIL mission that when it does not happen, the norms of the mandate are not internalized by the local population, and the mission must then turn to material incentives to obtain compliance. Furthermore, we see that coercion is not an available option for the UNIFIL mission in light of strong local support for Hezbullah. While the UNIFIL mission has been given perhaps an impossible mandate, this issue is faced by other international interventions; local perceptions will not always gel with international ones, not least because the "local" is heterogeneous and offers myriad different views of the role and purpose of the mission.

To be sure, there is an effect of source legitimacy of the United Nations on UNIFIL; it is highly doubtful that a force composed of individual states, or a "coalition of the willing," would have been able to gain any kind of foothold in South Lebanon. But local legitimacy is different from source legitimacy. This point has already been noted in the literature on peace operations; while a peace operation can possess legitimacy in the international community and among audiences at the national level, at the subnational level it is not guaranteed.

By raising the issue of how credibility functions, the limitations of credibility have been exposed. In the literature on peace operations, there remain many questions about what local legitimacy is or isn't, how to win it, and what kind of social capital it affords a peacekeeping operation. I argue that ofttimes what is described as local legitimacy in the literature is in fact credibility. Based on my definition of credibility, I raise the question of whether it is actually possible for an international intervention to ever really win local legitimacy.

Questions that require further research include the relationship between trust and legitimacy as well as a comparative study of various peace operations to help establish the reliability of my findings on credibility. A final question that this case study has been unable to answer is the power of source legitimacy on credibility. While local legitimacy and credibility can be distinguished from one another, it may not be the case with source legitimacy and credibility, which doubtless exercise some influence.

The use of force and its lack of utility in the UNIFIL environment are another important finding of this research. UNIFIL is unable to use force in the area of operation because were it to do so, it would necessarily alienate most of the local population, even those individuals who might be more favorably disposed to UNIFIL in the first place. Despite calls by Israel and the United States for UNIFIL to employ a more forceful posture and rid the area of alleged Hezbullah weapons, in this environment deterrence is not an option.[1] As such, winning cooperation from the local population has necessarily been through the use of nonviolent means. UNIFIL aside, recent history has shown that peace enforcement does not work in Lebanon. The Multinational Forces (I and II) and the Israeli and Syrian occupations were all ejected from Lebanon when trying to enforce peace. Local perceptions of the international interests at play in these attempts to enforce calm rendered all of them illegitimate, and by employing credibility in the way that it has, UNIFIL has survived precisely because it does not try to impose the will of some international actors in the area of operation.

Ultimately, the issue of Hezbullah's weapons is a national debate that needs to be solved by national solutions, not by international interposition. The most important role UNIFIL can play is to work to restrain the parties by shining an international spotlight on the area and continue to work toward the creation of everyday peace by helping the Lebanese build national institutions and infrastructure in an area that has repeatedly been torn apart by war.

Four types of credibility have been identified in this book—responsiveness, material, technical, and security. Unpacking the concept of credibility enables us to understand the different ways that peace operations serve the community and build relationships and the benefits that each of these types of credibility bring to the mission. Each element of credibility can be won or lost individually, and when establishing a mission, credibility will not immediately be present. Credibility is established over time and requires sustaining with evidence, and it is not something that is earned upon arrival with an initial show of weapons or money.

Scholarship on local legitimacy argues that a mission's legitimacy can increase or decrease over time.[2] One benefit of increasing our understanding of credibility in a peace operation is that it enables us to identify a strategy for bridging a legitimacy gap. Thus, when legitimacy for an intervention waxes and wanes, or is not present, credibility may ultimately be the factor that enables the force to function and therefore maintain stable conditions. Understanding what credibility can do for an international intervention is important and valuable, especially in light of the conflicts raging in Iraq, Syria, and Yemen.

A question that arises, then, is should peace operations seek credibility only under certain conditions? If they did so, and abandoned any pretension of seeking legitimacy, would something be lost? In practical terms, it is unlikely, because credibility is built up through a variety of actions that contribute to the material well-being of the community. But in terms of how staff conceive of their purpose and the source legitimacy of the

United Nations, it is possible that resorting to seeking only credibility might result in a loss of passion and cynicism from UN staff.

Finally, this research has also shown that despite scholarly discussion on local legitimacy, we still do not understand what kind of purchase it affords a mission. What does a "stock of goodwill" afford a peace operation? How many mistakes can a peace operation make before it loses legitimacy? I believe it is right to talk about the difference between international (source) legitimacy and local legitimacy, but I argue that the concept of local legitimacy may at times be credibility, which plays a very different role in the functionality of missions.

Temporality

A second theme that emerges from this book is the role of time. The continuity of the UNIFIL mission plays a big part in contributing to the management of smooth relations between the named parties (Israel and the Lebanese government) and their representatives (the IDF and the LAF). Over time, long-term UNIFIL staff have built relations with groups at both the local and the national levels that enable them to work collaboratively and generate solutions. Continuity also generates institutional memory, which, for example, means that political affairs officers understand "the rules" that govern the perceptions of both parties. They have demonstrated to both sides their impartiality and competence, which has been key to enabling stand-downs at critical moments because the parties regard them as "honest brokers" and have confidence in them. Temporality also facilitates consistency of effort, which is important in moving forward toward a sustainable peace. Political affairs officers' efforts in capacity building the Lebanese Armed Forces are starting to reap rewards, but only after years of effort; it is not something that can be executed as a short-term goal.

The short-term tenure of military staff that results in constant rotations is acknowledged to be a problem both on the ground and at the top in terms of replacement of force commanders. This heavy rotation negatively affects UNIFIL staff and civilians alike. The LAF, the strategic partner of UNIFIL, dislikes having to reeducate a new force commander every two years about institutional norms and local culture. Civilians complain that it is hard to get to know the battalions because no sooner have they arrived than they leave again. LAF officers noted that without the presence of certain long-term staff in the political affairs office, little progress would have been made both in capacity building the LAF and in generating preventative solutions for discussion at the tripartite meetings. At the local level, the long-term nature of civil affairs officer appointments also enables them to witness shifts in the local environment, such as the increase in Syrian refugees, and to build lasting relationships. This point was most noticeable among civilian respondents who were pro-Hezbullah. Even when they disagreed in principle with the UNIFIL mission objectives, many appeared to have a deep personal liking for the UNIFIL civil affairs officers they knew.

There is no substitute for building confidence over time. While liaison officers can use honesty and common sense to manage incoming crises to "firefight," they are not capable of generating preventative measures, in part because they have not been given access to key individuals through which to exercise influence and in part because they have not built a track record with the parties. Ultimately, a peace operation will always be faced with the difficulty of gauging how long a mission should be present. However, the UNIFIL mission shows us that time is a crucial component in helping to prevent flare-ups and in obtaining a measure of compliance from civilians in an area where Western-led institutions are regarded with intense suspicion. The local population may evaluate UNIFIL on the basis of the material benefits they obtain, but they also acknowledge how much UNIFIL has done for the area over time. Time then helps to mitigate the problem of "self-interest" referred to in chapter 1, although it does not obtain local legitimacy for the mission.

In regard to international interventions, there has been discussion, particularly in the case of Iraq and Afghanistan, of the need to commit to the long term for genuine reform to occur.[3] The case of UNIFIL highlights the important and useful role that long-term staff members play and therefore illustrates that when established, peace operations should ensure they retain some long-serving staff in the course of the mission's life. The

UN's recruitment policies have been criticized for nepotism and sloth; my research shows the particular need to employ more staff with local knowledge, which would help to resolve this problem.[4]

The Broader Picture

The third theme is that the research outlined in this book revealed a number of interesting empirical findings about how peace operations function—for example, how everyday small actions on the Blue Line are effectively preventing the escalation of incidents that could swiftly turn into conflict. Examining how UNIFIL monitors the Blue Line also highlights the complex network of relationships that exist between international and local actors in a peace operation—for example, language can constrain negotiations between different contingents in relation to how to manage a situation on the ground. Peace operations are fractured communities in the sense that battalions are often isolated and their only contact with other peacekeepers can be through headquarters. Building networks within the mission can therefore be just as useful as building networks among the local community to get the best results on a given day.

Understanding the microprocesses of a peace operation also helps us to examine the qualitative nature of the relationships that peace operations have with the local community. It illustrates how local actors can act as gatekeepers of a local community and impede UN access to civilians. Furthermore, a close examination of local civilians' conception of UNIFIL reveals an interesting contradiction: the political objections to the mandate that guide many local perceptions of UNIFIL versus a local longing for peace or warm relations (or both) with a particular UNIFIL battalion or individual. Interestingly, while this book highlights the material nature of the relationship between UNIFIL and the local population, it also shows how little things, such as the nonmaterial contribution of UNIFIL, or the smallest gesture can go further in winning hearts and minds than large expenditures. So while material interests may be what ultimately drive local considerations about whether to comply with UNIFIL's requests, this relationship is a nuanced one, overlaid by quality relationships generated over time.

Maintaining Stable Conditions

As I noted earlier, perceptions of UNIFIL are woven into civilian feelings about peace. In many ways, UNIFIL has tapped into the people's desire for peace by providing a steady and reliable presence.

> Well, I think the majority of the people, you know, irrespective of who they might support, I think the majority of people in every country you go to, they just want normality. People just want to get back to normality. It's just like everybody else, you know. You just want your kids to grow up and go to school; you want to go on a holiday. And that's what most of the people in the South are striving for, and they know, I think realistically, in their heart and soul that while the resistance is necessary in their minds, and probably is necessary, they know that they have to move beyond that too. They would like things to be normal and let the state cater to their security and their needs.[5]

A fourth theme of this book, then, is the maintenance of stable conditions. While the UNIFIL operation is unable to influence political actors to generate a peaceful solution to the ongoing conflict, it has created conditions conducive to peace. "Everyday peace" has been described as "the routinized practices used by individuals and collectives as they navigate their way through life in a deeply divided society that may suffer from ethnic or religious cleavages and be prone to episodic direct violence in addition to chronic or structural violence."[6] While these routinized practices exist in Lebanon, there is also a "normalization of peace"—meaning people are able to live their lives with minimal disruption from conflict or postconflict issues.[7] As one political affairs officer noted, "We have had ten years of peace. In another ten years we will have a generation of people who have only known peace."[8] Elise Boulding describes the culture of peace as being a socialization process: "It cannot be said that humans are innately peaceful or aggressive. Both capacities are there. It is socialization, the process by which society rears its children and shapes the attitudes and behaviors of its members of all ages, that determines how peacefully or violently individuals and institutions handle the problems that every human community faces in the daily work of maintaining itself."[9]

Ultimately, while sectarian political rhetoric remains present in Lebanon, socialization can take other forms. In the absence of a political solution to the conflict, and while it is not yet understood what effect this kind of intervention has on a local community, it is possible that having led a normal life for a protracted period, the local community will gradually lose interest in war and may be harder to mobilize in support of war. Hence, the normalization of peace in everyday life may lead to a change in normative ideas about the utility of war versus a peaceful life.

Predictability in Security

The fifth theme relates to predictability in the security environment. The routine actions of the UNIFIL mission—whether it be responding to each and every transgression of the Blue Line or conducting regular patrols in the villages—have created a kind of predictable security order. In a highly insecure environment, generating predictability is better than unpredictability, even if it means that some actors are able to take advantage of it and circumvent the mission. An unpredictable security environment is dangerous, as it allows for accidental confrontations with Hezbullah, which is not in the interests of the mission. A military showdown of any sort with Hezbullah would result in a contest for local legitimacy between UNIFIL and Hezbullah, and this competition is not one that UNIFIL could win.

Conclusion

While high theory or grand theory may be able to posit a great many things about the way the human race works, at the granular level we can observe whether these theories play out. The UNIFIL case has highlighted what credibility is and the role it plays in helping a peacekeeping mission function on the ground. It has isolated the difference between local credibility and local legitimacy and raises the question of whether local legitimacy has been confused for credibility at the local level in peacekeeping missions. In doing so, many questions remain unanswered. We still do not understand a great deal about the purchase that local legitimacy affords peacekeeping missions in terms of how much leverage it provides, its relationship with trust, and how it can be won.

In sum, the deviant case of the UNIFIL mission in South Lebanon raises several issues for further research. First, we need to develop a better understanding of the second-order success factors of legitimacy and credibility as individual concepts in peacebuilding in order to understand their utility. Second, we need to clarify the relationship between credibility and source legitimacy in peace operations. Third, in the discipline of political science we need to think more deeply about the nature of credibility to understand its role in international relations.

Notes

Bibliography

Index

Notes

Introduction

1. Interview with civilian, Hebbariyeh, South Lebanon, June 18, 2013.

2. Interview with civilian, Marja'youn, South Lebanon, Aug. 27, 2013.

3. Interview with civilian, al-Tiri, South Lebanon, Oct. 8, 2013.

4. Interview with UNIFIL civil affairs officer, Naqoura, South Lebanon, Aug. 13, 2013.

5. John Galtung, *Peace by Peaceful Means: Peace and Conflict, Development and Civilization*, 30; Charles T. Call and Elizabeth M. Cousens, "Ending Wars and Building Peace: International Responses to War-Torn Societies."

6. UNSC Resolution 425, Mar. 19, 1978, para. 3.

7. United Nations Department of Peacekeeping Operations, *Handbook on United Nations Multidimensional Peacekeeping Operations*.

8. Some of these missions remain in place in the absence of a resolution to the conflicts that triggered the interventions in the first place.

9. Alex J. Bellamy and Paul D. Williams, *Understanding Peacekeeping*, 75.

10. UNSC Resolution 1701, Aug. 11, 2006, 2–3.

11. United Nations, *United Nations Peacekeeping Operations: Principles and Guidelines*.

12. I define the term *normalization of peace* as a form of everyday peace and the ability to live a normal life without having to contend with constant security threats.

13. Michael Barnett and Martha Finnemore, *Rules for the World: International Organizations in Global Politics*.

14. Beatrice Pouligny, *Peace Operations Seen from Below: UN Missions and Local People*; Severine Autesserre, *The Trouble with the Congo: Local Violence and the Failure of International Peacebuilding*; Roland Paris, *At War's End: Building Peace and Conflict*.

15. David Hirst, *Beware of Small States: Lebanon, Battleground of the Middle East*; Sandra McKay, *Mirror of the Arab World: Lebanon in Conflict*.

16. Karim Makdisi et al., "UNIFIL II: Emerging and Evolving European Engagement in Lebanon and the Middle East"; Karim Makdisi, "Constructing Security Council

Resolution 1701 for Lebanon in the Shadow of the War on Terror"; Nubar Hovsepian, ed., *The War on Lebanon: A Reader*; Hitoshi Nasu, "The Responsibility to React? Lessons from the Security Council's Response to the Southern Lebanon Crisis of 2006"; Bruce Jones and Andrew Hart, "Keeping Middle East Peace?"; Sylvia Christine Hamieh and Roger Mac Ginty, "A Very Political Reconstruction: Governance and Reconstruction in Lebanon after the 2006 War"; Paul Kingston, "The Pitfalls of Peacebuilding from Below"; Marie-Joelle Zahar, "Liberal Interventions, Illiberal Outcomes: The United Nations, Western Powers and Lebanon"; Roger Mac Ginty, "Reconstructing Post-war Lebanon: A Challenge to the Liberal Peace?"; Karen Abi-Ezzi, "Lebanon: Confessionalism, Institution Building, and the Challenges of Securing Peace."

17. Ray Murphy, *UN Peacekeeping in Lebanon, Somalia and Kosovo*; Ronald Hatto, "UN Command and Control Capabilities: Lessons from UNIFIL's Strategic Military Cell."

18. Janja Vuga, "Cultural Differences in Multinational Peace Operations: A Slovenian Perspective"; Michael Liégeois, "Making Sense of a Francophone Perspective on Peace Operations: The Case of Belgium as a Minofrancophone State"; Chiara Ruffa, "What Peacekeepers Think and Do: An Exploratory Study of French, Ghanaian, Italian, and South Korean Armies in the United Nations Interim Force in Lebanon."

19. These are the United Nations Peacekeeping Force in Cyprus (UNFICYP), the United Nations Military Observer Group in India and Pakistan (UNMOGIP), UNDOF in Syria, and UNTSO in Israel.

20. Murphy, *UN Peacekeeping*.

21. United Nations, *United Nations Peacekeeping Operations*.

22. Bellamy and Williams, *Understanding Peacekeeping*, 14–18.

23. United Nations, *United Nations Peacekeeping Operations*, 18.

24. Norrie MacQueen, *Peacekeeping and the International System*.

25. Bellamy and Williams, *Understanding Peacekeeping*.

26. Sir Marrack Goulding, "The Evolution of United Nations Peacekeeping."

27. See the full list in John G. Cockell, "Conceptualising Peacebuilding: Human Security and Sustainable Peace."

28. United Nations, *United Nations Peacekeeping Operations*, 18.

29. Cockell, "Conceptualising Peacebuilding"; John Braithwaite, "Evaluating the Timor-Leste Peace Operation"; Call and Cousens, "Ending Wars and Building Peace."

30. Roger Mac Ginty, *International Peacebuilding and Local Resistance: Hybrid Forms of Peace*; Oliver P. Richmond, *The Transformation of Peace*; Oliver P. Richmond, *A Post-Liberal Peace*.

31. Autesserre, *Trouble with the Congo*; Adam Moore, *Peacebuilding in Practice*; Thania Paffenholz, *Civil Society and Peacebuilding: A Critical Assessment*; Pouligny, *Peace Operations Seen from Below*.

32. Roland Paris, "Saving Liberal Peacebuilding," 343.

33. John Gerring, *Case Study Research: Principles and Practices*, 105.

34. The UNIFIL mission currently has 10,200 troops, but is mandated for up to 15,000. In comparison, UNDOF has only 1,243 troops, and UNFICYP has 857. UNTSO and UNMOGIP are observer missions only with no peacekeeping troops.

35. As of August 31, 2016. European troop contributing countries include Austria, Belgium, Croatia, Cyprus, Finland, France, Germany, Greece, Hungary, Ireland, Italy, and Spain. The largest contributors are Finland, Ireland, Italy, and Spain. See United Nations Peacekeeping, "Country Contributions Detailed by Mission."

36. Bellamy and Williams, *Understanding Peacekeeping.*

37. As of August 31, 2016. See United Nations Peacekeeping, "Contributors to United Nations Peacekeeping Operations."

38. Autesserre, *Trouble with the Congo.*

39. Zoe Bray, "Ethnographic Approaches," 314.

40. Della Porta and Keating argue that qualitative methods enable the researcher to understand the "why and how" of a research topic more than the "what, where and when" obtained from quantitative methodology. See Donatella della Porta and Michael Keating, *Approaches and Methodologies in the Social Sciences: A Pluralist Perspective.*

41. Mark Neufeld, "Relexivity and International Relations Theory," 54–55.

42. Pouligny, *Peace Operations Seen from Below*; Autesserre, *Trouble with the Congo.*

43. In this area of Beirut most people speak only Arabic and very little English.

44. Owing to political issues, it was not possible to observe or interview members of the IDF.

45. Della Porta and Keating, *Approaches and Methodologies.*

46. For example, see Autesserre, *Trouble with the Congo.*

47. In this book, I quote Nicholas Blanford, from his book, not from our interview. The former spokesman for UNIFIL Timur Göksel allowed his remarks to go on the record.

48. Autesserre, *Trouble with the Congo.*

1. The Role of Credibility in Peacekeeping

1. Interview with political affairs officer, Beirut, Lebanon, Nov. 15, 2013.

2. United Nations, *United Nations Peacekeeping Operations.*

3. Robert Powell, "Anarchy in International Relations Theory: The Neorealist-Neoliberal Debate."

4. Robert Powell, *Nuclear Deterrence Theory: The Search for Credibility*; Thomas C. Schelling, *Arms and Influence.*

5. William W. Kaufman, *The Requirements of Deterrence.*

6. Schelling, *Arms and Influence.*

7. Robert Jervis, *Perception and Misperception in International Politics*; Alexander George and Richard Smoke, *Deterrence in American Foreign Policy: Theory and Practice*; Vesna Danilovic, "The Sources of Threat Credibility in Extended Deterrence"; James

D. Fearon, "Domestic Political Audiences and the Escalation of International Disputes"; James D. Fearon, "Signaling Foreign Policy Interests: Tying Hands Versus Sinking Costs."

8. George W. Downs and Michael A. Jones, "Reputation, Compliance, and International Law"; Daniel W. Drezner, "Ten Things to Read about Reputation in International Relations"; Daryl Press, *Calculating Credibility: How Leaders Assess Military Threats*; Mark Crescenzi, "Reputation and International Conflict."

9. See, for example, Kenneth Oye, ed., *Cooperation under Anarchy*; Robert Axelrod, *The Evolution of Cooperation*; and Michael D. Bordo and Ronald MacDonald, *Credibility and the International Monetary Regime: A Historical Perspective*.

10. Axelrod, *The Evolution of Cooperation*.

11. Arthur A. Stein, "Coordination and Collaboration: Regimes in an Anarchic World"; Robert O. Keohane, *After Hegemony: Cooperation and Discord in the World Political Economy*.

12. Keohane, *After Hegemony*.

13. Stephen D. Krasner, *International Regimes*, 2; John J. Mearsheimer, "The False Promise of International Institutions," 8.

14. Janice Gross Stein, "Threat Perceptions in International Relations"; Jonathan Mercer, "Emotional Beliefs."

15. Anne Sartori, *Deterrence by Diplomacy*.

16. Alvin Tze Tien Tan, "Sovereign Credibility in International Political Economy."

17. The actor here is the UNIFIL mission.

18. Peter A. Hall and Rosemary C. R. Taylor, "Political Science and the Three New Institutionalisms," 949.

19. Ibid., 948.

20. Evan Schofer et al., "Sociological Institutionalism and World Society," 62.

21. John Dowling and Jeffrey Pfeffer, "Organizational Legitimacy: Social Values and Organizational Behaviour," 122.

22. Barnett and Finnemore, *Rules for the World*, 43.

23. Dowling and Pfeffer, "Organizational Legitimacy," 135.

24. Ian Hurd, "Legitimacy and Authority in International Politics."

25. Ibid., 381.

26. Ian Clark, "Legitimacy in a Global Order."

27. Mark C. Suchman, "Managing Legitimacy: Strategic and Institutional Approaches."

28. John Gerard Ruggie, "International Regimes, Transactions, and Change: Embedded Liberalism in the Postwar Economic Order," 382; Hurd, "Legitimacy and Authority," 388.

29. Hurd, "Legitimacy and Authority," 388.

30. Barnett and Finnemore, *Rules for the World*, 21.

31. Ibid., 7.

32. Ibid., 9.

33. Ibid., 19.

34. Joel Oestreich, ed., *International Organizations as Independent Actors: A Framework for Analysis.*

35. For instance, Tomz found public opinion matters to leaders when deciding whether to support foreign policy. See Michael Tomz, "Domestic Audience Costs in International Relations: An Experimental Approach." Chapman found that public perceptions of the interests of the states involved affect audience perceptions of the legitimacy of the decisions of international organizations. See Terence L. Chapman, "Audience Beliefs and International Organization Legitimacy."

36. Ian Hurd, "Legitimacy, Power, and the Symbolic Life of the UN Security Council."

37. Michael Pugh, "The Social-Civil Dimension"; Oliver P. Richmond, "The Romanticisation of the Local: Welfare, Culture and Peacebuilding"; Ole Jacob Sending, "Why Peacebuilders Fail to Secure Ownership and Be Sensitive to Context"; Sarah B. K. von Billerbeck, "Local Ownership and UN Peacebuilding: Discourse versus Operationalization."

38. Richmond, "Romanticisation of the Local."

39. Oliver P. Richmond and Jason Franks, *Liberal Peace Transitions: Between Statebuilding and Peacebuilding.*

40. Mac Ginty, *International Peacebuilding and Local Resistance*; Thania Paffenholz, "What Civil Society Can Contribute to Peacebuilding."

41. See, for example, Nathan C. Funk and Abdul Aziz Said, "Localizing Peace: An Agenda for Sustainable Peacebuilding."

42. Sung Yong Lee and Alpaslan Ozerdem, *Local Ownership in International Peacebuilding: Key Theoretical and Practical Issues*; Roger Mac Ginty, "Where Is the Local? Critical Localism and Peacebuilding."

43. Oliver P. Richmond, "Beyond Local Ownership in the Architecture of International Peacebuilding."

44. Hanna Leonardsson and Gustave Rudd, "The 'Local Turn' in Peacebuilding: A Literature Review of Effective and Emancipatory Local Peacebuilding."

45. Severine Autesserre, *Peaceland: Conflict Resolution and the Everyday Politics of International Intervention.*

46. Thania Paffenholz, "Unpacking the Local Turn in Peacebuilding: A Critical Assessment towards an Agenda for Future Research."

47. Kristoffer Liden, "Building Peace between Global and Local Politics: The Cosmopolitical Ethics of Liberal Peacebuilding," 618.

48. Roger Mac Ginty and Oliver Richmond, "The Fallacy of Constructing Hybrid Liberal Orders: A Reappraisal of the Hybrid Turn in Peacebuilding," 220; Mac Ginty, *International Peacebuilding*, 73.

49. Mac Ginty and Richmond, "Fallacy of Constructing Hybrid Liberal Orders."

50. Gearoid Millar, "Disaggregating Hybridity: Why Hybrid Institutions Do Not Produce Predictable Experiences of Peace"; Mac Ginty and Richmond, "Fallacy of Constructing Hybrid Liberal Orders."

51. Joanne Wallis, Renee Jeffrey, and Lia Kent, "Political Reconciliation in Timor Leste, Solomon Islands and Bougainville: The Dark Side of Hybridity."

52. Jenny H. Peterson, "A Conceptual Unpacking of Hybridity: Accounting for Notions of Power, Politics and Progress in Analyses of Aid-Driven Interfaces."

53. Chetan Kumar and Jos De la Haye, "Hybrid Peacemaking: Building National 'Infrastructures for Peace.'"

54. Suthaharan Nadarajah and David Rampton, "The Limits of Hybridity and the Crisis of Liberal Peace."

55. Peterson, "Conceptual Unpacking of Hybridity."

56. Kate Meagher, Tom De Herdt, and Kristof Titeca, "Unravelling Public Authority: Paths of Hybrid Governance in Africa."

57. Richmond, A Post-Liberal Peace; Robert Cox, "Social Forces, States and World Orders: Beyond International Relations Theory"; David Roberts, "Post-conflict Peacebuilding, Liberal Irrelevance and the Locus of Legitimacy"; David Roberts, "Beyond the Metropolis? Popular Peace and Post-conflict Peacebuilding."

58. Roberts, "Post-conflict Peacebuilding," 414.

59. Richmond, "Romanticisation of the Local"; Jens Narten, "Post-conflict Peacebuilding and Local Ownership: Dynamics of External-Local Interaction in Kosovo under United Nations Administration."

60. Nathan C. Funk, "Building on What's Already There: Valuing the Local in International Peacebuilding"; Richmond, "Romanticisation of the Local."

61. Paris, "Saving Liberal Peacebuilding," 354; Richmond, "Romanticisation of the Local"; Roberts, "Beyond the Metropolis?," 2542; Elisa Randazzo, "The Paradoxes of the 'Everyday': Scrutinizing the Local Turn in Peacebuilding."

62. Stefanie Kappler and Oliver Richmond, "Peacebuilding and Culture in Bosnia and Herzegovina: Resistance or Emancipation?"; Autesserre, Trouble with the Congo; Pouligny, Peace Operations Seen from Below.

63. Timothy Donais, "Empowerment or Imposition? Dilemmas of Local Ownership in Post-conflict Peacebuilding Processes."

64. David Chandler, "Resilience and the 'Everyday': Beyond the Paradox of 'Liberal Peace.'"

65. Mark Philps, "Peacebuilding and Corruption"; Narten, "Post-conflict Peacebuilding and Local Ownership"; Funk, "Building on What's Already There"; Donais, "Empowerment or Imposition?"

66. United Nations, United Nations Peacekeeping Operations, 36.

67. Ibid., 36.

68. Ibid., 37.

69. Hurd, "Legitimacy and Authority."

70. Jeni Whalan, *How Peace Operations Work: Power, Legitimacy and Effectiveness.*

71. Ibid.; private correspondence with Jeni Whalan, 2016.

72. Whalan, *How Peace Operations Work*, 63–64.

73. Ibid., 65.

74. Ibid., 67.

75. Ibid., 69.

76. United Nations, *United Nations Peacekeeping Operations*, 36.

77. Whalan, *How Peace Operations Work*, 68.

78. Ibid., 207.

79. Ibid., 68.

80. Chapman, "Audience Beliefs," 740.

81. Whalan, *How Peace Operations Work*, 65.

82. Ibid.; Tom R. Tyler, "Trust and Legitimacy: Policing in the USA and Europe"; James Hawdon, "Legitimacy, Trust, Social Capital, and Policing Styles: A Theoretical Assessment"; Sofie Marien and Marc Hooghe, "Does Political Trust Matter? An Empirical Investigation into the Relation between Political Trust and Support for Law Compliance."

83. *Oxford English Dictionary*, s.v. "credibility."

84. Hurd, "Legitimacy and Authority," 387.

85. United Nations, *United Nations Peacekeeping Operations*, 38.

86. Ibid.

87. Pouligny, *Peace Operations Seen from Below.*

88. United Nations, *United Nations Peacekeeping Operations*, 38.

89. Autesserre, *Peaceland.*

90. Interview with senior UNIFIL political affairs officer, Tyre, South Lebanon, July 9, 2016.

91. Autesserre, *Peaceland*, 25.

92. Jonathan Mercer, "Rationality and Psychology in International Politics," 95.

93. Tyler, "Trust and Legitimacy"; Hawdon, "Legitimacy, Trust, Social Capital, and Policing Styles"; Marien and Hooghe, "Does Political Trust Matter?"

2. The UNIFIL Mission in Context

1. Alan James, "Painful Peacekeeping: The United Nations in Lebanon, 1978–1982"; Hatto, "UN Command and Control Capabilities"; Nicholas Blanford, *Warriors of God: Inside Hezbollah's Thirty-Year Struggle against Israel*; Lamis Andoni, "UNIFIL 'on Shaky Ground' in Lebanon."

2. See, for example, United Nations, *United Nations Peacekeeping Operations.*

3. Interview with former UNIFIL spokesman Timur Göksel, Beirut, Lebanon, May 21, 2013.

4. The second mandate repeated many of the mistakes of the first.

5. On May 14, 1948, when the formation of the independent state of Israel was announced, Lebanon, along with other Arab states (Egypt, Iraq, Jordan, Saudi Arabia, Syria, and Yemen), declared it was in a state of war with Israel. Owing to internal tensions, however, Lebanon as a state never actually went to war against Israel. The first UN peace operation established—the United Nations Truce Supervision Organization—was able to swiftly supervise a truce between Lebanon and Israel that continued to exist until 1978. See UNSC Resolution 425, Mar. 19, 1978.

6. Brenda M. Seaver, "The Regional Sources of Power-Sharing Failure: The Case of Lebanon."

7. UNSC Resolution 425, Mar. 19, 1978, 5.

8. UNSC Resolution 426, Mar. 19, 1978.

9. UNSC Resolution 427, May 3, 1978.

10. Iranian troops were withdrawn after the 1979 revolution and replaced by troops from France, Nepal, and Norway.

11. James, "Painful Peacekeeping."

12. Ibid.

13. Maureen Boerma, "The United Nations Interim Force in the Lebanon: Peacekeeping in a Domestic Conflict."

14. Oren Barak, *The Lebanese Army: A National Institution in a Divided Society*; Aram Nerguizian, "Between Sectarianism and Military Development: The Paradox of the Lebanese Armed Forces."

15. Carole Dagher, "Lebanon Holds First Municipal Elections in 35 Years"; Associated Press, "Lebanon: Eve of Third Round of First Municipal Elections in 35 Years," July 21, 2015.

16. It should be noted that there is no specific mention of peacekeeping missions in the UN Charter itself.

17. James, "Painful Peacekeeping," 623.

18. Boerma, "United Nations Interim Force in the Lebanon."

19. Brynjar Lia, "Islamist Perceptions of the United Nations and Its Peacekeeping Missions: Some Preliminary Findings."

20. Ramesh Thakur, *International Peacekeeping in Lebanon: United Nations Authority and Multinational Force*; James, "Painful Peacekeeping"; Lia, "Islamist Perceptions of the United Nations"; Ray Murphy, "United Nations Peacekeeping in Lebanon and Somalia, and the Use of Force"; E. D. Doyle, "Reflections of a UN Peacekeeper: The Changing Fortunes of Conflict Control"; Makdisi et al., "UNIFIL II."

21. James, "Painful Peacekeeping."

22. Makdisi et al., "UNIFIL II."

23. Interview with Göksel.

24. Interview with civilian, Hebbariyeh, South Lebanon, June 18, 2013.

25. Interview with civilian, Blat, South Lebanon, May 29, 2013.

26. Interview with Göksel.

27. Ibid.

28. Interview with civilian, Qlayli, South Lebanon, Aug. 22, 2013.

29. Interview with Göksel.

30. Hezbullah sustained a campaign of violent resistance, often using roadside bombs on Israeli patrols. Doing so helped to embolden domestic civilian resistance, which also placed pressure on Israel to withdraw. See Blanford, *Warriors of God*. Within Israel itself there was also pressure from domestic audiences for the Israelis to withdraw, in particular a group known as the "Four Mothers."

31. The LAF was not confident that it would be accepted in the South alongside the presence of Hezbullah. There also remained a desperate shortage of equipment for the LAF that (as noted later) prevented full deployment during this period. See Oren, *Lebanese Army*; and Nerguizian, "Between Sectarianism and Military Development."

32. Anthony Shadid, "Inside Hezbollah, Big Miscalculations," *New York Times*, Oct. 8, 2006.

33. Stephen Zunes, "Washington's Proxy War"; Irene L. Gendzier, "Exporting Death as Democracy: US Foreign Policy in Lebanon."

34. Shadid, "Inside Hezbollah, Big Miscalculations."

35. Richard Falk and Asli Bali, "International Law and the Vanishing Point."

36. Robert Fisk, "Lebanon Death Toll Hits 1,300," *Independent*, Aug. 17, 2006; Economist Intelligence Unit, *Country Report—Lebanon*.

37. UNSC Resolution 1701, Aug. 11, 2006.

38. Private correspondence with senior political affairs officer, Dec. 22, 2016.

39. Makdisi, "Constructing Security Council Resolution 1701"; Falk and Bali, "International Law and the Vanishing Point."

40. Falk and Bali, "International Law and the Vanishing Point"; Makdisi, "Constructing Security Council Resolution 1701"; Phyllis Bennis, "The Lebanon War in the UN, the UN in the Lebanon War"; Gendzier, "Exporting Death as Democracy."

41. Gendzier, "Exporting Death as Democracy"; Bennis, "Lebanon War in the UN"; Frida Berrigan and William D. Hartung, "US Military Assistance and Arms Transfers to Israel."

42. Falk and Bali, "International Law and the Vanishing Point," 217.

43. Makdisi, "Constructing Security Council Resolution 1701"; Falk and Bali, "International Law and the Vanishing Point"; Warren Hoge and Steven Erlanger, "The Cease-Fire: UN Council Backs Measure to Halt War in Lebanon," *New York Times*, Aug. 12, 2006.

44. Zunes, "Washington's Proxy War"; Jones and Hart, "Keeping Middle East Peace?"

45. Falk and Bali, "International Law and the Vanishing Point."

46. Ibid.; Makdisi, "Constructing Security Council Resolution 1701"; Zunes, "Washington's Proxy War."

47. UNSC Resolution 1701, 1.

48. Falk and Bali, "International Law and the Vanishing Point."

49. Makdisi, "Constructing Security Council Resolution 1701."

50. Falk and Bali, "International Law and the Vanishing Point."

51. UNSC Resolution 1701, 1.

52. Falk and Bali, "International Law and the Vanishing Point"; Nasu, "Responsibility to React?"

53. Falk and Bali, "International Law and the Vanishing Point."

54. It should be noted that while Hezbullah is not explicitly named in Resolution 1701, the force is tasked with clearing the area of all illegal weapons not belonging to the state of Lebanon. A recent debate on the renewal of Resolution 1701 (2017) highlighted that there is an understanding in the international community that clearing Hezbullah's weapons is part of UNIFIL's job. See "U.S. Envoy to U.N. Takes Jab at UNIFIL Head Beary," *Daily Star* (Beirut), Aug. 26, 2017.

55. UNSC Resolution 1701, 2.

56. Ibid., 2.

57. Falk and Bali, "International Law and the Vanishing Point." In comparison, the mandate called for Israel to stop all offensive military action, which enabled it to retain its troops on Lebanese soil and conduct some commando operations in the Beqaa Valley a week after the cease-fire, under the cover of its right of self-defense. This issue again raises questions about the legitimacy of states claiming the right of self-defense in order to engage in disproportionate acts of aggression toward other states.

58. Thierry Tardy, "A Critique of Robust Peacekeeping in Contemporary Peace Operations"; Jones and Hart, "Keeping Middle East Peace?"

59. A useful comparison can be found in the Democratic Republic of Congo, an area the size of western Europe, where the UN has stationed just over nineteen thousand troops. The area south of the Litani River is two-thirds the size of the US state of Connecticut.

60. UNSC Resolution 1701, 2.

61. See, for example, UNSC Resolution 1773, Aug. 24, 2007.

62. UNSC Resolution 1365, July 31, 2001.

63. See, for example, UNSC Resolution 1937, Aug. 30, 2010.

64. See, for example, UNSC Resolution 1773, Aug. 24, 2007.

65. In 2017 for the first time since 2006, there was a strong push by the United States to strengthen the mandate with the specific purpose of routing out Hezbullah weapons. After strong debate, this initiative was rejected by the Security Council, and the mandate remains the same. The mandate has been renewed, and the only change is that the

secretary-general has been asked to look into ways to increase UNIFIL's visibility in the area of operation. See UNSC Resolution 2373, Aug. 30, 2017.

66. United Nations Interim Force in Lebanon, "Peacekeeping Fact Sheet," Aug. 31, 2016, http://www.un.org/en/peacekeeping/resources/statistics/factsheet.shtml#IFIL.

67. The main troop contributing countries currently are Indonesia (1,296), Italy (1,231), India (899), Ghana (870), Nepal (868), Malaysia (826), France (790), Spain (609), China (418), and the Republic of Korea (332). Brazil provides Maritime Task Force flagship with an on-board helicopter. The complete list of UNIFIL troop contributing countries is as follows: Armenia, Austria, Bangladesh (MTF), Belarus, Belgium, Brazil (MTF flagship), Brunei, Cambodia, China, Croatia, Cyprus, El Salvador, Estonia, Fiji, Finland, France, Former Yugoslav Republic of Macedonia, Germany (MTF), Ghana, Greece (MTF), Guatemala, Hungary, India, Indonesia (MTF), Ireland, Italy, Kenya, Korea, Malaysia, Mexico, Nepal, Nigeria, Qatar, Serbia, Sierra Leone, Slovenia, Spain, Sri Lanka, Tanzania, and Turkey (MTF). For further detail, see the UNIFIL press kit on the UNIFIL website: http://unifil.unmissions.org/.

68. Joachim Alexander Koops et al., *The Oxford Handbook of United Nations Peacekeeping Operations*.

69. UNIFIL has constructed 215 points along the Blue Line and verified 194 with both the named parties (with the remaining 21 markers awaiting verification). In 2014 UNIFIL also had a further 20 markers under construction. Private correspondence, UNIFIL political affairs officer, May 8, 2017.

70. The issue of Palestinian prisoners in Israeli jails concerns Hezbullah and not the Lebanese government.

71. The issues of the occupation of Ghajar, Lebanese prisoners in Israeli jails, and Israeli air and sea violations are raised in every secretary-general report on Resolution 1701. See, for example, United Nations Secretary-General, "Report of the Secretary-General on the Implementation of Security Council Resolution 1701 (2006)," S/2013/650, Nov. 13, 2013.

72. This number has been increasing during the Syrian crisis.

73. Augustus Richard Norton, "The Role of Hezbollah in Lebanese Domestic Politics."

74. This concern is also a consideration with the influx of Syrian refugees into the country.

75. Agence-France Presse in Beirut, "Lebanon Accused of Turning Away Some Palestinian Syrian Refugees," *Guardian*, May 6, 2014.

76. See, for example, Nicholas Noe, ed., *Voice of Hezbollah: The Statements of Sayyed Hassan Nasrallah*.

77. See, for example, Naim Qassem, *Hizbullah: The Story from Within*, 261–310. While Hezbullah does not expressly state that Israel should be destroyed, it is implied in Hezbullah's approach to resistance against Israel and its refusal to accept the two-state solution.

78. Interview with UNIFIL political affairs officer, Beirut, Lebanon, Nov. 30, 2013.

79. Blanford, *Warriors of God*; Hirst, *Beware of Small States*.

80. See, for example, William Wunderle and Andre Briere, *US`Foreign Policy and Israel's Qualitative Military Edge: The Need for a Common Vision*.

81. For example, in 2005 Israel is widely acknowledged to have bombed a site in northern Syria that was believed to be enriching uranium. See David E. Sanger and Mark Mazzetti, "Israel Struck Syrian Nuclear Project, Analysts Say," *New York Times*, Oct. 14, 2007; and Erich Follath and Holger Stark, "The Story of 'Operation Orchard': How Israel Destroyed Syria's Al Kibar Nuclear Reactor." The Iran-Israel debate on nuclear weapons for Iran is well known and is not discussed here.

82. Israel bombed a suspected Hezbullah arms convoy in the Beqaa Valley in 2014. See Rakan al-Faikh, "Israeli Strike on Hezbollah Missiles Killed Four," *Daily Star* (Beirut), Feb. 26, 2014.

83. Private conversation with a UNIFIL officer, South Lebanon, 2013.

84. The major political parties in Lebanon are Hezbullah (Shia), Amal (Shia), Kataeb Party (Maronite Christian), the Free Patriotic Movement (FPM) (Christian), the Lebanese Forces (Maronite Christian), the Future Movement (Sunni), and the Progressive Socialist Party (Druze). There are eighteen officially recognized religious sects within Lebanon.

85. A configuration of political support marched in on March 14, 2005, to demand that Syria leave Lebanon after the assassination of then prime minister Rafiq Hariri on February 14, 2005.

86. For reference, voting in Lebanon still occurs largely along sectarian lines. The Lebanese Forces and the Kataeb Party draw their support mostly from the Christian population, and the Future Movement is the dominant Sunni political party in Lebanon.

87. Elias Sakr, "Hariri Slams Hezbollah's Arms as March 14 Steps Up Rhetoric," *Daily Star* (Beirut), Feb. 19, 2011; Henrietta Wilkins, *The Making of Lebanese Foreign Policy: Understanding the Hezbollah Israeli War*.

88. Roschanack Shaery-Eisenlohr, *Shi'ite Lebanon: Transnational Religion and the Making of National Identities*; Blanford, *Warriors of God*; Augustus Richard Norton, *Hezbollah: A Short History*; McKay, *Mirror of the Arab World*.

89. Michael Slackman, "U.S.-Backed Alliance Wins in Lebanon," *New York Times*, June 7, 2009; Wilkins, *Making of Lebanese Foreign Policy*.

90. Wilkins, *Making of Lebanese Foreign Policy*.

91. The March 8 Grouping is named to mark the day that this political configuration marched, ostensibly to thank Syria for its assistance in Lebanon, but with a subtext of reminding Syria that it was time for Syrian troops to leave Lebanon.

92. Supporters of the resistance movement often make this comment to UNIFIL officers when they hold information sessions to educate local people about the Blue Line. Interview with UNIFIL civil affairs officer, Naqoura, South Lebanon, Aug. 13, 2013.

93. Possibly owing to the fact that Hezbullah did not want to be seen to be continuing to prosecute a war when so many civilians were dying as a result of it. It is also questionable how long Hezbullah could have held out against Israel in a long war. Therefore, peace had to be sought. See Noe, *Voice of Hezbollah*.

94. Ibid.

95. It should be noted that the Lebanese Army does not share this slogan; their slogan is "Dignity, Sacrifice and Loyalty." Joseph Haboush, "Praise, Support Pour in on Army Day," *Daily Star* (Beirut), Aug. 2, 2017. Hezbullah continues to propagate the tripartite slogan "Lebanon's Second Liberation Consolidates Trilogy of Army, Resistance, People."

96. Norton, "Role of Hezbollah"; A. Nizar Hazmeh, "Lebanon's Hizbullah: From Islamic Revolution to Parliamentary Accommodation."

97. Qassem, *Hizbullah*.

98. Ibid. The IDF withdrew from northern Ghajar in 2000 and then reoccupied it during the 2006 war and continue to do so to this day. While Hezbullah consistently mentions the Kfar Shouba Hills as contested territory, the UN does not refer to them as such. Hezbullah also continues to stress the need for Israel to hand over all Lebanese prisoners that were imprisoned in Israel during the Israeli occupation.

99. Blanford, *Warriors of God*. While Hezbullah did not technically "win" the war against Israel in 2006, neither did it lose; rather, it created a stalemate that generated human costs that Israel was unwilling to bear.

100. See, for example, "Give Me a Chance, and I Will F*** Hezbollah." The cables revealed that some leaders within this political faction had indirectly advised the Israelis to continue the bombing campaign in the South in order to eliminate Hezbullah from the area. This advice came from individuals who may or may not have been reflecting the wishes of their support base.

101. For details, see United Nations Secretary-General, "Report of the Secretary-General on the Implementation of Security Council Resolution 1701 (2006)," S/2015/147, Feb. 27, 2015, and S2016/189, Feb. 26, 2016.

102. Itamar Rabinovich, "Syria: The View from Israel," *Guardian*, Aug. 2, 2012; Michael Herzog, "New Israeli Policy Dilemmas in the Syrian Crisis"; Ehud Yaari, "Israel's Growing Role in Southern Syria."

103. Qassem, *Hizbullah*.

104. As of September 30, 2016, the United Nations High Commissioner for Refugees listed 1,017,433 million registered Syrian refugees. See UNHCR, "Syria Regional Refugee Response."

105. United Nations Secretary-General, "Report of the Secretary-General on the Implementation of Security Council Resolution 1701 (2006)," S/2016/572, June 24, 2016, 2.

106. Marisa Sullivan, "Hezbollah in Syria."

107. United Nations General Assembly, "Identical Letters Dated 13 June 2012 from the Chargé d'Affaires a.i. of the Permanent Mission of Lebanon to the United Nations Addressed to the Secretary-General and the President of the Security Council," A/66/849?S/2012/477, June 21, 2012; Sami Nader, "Lebanese Independence from 1943 Pact to Baabda Declaration."

108. Haytham Mouzahem, "Lebanese President Provokes Outcry with Hezbollah Comment." Aoun's political party has a memorandum of understanding with Hezbullah.

109. Nicholas Blanford, "Hizbullah Silence on Israeli Raids Conveys Burdens at Home, in Syria," *Daily Star* (Beirut), Feb. 26, 2014.

3. Credibility in Interstate Conflict

1. Interview with UNIFIL political affairs officer, Beirut, Lebanon, Aug. 30, 2013.

2. It should be noted that this refers to non-Hezbullah violations. Hezbullah violations are usually conducted at night and usually circumvent both the IDF and the UNIFIL monitoring systems.

3. Daniel Meier, "The South Border: Drawing the Line in Shifting (Political) Sands."

4. Between 350 and 400 patrols of the Blue Line are conducted each day, of which around 16 to 20 are conducted with the LAF. Interview with LAF officer, Beirut, Lebanon, Aug. 28, 2013.

5. Interview with LAF officer, Beirut, Lebanon, Aug. 28, 2013.

6. Interview with UNIFIL political affairs officer, Beirut, Lebanon, Aug. 30, 2013.

7. See, for example, United Nations Secretary-General, "Report of the Secretary-General on the Implementation of Security Council Resolution 1701 (2006)," S/2013/120, Feb. 27, 2013, 4; and S/2013/650, Nov. 13, 2013, 5. Figures vary, especially during the Syrian crisis; the LAF has been extremely stretched across the country and has withdrawn some troops from the area of operation.

8. United Nations, *United Nations Peacekeeping Operations*, 35; Edward Newman and Oliver Richmond, eds., *Challenges to Peacebuilding: Managing Spoilers during Conflict Resolution.*

9. How Hezbullah is able to circumvent IDF and UNIFIL surveillance remains unknown.

10. See Blanford, *Warriors of God*, chap. 11. Blanford discusses Israel's possession of a number of surveillance mechanisms within the state of Lebanon, which is a violation of Lebanese sovereignty. On a number of occasions, Hezbullah and LAF have discovered these mechanisms and dismantled them.

11. These levels of seriousness were confirmed by UNIFIL staff.

12. All shepherds in Lebanon appear to be male.

13. Interview with UNIFIL political affairs officer, Beirut, Lebanon, Aug. 30, 2013.

14. The area of Shebaa is contested between Lebanon and Syria and occupied (on the Syrian side) by Israel. As such, physical marking of the Blue Line has not yet occurred.

15. Interview with UNIFIL peacekeeper (public information), Blat, South Lebanon, May 29, 2013.

16. Rajana Hamyeh, "Clearing Cluster Bombs and Landmines: Lebanon's Long and Winding Road," *al-Akhbar*, Sept. 13, 2011; Mines Advisory Group, http://www.maginter national.org/where-mag-works/lebanon/#.UtJ3HvYjRzI; "About UNMAS in Lebanon."

17. Interview with UNIFIL political affairs officer, Beirut, Lebanon, Nov. 15, 2013.

18. Interview with UNIFIL peacekeeper (public information), al-Tiri, South Lebanon, Nov. 20, 2013.

19. United Nations Secretary-General, "Report of the Secretary-General," S/2013/120.

20. Mohammed Zaatari, "Israeli Soldiers Kidnap Lebanese Goats," *Daily Star* (Beirut), May 9, 2014; Stephen Dockery, "Goats Taken by Israeli Forces Returned," *Daily Star* (Beirut), July 18, 2012.

21. Interview with UNIFIL political affairs officer, Beirut, Lebanon, Aug. 30, 2013.

22. Interview with UNIFIL peacekeeper (public information), Qlay'aa, South Lebanon, Aug. 29, 2013.

23. United Nations Secretary-General, "Report of the Secretary-General on the Implementation of Security Council Resolution 1701 (2006)," S/2014/438, June 26, 2014, 5.

24. Interview with UNIFIL peacekeeper (public information), Al Tiri, South Lebanon, Nov. 20, 2013.

25. Nicholas Blanford, "Whose Water Is It Anyways? Resentment Pools on Israel-Lebanon Border," *Christian Science Monitor*, May 6, 2014.

26. Tarek Abou Hamdan, "A Lebanese Resort Emerges on Anxious Israel's Border"; Ana Maria Luca, "Much Ado about a Summer Resort."

27. See, for example, United Nations Secretary-General, "Report of the Secretary-General," S/2013/650.

28. Interview with civilian, Wazzani, South Lebanon, Aug. 27, 2013.

29. United Nations Secretary-General, "Report of the Secretary-General on the Implementation of Security Council Resolution 1701 (2006)," S/2015/147, Feb. 27, 2015, 5.

30. United Nations Secretary-General, "Report of the Secretary-General," S/2013/650, 5.

31. Interview with UNIFIL political affairs officer, Beirut, Lebanon, Aug. 30, 2013. In 2018, the Israelis have begun to construct more walls along the border.

32. "UNIFIL Complains to UN over Israel Overflights," *Daily Star* (Beirut), May 8, 2013; "IAF Jets Fly Mock Raids over South Lebanon After Mysterious Aircraft Shot Down over Israel," *Haaretz*, Oct. 7, 2012.

33. See, for example, United Nations Secretary-General, "Report of the Secretary-General," S/2013/120, 3.

34. Interview with UNIFIL liaison officer, Naqoura, South Lebanon, July 7, 2016.

35. United Nations Secretary-General, "Report of the Secretary-General on the Implementation of Security Council Resolution 1701 (2006)," S/2014/784, Nov. 5, 2014, 5.

36. For example, in 2011 ten cases were reported, but in 2013 only one and in 2014 three or four. However, interviews revealed that incidents have taken place but are not deemed serious enough to be included in the report. See United Nations Secretary-General, "Report of the Secretary-General on the Implementation of Security Council Resolution 1701 (2006)," 2006–16.

37. Israel's Iron Dome is a mobile all-weather air defense system developed by Rafael Advanced Defence Systems. The system is designed to intercept and destroy short-range rockets and artillery shells fired from distances of four to seventy kilometers away and whose trajectory would take them to a populated area.

38. Interview with UNIFIL political affairs officer, Naqoura, South Lebanon, Oct. 10, 2013.

39. United Nations Secretary-General, "Report of the Secretary-General," S/2013/650, 3.

40. United Nations Secretary-General, "Report of the Secretary-General on the Implementation of Security Council Resolution 1701 (2006)," S/2013/381, June 26, 2013. As explained in chapter 4, the LAF must avoid being seen as partial by any one sect. As LAF officers view themselves as trying to win hearts and minds in the south, they are disinclined to place too much pressure on Hezbullah.

41. United Nations Secretary-General, "Report of the Secretary-General," S/2013/381, 3.

42. "Lebanon Files Complaint to U.N. over Israeli Spying," *Daily Star* (Beirut), Jan. 8, 2014.

43. MacQueen, *Peacekeeping and the International System*, 134.

44. United Nations Secretary-General, "Report of the Secretary-General," S/2013/381, 7.

45. United Nations Secretary-General, "Report of the Secretary-General on the Implementation of Security Council Resolution 1701 (2006)," S/2014/130, Feb. 26, 2014, 2–3.

46. Interview with LAF officer, Beirut, Lebanon, Aug. 28, 2013.

47. Interview with UNIFIL political affairs officer, Beirut, Lebanon, Aug. 30, 2013.

48. Ibid.

49. Interview with UNIFIL political affairs officer, Beirut, Lebanon, Aug. 30, 2013.

50. Ibid.

51. Interview with UNIFIL political affairs officer, Beirut, Lebanon, Nov. 15, 2013.

52. UNSC Resolution 425, Mar. 25, 1978.

53. See, for example, Frederic C. Hof, "A Practical Line: The Line of Withdrawal from Lebanon and Its Potential Applicability to the Golan Heights"; Brendan O'Shea,

"Lebanon's 'Blue Line': A New International Border or Just Another Cease-Fire Zone?";
Meier, "South Border."

54. Meier, "South Border."

55. Hof, "Practical Line."

56. Ibid.

57. O'Shea, "Lebanon's 'Blue Line.'"

58. Meier, "South Border," 363.

59. United Nations Secretary-General, "Report of the Secretary-General on the Implementation of Security Council Resolution 1701 (2006)," S/2016/572, June 24, 2016. Marking the line involves three stages. First, each of the parties conducts separate "on-site" visits to each marked point agreed upon, a demining process takes place for mined areas, and measuring occurs in the presence of UNIFIL using instruments with the same level of precision. Second, the parties have to agree on the measurement and location of a blue barrel marker. Third, the parties must agree how to erect the barrel and what to state on it and provide the Joint Geographic Information Service permission to do it. See Meier, "South Border," 364–65.

60. Interview with UNIFIL liaison officer, Naqoura, South Lebanon, July 7, 2016.

61. Ibid.

62. Ibid.

63. At times this issue arises because of language differences, which can hinder urgent communications.

64. Interview with UNIFIL political affairs officer, Beirut Lebanon, Nov. 15, 2013.

65. Mercer, "Rationality and Psychology."

66. Interview with UNIFIL liaison officer, Naqoura, South Lebanon, July 7, 2016.

67. Interview with UNIFIL political affairs officer, Beirut, Lebanon, Nov. 15, 2013.

68. Correspondence with senior UNIFIL political affairs officer, Naqoura, South Lebanon, Oct. 11, 2016.

69. Ibid.

70. Ibid.

71. Ibid.

72. Interview with UNIFIL liaison officer, Naqoura, South Lebanon, July 7, 2016.

73. Interview with UNIFIL political affairs officer, Beirut, Lebanon, Nov. 15, 2013.

74. Ibid.

75. See, for example, United Nations Secretary-General, "Report of the Secretary-General," S/2013/120; S/2013/381; S/2013/650.

76. Interview with UNIFIL liaison officer, Naqoura, South Lebanon, July 7, 2016.

77. Ibid.

78. *Strategic corporal* is a military term and refers to the decision maker on the ground on the day that events unfold.

79. Interview with UNIFIL political affairs officer, Beirut, Lebanon, Nov. 15, 2013.

80. An area of the Blue Line where the markings have not been agreed upon.

81. United Nations Secretary-General, "Fourteenth Report of the Secretary General on the Implementation of Resolution 1701 (2006)," S/2010/565, Nov. 1, 2010.

82. Interview with UNIFIL political affairs officer, Beirut Lebanon, Nov. 15, 2013.

83. Ibid.

84. Ibid. Again here, trust should be regarded as confidence.

85. "Criticism and Two Indonesian Soldiers Flee Lebanese, Israeli Battle in Taxi," Agence France Press, Aug. 5, 2010.

86. Interview with UNIFIL political affairs officer, Beirut, Lebanon, Nov. 15, 2013.

87. Discussed in more detail in chapter 5.

88. Interview with UNIFIL political affairs officer, Beirut, Lebanon, Nov. 15, 2013.

89. Ibid.

90. In South Lebanon, several militias are active, but most are pro-Palestinian factions, such as the Popular Front for the Liberation of Palestine-General Command, Fatah al-Islam, Jabha Shabiyah LiTahrir Falasteen, and Jamaah Islamiyeh. Occasionally, one of these groups will launch a rocket into northern Israel, but these missiles are usually intercepted by Israel's Iron Dome. On these occasions, Israel may respond in kind, but it will be a proportionate response and UNIFIL is forewarned as to where they will strike.

91. United Nations Secretary-General, "Report of the Secretary General," S/2013/565.

92. Interview with UNIFIL political affairs officer, Beirut, Lebanon, Aug. 30, 2013. The MNF is the peacekeeping force composed of American, British, and Italian soldiers that was stationed in Lebanon during the civil war to oversee the withdrawal of the Palestine Liberation Organization from Beirut in 1983. The MNF had a robust mandate, and it quickly became embroiled in the conflict. The force withdrew from Lebanon in March 1984 after the bombing of the US Marine barracks in Beirut in October 1983. See Thakur, *International Peacekeeping in Lebanon*.

93. Interview with UNIFIL political affairs officer, Beirut, Lebanon, Nov. 15, 2013.

4. Credibility with National Institutions

1. As noted earlier, the different levels of analysis I have used often overlap, but I have retained them to more easily explicate and describe UNIFIL's myriad projects on the ground.

2. Interview with UNIFIL political affairs officer, Beirut, Lebanon, Aug. 30, 2013.

3. Based on interviews with UNIFIL political affairs officers.

4. Based on interviews with UNIFIL civil affairs officers.

5. UNSC Resolution 1559, Sept. 2, 2004, 1; UNSC Resolution 1680, May 17, 2006.

6. UNSC Resolution 1701, Aug. 11, 2006, preamble, para. 5, 3, 8, 12.

7. Interview with UNIFIL civil affairs officer, Naqoura, South Lebanon, Aug. 13, 2013.

8. In the early 1970s, the Palestinians took over the area (known as "Fatahland"), which became too unstable to hold elections. Owing to the presence of the militias, who set up their own de facto authority south of the Litani River by use of guns, local government was unable to extend its authority over the area. The civil war and the Israeli occupation left the environment unsuitable for holding local elections. After the Israelis left the area in 2000, Hezbullah operated as the de facto authority because the LAF was not present. The decision by Hezbullah's military wing to officially pull back to north of the Litani River meant that political space for a legitimate form of local government authority opened up.

9. Interview with UNIFIL civil affairs officer, Naqoura, South Lebanon, Aug. 13, 2013.

10. Ibid.

11. Interview with civilian, Marja'youn, South Lebanon, Aug. 27, 2013.

12. Interview with UNIFIL civil affairs officer, Naqoura, South Lebanon, Aug. 13, 2013.

13. Interview with civilian, al-Tiri, South Lebanon, Oct. 8, 2013.

14. Interview with UNIFIL civil affairs officer, Naqoura, South Lebanon, Aug. 13, 2013.

15. Ibid.

16. Ibid.

17. Designed to win hearts and minds on the ground, quick impact projects are short-term schemes that are financed by UN peace operations to assist local populations with reconstruction. They usually have a turnaround time of less than four months so that rotating troop contingents can obtain the benefits of local goodwill as quickly as possible. See chapter 5 for details.

18. Interview with UNIFIL civil affairs officer, Naqoura, South Lebanon, Aug. 13, 2013.

19. Even throughout the civil war. See Theodor Hanf, *Coexistence in Wartime Lebanon: Decline of a State and Rise of a Nation*; and Paul Salem, "Can Lebanon Survive the Syrian Crisis?"

20. Interview with civilian, Wazzani, South Lebanon, Aug. 27, 2013.

21. Interview with civilian, Deir Mimas, South Lebanon, Aug. 27, 2013.

22. Interview with civilian, Marja'youn, South Lebanon, Aug. 27, 2013.

23. Interview with UNIFIL civil affairs officer, Tyre, South Lebanon, Dec. 6, 2016.

24. Interview with UNIFIL civil affairs officer, Naqoura, South Lebanon, Aug. 13, 2013.

25. As the local record keeper of the village, the *mukhtar* records all the births, deaths, and marriage details of each family. Depending on the size of the village, he may also perform some other administrative duties.

26. Interview with UNIFIL civil affairs officer, Naqoura, South Lebanon, Aug. 13, 2013.

27. Ibid.

28. Ibid.

29. Interview with civilian, al-Tiri, South Lebanon, Oct. 8, 2013.

30. Interview with UNIFIL political affairs officer, Beirut, Lebanon, Nov. 15, 2013.

31. Interview with UNIFIL political affairs officer, Naqoura, South Lebanon, Oct. 10, 2013.

32. Hezbullah has stated that it does not separate its military wing from its political wing. See Nasser Chararah, "No Separation in Hezbollah Military and Political Wings."

33. UNSC Resolution 1701, 1–2.

34. Ibid., 2.

35. Interview with UNIFIL political affairs officer, Beirut, Lebanon, Aug. 30, 2013.

36. Frederic C. Hof, *Galilee Divided: The Israel-Lebanon Frontier, 1916–1984*; Oren, *Lebanese Army*.

37. See Oren, *Lebanese Army*.

38. See Timur Göksel, "'Mr UNIFIL' Reflects on a Quarter Century of Peacekeeping in South Lebanon."

39. Oren, *Lebanese Army*, chap. 11.

40. Interview with UNIFIL public information officer, Aug. 13, 2013.

41. Nerguizian, "Between Sectarianism and Military Development."

42. Are John Knudsen, *Lebanese Armed Forces: A United Army for a Divided Country?*

43. United Nations Secretary-General, "Report of the Secretary-General on the Implementation of Security Council Resolution 1701 (2006)," S/2016/572, June 24, 2016.

44. Interview with UNIFIL political affairs officer, Naqoura, South Lebanon, Oct. 10, 2013.

45. Secretary-general reports include incidents that occur between locals and UNI-FIL. See United Nations Secretary-General, "Report of the Secretary-General on the Implementation of Security Council Resolution 1701 (2006)," 2006–16.

46. Robert A. Rubinstein, *Peacekeeping under Fire*.

47. UNSC Resolution 1701, para. 3, 8.

48. Interview with civilian, Wazzani, South Lebanon, Aug. 27, 2013.

49. Interview with civilian, al-Amriyeh, South Lebanon, Aug. 21, 2013.

50. Interview with LAF officer, Beirut, Lebanon, Aug. 28, 2013.

51. Interview with UNIFIL peacekeeper, Kfar Hammam, South Lebanon, July 24, 2013.

52. Interview with UNIFIL peacekeeper (public information), al-Tiri, South Lebanon, Nov. 20, 2013.

53. Interview with UNIFIL political affairs officer, Beirut, Lebanon, Nov. 15, 2013.

54. Interview with civilian, Blat, South Lebanon, May 29, 2013.

55. Interview with LAF officer, Beirut, Lebanon, Aug. 28, 2013.

56. Interview with UNIFIL political affairs officer, Beirut, Lebanon, Aug. 30, 2013.

57. Ibid.

58. Ibid.

59. Ibid.

60. Interview with UNIFIL political affairs officer, Beirut, Lebanon, Nov. 15, 2013.

61. Interview with LAF officer, Beirut, Lebanon, Aug. 28, 2013.

62. Interview with LAF officer, Beirut, Lebanon, Sept. 30, 2013.

63. Interview with UNIFIL public information officer, Naqoura, South Lebanon, Aug. 13, 2013.

64. Interview with LAF officer, Beirut, Lebanon, Aug. 28, 2013.

65. Ibid.

66. Interview with UNIFIL political affairs officer, Naqoura, South Lebanon, Oct. 10, 2013. It should be noted in 2017, the LAF brought additional troops down to the South at the request of the UNSC after the renewal of Resolution 1701. "UNIFIL Welcomes Deployment of Additional Troops on Lebanon's Southern Border," Asharq al-Awsat, Sept. 23, 2017, https://eng-archive.aawsat.com/theaawsat/news-middle-east/unifil-welcomes-deployment-additional-troops-lebanons-southern-border.

67. Nerguizian, "Between Sectarianism and Military Development."

68. Joe Dyke, "Strengthen the Lebanese Armed Forces: Lebanon's Most Popular Institution Needs More Support." In the UNIFIL mission, the troop contributing countries do not include any Arab or neighboring states that might have conflicting interests, unlike other UN missions where doing so has been a problem. See, for example, Peter Albrecht and Cathy Haenlein, "Sierra Leone's Post-conflict Peacekeepers: Sudan, Somalia and Ebola."

69. Interview with UNIFIL political affairs officer, Beirut, Lebanon, Nov. 15, 2013.

70. Wunderle and Briere, *US Foreign Policy.*

71. Interview with UNIFIL political affairs officer, Beirut, Lebanon, Nov. 15, 2013.

72. Ibid.

73. Ibid.

74. Ibid.

5. Credibility through Aid

1. Interview with civilian, Marja'youn, South Lebanon, Aug. 27, 2013.

2. MacQueen, *Peacekeeping and the International System*; Rubinstein, *Peacekeeping under Fire.*

3. United Nations Secretary-General, "Report of the Secretary-General on the Implementation of Security Council Resolution 1701 (2006)," S/2007/641, Oct. 30, 2007.

4. Blanford, *Warriors of God*, 422–23.

5. Ibid.

6. This assault has not been the only improvised explosive device attack on UNIFIL patrols since 2006, but it was by far the most serious. Other attacks have been launched, such as on a Tanzanian patrol in July 2007, but there were no fatalities or serious injuries. The perpetrators of this attack were suspected as being members of a radical Palestinian group Fatah al-Islam. See United Nations Secretary-General, "Report of the Secretary-General on the Implementation of Security Council Resolution 1701 (2006)," S/2007/641, Oct. 30, 2007.

7. United Nations Secretary-General, "Report of the Secretary-General on the Implementation of Security Council Resolution 1701 (2006)," S/2013/120, Feb. 27, 2013.

8. Interview with UNIFIL peacekeeper (public information), al-Tiri, South Lebanon, Nov. 20, 2013.

9. Ibid.

10. Ibid.

11. Interview with civilian, Deir Mimas, South Lebanon, Aug. 27, 2013.

12. Interview with UNIFIL civil affairs officer, Tyre, South Lebanon, Dec. 6, 2016.

13. Interview with UNIFIL CIMIC officer, Naqoura, South Lebanon, Aug. 13, 2013.

14. Interview with civilian, Tayrdebba, South Lebanon, Oct. 10, 2013.

15. Interview with UNIFIL political affairs officer, Naqoura, South Lebanon, Oct. 10, 2013.

16. Interview with UNIFIL peacekeeper (medical officer), Qlayaa, South Lebanon, Aug. 29, 2013.

17. Interview with civilian, Yatar, South Lebanon, July 7, 2016.

18. Interview with civilian, Kfar Hammam, South Lebanon, July 24, 2013.

19. Interview with UNIFIL peacekeeper (public information), Blat, South Lebanon, July 24, 2013.

20. Interview with UNIFIL peacekeeper (battalion commander), Blat, South Lebanon, May 29, 2013.

21. Interview with civilian, Deir Mimas, South Lebanon, Aug. 27, 2013; interview with UNIFIL peacekeeper (CIMIC), Nov. 20, 2013; interview with civilian, Tayrdebba, South Lebanon, Oct. 10, 2013.

22. Interview with UNIFIL CIMIC officer, al-Tiri, South Lebanon, Nov. 20, 2013.

23. Interview with civilian, Tayrdebba, South Lebanon, Oct. 10, 2013.

24. Interview with civilian, al-Amriyeh, South Lebanon, Aug. 27, 2013.

25. With the exception of the Indian and Ghanaian battalions who historically have always received money from headquarters.

26. Interview with civilian, Blat, South Lebanon, May 29, 2013.

27. Interview with UNIFIL civil affairs officer, Naqoura, South Lebanon, Aug. 13, 2013.

28. Interview with civilian, Blat, South Lebanon, May 29, 2013.

29. Interview with civilian, Tayrdebba, South Lebanon, Oct. 10, 2013.

30. Ibid.

31. Interview with UNIFIL peacekeeper (public information), Blat, South Lebanon, May 29, 2013.

32. Interview with UNIFIL peacekeeper (CIMIC), al-Tiri, South Lebanon, Nov. 20, 2013.

33. Interview with UNIFIL peacekeeper (public information), Blat, May 29, 2013.

34. Interview with UNIFIL peacekeeper (CIMIC), al-Tiri, South Lebanon, Nov. 20, 2013.

35. Ibid.

36. Interview with UNIFIL peacekeeper (public information), Qlayaa, South Lebanon, Aug. 29, 2013.

37. Interview with UNIFIL peacekeeper (CIMIC), al-Tiri, South Lebanon, Nov. 20, 2013.

38. Interview with UNIFIL peacekeeper (public information), Qlayaa, South Lebanon, Aug. 29, 2013.

39. Interview with UNIFIL CIMIC officer, Naqoura, South Lebanon, Aug. 13, 2013.

40. Interview with civilian, Wazzani, South Lebanon, Aug. 27, 2013.

41. Interview with UNIFIL peacekeeper (CIMIC), al-Tiri, South Lebanon, Nov. 20, 2013.

42. Interview with UNIFIL peacekeeper (public information), Qlayaa, South Lebanon, Aug. 29, 2013.

43. Interview with UNIFIL civil affairs officer, Naqoura, South Lebanon, Aug. 13, 2013.

44. Ibid.

45. Interview with UNIFIL peacekeeper (battalion commander), Blat, South Lebanon, July 24, 2013; interview with UNIFIL civil affairs officer, Naqoura, South Lebanon, Aug. 13, 2013.

46. Interview with UNIFIL peacekeeper (public information), Blat, South Lebanon, May 29, 2013.

47. Interview with UNIFIL peacekeeper (CIMIC), Qlayaa, South Lebanon, Aug. 29, 2013.

48. Interview with UNIFIL peacekeeper (CIMIC), al-Tiri, South Lebanon, Nov. 20, 2013.

49. Interview with civilian, Marja'youn, South Lebanon, Aug. 27, 2013. It is important to note that not all Shi'a towns or villages politically support Hezbullah; many support Amal (another Shi'ite political party) and Amal politicians do not always subscribe to the same views on UNIFIL as Hezbullah.

50. Ibid.

51. Interview with UNIFIL peacekeeper (CIMIC), Qlayaa, South Lebanon, Aug. 29, 2013.

52. Interview with civilian, Blat, South Lebanon, May 29, 2013.

53. Interview with UNIFIL civil affairs officer, Tyre, South Lebanon, Dec. 6, 2016.

54. Interview with UNIFIL civil affairs officer, Naqoura, South Lebanon, Aug. 13, 2013.

55. Interview with UNIFIL civil affairs officer, Naqoura, South Lebanon, Aug. 13, 2013.

56. Interview with UNIFIL political affairs officer, Beirut, Lebanon, Nov. 15, 2013.

57. Interview with civilian, Blat, South Lebanon, 29 May 2013.

58. Interview with civilian, Blat, South Lebanon, May 29, 2013.

59. Interview with UNIFIL political affairs officer, Naqoura, South Lebanon, Oct. 10, 2013.

60. Interview with UNIFIL civil affairs officer, Naqoura, South Lebanon, Aug. 13, 2013.

61. Interview with civilian, al-Tiri, South Lebanon, Oct. 8, 2013.

62. Interview with civilian, Blat, South Lebanon, May 29, 2013.

63. Interview with UNIFIL political affairs officer, Beirut, Lebanon, Nov. 15, 2013; interview with UNIFIL political affairs officer, Naqoura, South Lebanon, Oct. 10, 2013.

64. Interview with UNIFIL peacekeeper (CIMIC), Aug. 29, 2013; interview with UNIFIL political affairs officer, Beirut, Lebanon, Nov. 15, 2013.

65. Interview with UNIFIL political affairs officer, Naqoura, South Lebanon, Oct. 10, 2013.

66. Interview with UNIFIL public information officer, Naqoura, South Lebanon, Aug. 13, 2013. Again here, I believe the officer is referring to confidence rather than trust (as outlined in chapter 1).

67. Interview with civilian, Hebbariyah, South Lebanon, June 18, 2013; interview with UNIFIL civilian, Blat, South Lebanon, May 29, 2013; interview with civilian, Tayrdebba, South Lebanon, Oct. 10, 2013.

68. Interview with UNIFIL civil affairs officer, Naqoura, South Lebanon, Aug. 13, 2013.

69. Interview with Timur Göksel, former UNIFIL spokesman, Beirut, Lebanon, May 21, 2013.

70. Interview with UNIFIL CIMIC officer, Naqoura, South Lebanon, Aug. 13, 2013.

71. Interview with UNIFIL civil affairs officer, Naqoura, South Lebanon, Aug. 13, 2013.

72. Interview with UNIFIL peacekeeper (public information), Blat, May 29, 2013.

73. Interview with UNIFIL peacekeeper (public information), Qlayaa, South Lebanon, Aug. 29, 2013.

74. Ruffa, "What Peacekeepers Think and Do."

75. Interview with civilian, Marja'youn, South Lebanon, Aug. 27, 2013.

76. Interview with UNIFIL civil affairs officer, Naqoura, South Lebanon, Aug. 13, 2013.

77. Vanessa Newby, "Power, Politics and Perception: The Impact of Foreign Policy on Civilian-Peacekeeper Relations."

78. Interview with UNIFIL civil affairs officer, Naqoura, South Lebanon, Aug. 13, 2013.

79. Ibid.

80. Ibid.

81. Ibid.

82. Ibid.

83. Ibid.

84. Interview with UNIFIL peacekeeper (public information), Qlayaa, South Lebanon, Aug. 29, 2013.

85. Interview with UNIFIL civil affairs officer, Naqoura, South Lebanon, Aug. 13, 2013.

Conclusion

1. Vanessa F. Newby, "Don't Ask the UN to Fight America's War with Hizbullah."

2. This erosion can happen for many reasons—for example, because of poor peace-keeper behavior on the ground, the length of time that a mission is present with little change in local conditions, or political rhetoric at the national or international level that discredits the mission.

3. Michael Wesley, "The State of the Art on the Art of Statebuilding"; Paris, *At War's End*.

4. Anthony Banbury, "I Love the UN but It Is Failing," *New York Times*, Mar. 18, 2016; Papa Louis Fall and Yishan Zhang, *Staff Recruitment in United Nations System Organizations, a Comparative Analysis and Benchmarking Framework: The Recruitment Process*; Chris MacGreal, "70 Years and Half a Trillion Dollars Later: What Has the UN Achieved?," *Guardian*, Sept. 7, 2015.

5. Interview with UNIFIL political affairs officer, Beirut, Lebanon, Nov. 15, 2013.

6. Roger Mac Ginty, "Everyday Peace: Bottom-Up and Local Agency in Conflict-Affected Societies," 549.

7. Such as poor infrastructure, roadblocks, acts of political violence, and so forth.

8. Interview with UNIFIL political affairs officer, Nov. 15, 2013.

9. Elise Boulding, "The Problems of Managing Human Difference," 446.

Bibliography

Abi-Ezzi, Karen. "Lebanon: Confessionalism, Institution Building, and the Challenges of Securing Peace." In *Beyond Settlement: Making Peace Last after Civil Conflict*, edited by Vanessa Shields and Nicholas D. J. Baldwin, 159–72. Madison, NJ: Fairleigh Dickinson Univ. Press, 2008.

"About UNMAS in Lebanon." United Nations Mine Action Support. http://www.mineaction.org/programmes/lebanon.

Albrecht, Peter, and Cathy Haenlein. "Sierra Leone's Post-conflict Peacekeepers: Sudan, Somalia and Ebola." *RUSI Journal* 160, no. 1 (2015): 26–36.

Andoni, Lamis. "UNIFIL 'on Shaky Ground' in Lebanon." *Al Jazeera*, Aug. 4, 2010. http://www.aljazeera.com/focus/2010/08/201083115627535963.html.

Autesserre, Severine. *Peaceland: Conflict Resolution and the Everyday Politics of International Intervention*. Cambridge: Cambridge Univ. Press, 2014.

————. *The Trouble with the Congo: Local Violence and the Failure of International Peacebuilding*. Cambridge: Cambridge Univ. Press, 2010.

Axelrod, Robert. *The Evolution of Cooperation*. New York: Basic Books, 1984.

Barak, Oren. *The Lebanese Army: A National Institution in a Divided Society*. New York: SUNY Press, 2009.

Barnett, Michael, and Martha Finnemore. *Rules for the World: International Organizations in Global Politics*. Ithaca, NY: Cornell Univ. Press, 2004.

Bellamy, Alex J., and Paul D. Williams. *Understanding Peacekeeping*. Cambridge: Polity Press, 2010.

Bennis, Phyllis. "The Lebanon War in the UN, the UN in the Lebanon War." In *The War on Lebanon: A Reader*, edited by Nubar Hovsepian, 225–42. Northampton, MA: Olive Branch Press, 2007.

Berrigan, Frida, and William D. Hartung. "US Military Assistance and Arms Transfers to Israel." In *The War on Lebanon: A Reader*, edited by Nubar Hovsepian, 243–51. Northampton, MA: Olive Branch Press, 2007.

Blanford, Nicholas. *Warriors of God: Inside Hezbollah's Thirty-Year Struggle against Israel.* New York: Random House, 2011.

Boerma, Maureen. "The United Nations Interim Force in the Lebanon: Peace-keeping in a Domestic Conflict." *Millennium: Journal of International Studies* 8, no. 1 (1979): 51–63.

Bordo, Michael D., and Ronald MacDonald. *Credibility and the International Monetary Regime: A Historical Perspective.* Cambridge: Cambridge Univ. Press, 2012.

Boulding, Elise. "The Problems of Managing Human Difference." *CrossCurrents* 48, no. 4 (1998–99): 445–57.

Braithwaite, John. "Evaluating the Timor-Leste Peace Operation." *Journal of International Peacekeeping* 16, nos. 3–4 (2012): 282–305.

Bray, Zoe. "Ethnographic Approaches." In *Approaches and Methodologies in the Social Sciences: A Pluralist Perspective*, edited by Donatella della Porta and Michael Keating, 296–315. Cambridge: Cambridge Univ. Press, 2008.

Call, Charles T., and Elizabeth M. Cousens. "Ending Wars and Building Peace: International Responses to War-Torn Societies." *International Studies Perspectives* 9, no. 1 (2008): 1–21.

Chandler, David. "Resilience and the 'Everyday': Beyond the Paradox of 'Liberal Peace.'" *Review of International Studies* 41, no. 1 (2015): 27–48.

Chapman, Terence L. "Audience Beliefs and International Organization Legitimacy." *International Organization* 63, no. 4 (2009): 733–64.

Chararah, Nasser. "No Separation in Hezbollah Military and Political Wings." *Al-Monitor*, July 26, 2013.

Clark, Ian. "Legitimacy in a Global Order." *Review of International Studies* 29, no. S1 (2003): 75–95.

Cockell, John G. "Conceptualising Peacebuilding: Human Security and Sustainable Peace." In *Regeneration of War-Torn Societies*, edited by Michael Pugh, 15–34. Basingstoke: Palgrave Macmillan, 2000.

Cox, Robert. "Social Forces, States and World Orders: Beyond International Relations Theory." *Millennium: Journal of International Studies* 10, no. 2 (1981): 126–55.

Crescenzi, Mark. "Reputation and International Conflict." *American Journal of Political Science* 51, no. 2 (2007): 382–96.

Dagher, Carole. "Lebanon Holds First Municipal Elections in 35 Years." *Washington Report on Middle East Affairs* (July–Aug. 1998).

Danilovic, Vesna. "The Sources of Threat Credibility in Extended Deterrence." *Journal of Conflict Resolution* 45, no. 3 (2001): 341–69.

della Porta, Donatella, and Michael Keating, eds. *Approaches and Methodologies in the Social Sciences: A Pluralist Perspective.* Cambridge: Cambridge Univ. Press, 2008.

Donais, Timothy. "Empowerment or Imposition? Dilemmas of Local Ownership in Post-conflict Peacebuilding Processes." *Peace and Change* 34, no. 1 (2009): 3–26.

Dowling, John, and Jeffrey Pfeffer. "Organizational Legitimacy: Social Values and Organizational Behaviour." *Pacific Sociological Review* 18, no. 1 (1975): 122–36.

Downs, George W., and Michael A. Jones. "Reputation, Compliance, and International Law." *Journal of Legal Studies* 31, no. S1 (2002): S95–S114.

Doyle, E. D. "Reflections of a UN Peacekeeper: The Changing Fortunes of Conflict Control." *International Peacekeeping* 10, no. 4 (2003): 24–39.

Drezner, Daniel W. "Ten Things to Read about Reputation in International Relations." *Foreign Policy* (May 27, 2009).

Dyke, Joe. "Strengthen the Lebanese Armed Forces: Lebanon's Most Popular Institution Needs More Support." *Executive Magazine* (Mar. 7, 2014).

Economist Intelligence Unit. *Country Report—Lebanon.* London: Economist Intelligence Unit, 2006.

Falk, Richard, and Asli Bali. "International Law and the Vanishing Point." In *The War on Lebanon: A Reader,* edited by Nubar Hovsepian, 208–24. Northampton, MA: Olive Branch Press, 2007.

Fall, Papa Louis, and Yishan Zhang. *Staff Recruitment in United Nations System Organizations, a Comparative Analysis and Benchmarking Framework: The Recruitment Process.* Geneva: United Nations Joint Inspection Unit, 2012.

Fearon, James D. "Domestic Political Audiences and the Escalation of International Disputes." *American Political Science Review* 88 (1994): 577–92.

———. "Signaling Foreign Policy Interests: Tying Hands versus Sinking Costs." *Journal of Conflict Resolution* 41, no. 1 (1997): 68–90.

Follath, Erich, and Holger Stark. "The Story of 'Operation Orchard': How Israel Destroyed Syria's Al Kibar Nuclear Reactor." Spiegel Online, Feb. 11, 2009. http://www.spiegel.de/international/world/the-story-of-operation-orchard-how-israel-destroyed-syria-s-al-kibar-nuclear-reactor-a-658663-druck.html.

Funk, Nathan C. "Building on What's Already There: Valuing the Local in International Peacebuilding." *International Journal* 67, no. 2 (2012): 391–408.

Funk, Nathan C., and Abdul Aziz Said. "Localizing Peace: An Agenda for Sustainable Peacebuilding." *Peace and Conflict Studies* 17, no. 1 (2010): 101–43.

Galtung, Johan. *Peace by Peaceful Means: Peace and Conflict, Development and Civilization.* London: Sage, 1996.

Gendzier, Irene L. "Exporting Death as Democracy: US Foreign Policy in Lebanon." In *The War on Lebanon: A Reader,* edited by Nubar Hovsepian, 119–32. Northampton, MA: Olive Branch Press, 2007.

George, Alexander, and Richard Smoke. *Deterrence in American Foreign Policy: Theory and Practice.* New York: Columbia Univ. Press, 1974.

Gerring, John. *Case Study Research: Principles and Practices.* Cambridge: Cambridge Univ. Press, 2007.

"Give Me a Chance, and I Will F*** Hezbollah." *Al-Akhbar,* May 2011. http://www.al-akhbar.com/2006war_cables.

Göksel, Timur. "'Mr UNIFIL' Reflects on a Quarter Century of Peacekeeping in South Lebanon." *Journal of Palestine Studies* 36, no. 3 (2007): 50–77.

Goulding, Sir Marrack. "The Evolution of United Nations Peacekeeping." *International Affairs* 69, no. 3 (1993): 451–64.

Gross Stein, Janice. "Threat Perceptions in International Relations." In *Oxford Handbook of Political Psychology,* edited by Leonie Huddy, David Sears, and Jack Levy. 2nd ed. Oxford: Oxford Univ. Press, 2013.

Hall, Peter A., and Rosemary C. R. Taylor. "Political Science and the Three New Institutionalisms." *Political Studies* 44, no. 5 (1996): 936–57.

Hamdan, Tarek Abou. "A Lebanese Resort Emerges on Anxious Israel's Border." *Al-Monitor,* Oct. 19, 2012. http://www.al-monitor.com/pulse/culture/2012/10/the-south-lebanon-resort-village-attracting-tourists-meters-from-the-enemy.html.

Hamieh, Sylvia Christine, and Roger Mac Ginty. "A Very Political Reconstruction: Governance and Reconstruction in Lebanon after the 2006 War." *Disasters* 34, no. S1 (2010): S103–S123.

Hanf, Theodor. *Coexistence in Wartime Lebanon: Decline of a State and Rise of a Nation.* London: I. B. Tauris, 2015.

Hatto, Ronald. "UN Command and Control Capabilities: Lessons from UNIFIL's Strategic Military Cell." *International Peacekeeping* 16, no. 2 (2009): 186–98.

Hawdon, James. "Legitimacy, Trust, Social Capital, and Policing Styles: A Theoretical Assessment." *Police Quarterly* 11, no. 2 (2008): 182–201.

Hazmeh, A. Nizar. "Lebanon's Hizbullah: From Islamic Revolution to Parliamentary Accommodation." *Third World Quarterly* 14, no. 2 (1993): 321–37.

Herzog, Michael. "New Israeli Policy Dilemmas in the Syrian Crisis." BICOM (Britain Israel Communications and Research Centre), June 11, 2013. http://www.bicom.org.uk/analysis/14915/.

Hirst, David. *Beware of Small States: Lebanon, Battleground of the Middle East.* London: Faber and Faber, 2010.

Hof, Frederic C. *Galilee Divided: The Israel-Lebanon Frontier, 1916–1984.* Boulder, CO: Westview Press, 1985.

———. "A Practical Line: The Line of Withdrawal from Lebanon and Its Potential Applicability to the Golan Heights." *Middle East Journal* 55, no. 1 (2001): 25–42.

Hovsepian, Nubar, ed. *The War on Lebanon: A Reader.* Northampton, MA: Olive Branch Press, 2007.

Hurd, Ian. "Legitimacy, Power, and the Symbolic Life of the UN Security Council." *Global Governance* 8, no. 1 (2003): 35–51.

———. "Legitimacy and Authority in International Politics." *International Organization* 53, no. 2 (1999): 379–408.

James, Alan. "Painful Peacekeeping: The United Nations in Lebanon, 1978–1982." *International Journal* 38, no. 4 (1983): 613–34.

Jervis, Robert. *Perception and Misperception in International Politics.* Princeton, NJ: Princeton Univ. Press, 1976.

Jones, Bruce, and Andrew Hart. "Keeping Middle East Peace?" *International Peacekeeping* 15, no. 1 (2008): 102–17.

Kappler, Stefanie, and Oliver Richmond. "Peacebuilding and Culture in Bosnia and Herzegovina: Resistance or Emancipation?" *Security Dialogue* 42, no. 3 (2011): 261–78.

Kaufman, William W. *The Requirements of Deterrence.* Princeton, NJ: Princeton Univ. Press, 1954.

Keohane, Robert O. *After Hegemony: Cooperation and Discord in the World Political Economy.* Princeton, NJ: Princeton Univ. Press, 1984.

Kingston, Paul. "The Pitfalls of Peacebuilding from Below." *International Journal* 67, no. 2 (2012): 333–50.

Knudsen, Are John. *Lebanese Armed Forces: A United Army for a Divided Country?* CMI Insight, no. 9. Bergen: Chr. Michelsen Institute, 2014.

Koops, Joachim Alexander, Norrie MacQueen, Thierry Tardy, and Paul D. Williams. *The Oxford Handbook of United Nations Peacekeeping Operations.* Oxford: Oxford Univ. Press, 2015.

Krasner, Stephen D. *International Regimes.* Ithaca, NY: Cornell Univ. Press, 1983.

Kumar, Chetan, and Jos De la Haye. "Hybrid Peacemaking: Building National 'Infrastructures for Peace.'" *Global Governance* 18, no. 1 (2012): 13–20.

"Lebanon's Second Liberation Consolidates Trilogy of Army, Resistance, People." *Al-Manar*, Aug. 31, 2017.

Lee, Sung Yong, and Alpaslan Ozerdem. *Local Ownership in International Peacebuilding: Key Theoretical and Practical Issues.* London: Routledge, 2015.

Leonardsson, Hanna, and Gustave Rudd. "The 'Local Turn' in Peacebuilding: A Literature Review of Effective and Emancipatory Local Peacebuilding." *Third World Quarterly* 36, no. 5 (2015): 825–39.

Lia, Brynjar. "Islamist Perceptions of the United Nations and Its Peacekeeping Missions: Some Preliminary Findings." *International Peacekeeping* 5, no. 2 (1998): 38–63.

Liden, Kristoffer. "Building Peace between Global and Local Politics: The Cosmopolitical Ethics of Liberal Peacebuilding." *International Peacekeeping* 16, no. 5 (2009): 616–34.

Liégeois, Michael. "Making Sense of a Francophone Perspective on Peace Operations: The Case of Belgium as a Minofrancophone State." *International Peacekeeping* 19, no. 3 (2012): 316–32.

Luca, Ana Maria. "Much Ado about a Summer Resort." *NOW Lebanon*, July 12, 2012. https://now.mmedia.me/lb/en/reportsfeatures/much_ado_about_a _summer_resort.

Mac Ginty, Roger. "Everyday Peace: Bottom-Up and Local Agency in Conflict-Affected Societies." *Security Dialogue* 45, no. 6 (2014): 548–64.

———. *International Peacebuilding and Local Resistance: Hybrid Forms of Peace.* Basingstoke: Palgrave Macmillan, 2011.

———. "Reconstructing Post-war Lebanon: A Challenge to the Liberal Peace?" *Conflict, Security & Development* 7, no. 3 (2007): 457–82.

———. "Where Is the Local? Critical Localism and Peacebuilding." *Third World Quarterly* 36, no. 5 (2015): 840–56.

Mac Ginty, Roger, and Oliver Richmond. "The Fallacy of Constructing Hybrid Liberal Orders: A Reappraisal of the Hybrid Turn in Peacebuilding." *International Peacekeeping* 23, no. 2 (2016): 219–39.

MacQueen, Norrie. *Peacekeeping and the International System*. Abingdon: Routledge, 2006.

Makdisi, Karim. "Constructing Security Council Resolution 1701 for Lebanon
in the Shadow of the War on Terror." *International Peacekeeping* 18, no. 1
(2011): 4–20.

Makdisi, Karim, Timur Göksul, Hans Bastian Hauck, and Stuart Reigeluth.
"UNIFIL II: Emerging and Evolving European Engagement in Lebanon
and the Middle East." Policy Paper no. 72. Lisbon: Euro-Mediterranean
Study Commission, 2009.

Marien, Sofie, and Marc Hooghe. "Does Political Trust Matter? An Empirical
Investigation into the Relation between Political Trust and Support for Law
Compliance." *European Journal of Political Research* 50, no. 2 (2011): 267–91.

McKay, Sandra. *Mirror of the Arab World: Lebanon in Conflict*. New York: W. W.
Norton, 2009.

Meagher, Kate, Tom De Herdt, and Kristof Titeca. "Unravelling Public Authority: Paths of Hybrid Governance in Africa." Research Brief no. 10. London:
London School of Economics, 2014.

Mearsheimer, John J. "The False Promise of International Institutions." *International Security* 19, no. 3 (1994–95): 5–49.

Meier, Daniel. "The South Border: Drawing the Line in Shifting (Political)
Sands." *Mediterranean Politics* 18, no. 3 (2013): 358–75.

Mercer, Jonathan. "Emotional Beliefs." *International Organization* 64, no. 1
(2010): 1–31.

———. "Rationality and Psychology in International Politics." *International Organization* 59, no. 1 (2005): 77–106.

Millar, Gearoid. "Disaggregating Hybridity: Why Hybrid Institutions Do Not
Produce Predictable Experiences of Peace." *Journal of Peace Research* 51,
no. 4 (2014): 501–14.

Moore, Adam. *Peacebuilding in Practice*. Ithaca, NY: Cornell Univ. Press, 2013.

Mouzahem, Haytham. "Lebanese President Provokes Outcry with Hezbollah
Comment." *Al-Monitor*, Mar. 3, 2017.

Murphy, Ray. "United Nations Peacekeeping in Lebanon and Somalia, and the
Use of Force." *Journal of Conflict & Security Law* 8, no. 1 (2003): 71–99.

———. *UN Peacekeeping in Lebanon, Somalia and Kosovo*. Cambridge: Cambridge Univ. Press, 2007.

Nadarajah, Suthaharan, and David Rampton. "The Limits of Hybridity and the
Crisis of Liberal Peace." *Review of International Studies* 41, no. 1 (2015): 49–72.

Nader, Sami. "Lebanese Independence from 1943 Pact to Baabda Declaration." *Al-Monitor*, Nov. 26, 2013. http://www.al-monitor.com/pulse/originals/2013 /11/lebanon-independence-baabda-declaration-syria.html.

Narten, Jens. "Post-conflict Peacebuilding and Local Ownership: Dynamics of External-Local Interaction in Kosovo under United Nations Administration." *Journal of Intervention and Statebuilding* 2, no. 3 (2008): 369–90.

Nasu, Hitoshi. "The Responsibility to React? Lessons from the Security Council's Response to the Southern Lebanon Crisis of 2006." *International Peacekeeping* 14, no. 3 (2007): 339–52.

Nerguizian, Aram. "Between Sectarianism and Military Development: The Paradox of the Lebanese Armed Forces." In *The Politics of Sectarianism in Postwar Lebanon*, edited by Bassel F. Salloukh, Rabie Barakat, Jinan S. al-Habbal, Lara W. Khattab, and Shoghig Mikaelian, 108–35. London: Pluto Press, 2015.

Neufeld, Mark. "Relexivity and International Relations Theory." *Millennium: Journal of International Studies* 22, no. 1 (1993): 53–76.

Newby, Vanessa F. "Don't Ask the UN to Fight America's War with Hizbullah." Lowy Interpreter, Lowy Institute, Aug. 30, 2017.

———. "Power, Politics and Perception: The Impact of Foreign Policy on Civilian-Peacekeeper Relations." *Third World Quarterly* OnlineFirst, June 19, 2019. http://dx.doi.org/10.1080/01436597.2017.1334542.

Newman, Edward, and Oliver Richmond, eds. *Challenges to Peacebuilding: Managing Spoilers during Conflict Resolution*. Tokyo: United Nations Univ. Press, 2006.

Noe, Nicholas, ed. *Voice of Hezbollah: The Statements of Sayyed Hassan Nasrallah*. London: Verso, 2007.

Norton, Augustus Richard. *Hezbollah: A Short History*. Princeton, NJ: Princeton Univ. Press, 2007.

———. "The Role of Hezbollah in Lebanese Domestic Politics." *International Spectator* 42, no. 4 (2007): 475–91.

Oestreich, Joel, ed. *International Organizations as Independent Actors: A Framework for Analysis*. London: Routledge, 2012.

Oren, Barak. *The Lebanese Army: A National Institution in a Divided Society*. New York: SUNY Press, 2009.

O'Shea, Brendan. "Lebanon's 'Blue Line': A New International Border or Just Another Cease-Fire Zone?" *Studies in Conflict & Terrorism* 27, no. 1 (2004): 19–30.

Oye, Kenneth, ed. *Cooperation under Anarchy*. Princeton, NJ: Princeton Univ. Press, 1986.

Paffenholz, Thania. *Civil Society and Peacebuilding: A Critical Assessment*. Boulder, CO: Lynne Rienner, 2010.

———. "Unpacking the Local Turn in Peacebuilding: A Critical Assessment towards an Agenda for Future Research." *Third World Quarterly* 36, no. 5 (2015): 857–74.

———. "What Civil Society Can Contribute to Peacebuilding." In *Civil Society and Peacebuilding: A Critical Assessment*, edited by Thania Paffenholz, 381–404. Boulder, CO: Lynne Rienner, 2010.

Paris, Roland. *At War's End: Building Peace and Conflict*. Cambridge: Cambridge Univ. Press, 2004.

———. "Saving Liberal Peacebuilding." *Review of International Studies* 36, no. 2 (2010): 337–65.

Peterson, Jenny H. "A Conceptual Unpacking of Hybridity: Accounting for Notions of Power, Politics and Progress in Analyses of Aid-Driven Interfaces." *Journal of Peacebuilding and Development* 7, no. 2 (2012): 9–22.

Philps, Mark. "Peacebuilding and Corruption." *International Peacekeeping* 15, no. 3 (2008): 310–27.

Pouligny, Beatrice. *Peace Operations Seen from Below: UN Missions and Local People*. London: Hurst, 2005.

Powell, Robert. "Anarchy in International Relations Theory: The Neorealist-Neoliberal Debate." *International Organization* 48, no. 2 (1994): 330–34.

———. *Nuclear Deterrence Theory: The Search for Credibility*. Cambridge: Cambridge Univ. Press, 1990.

Press, Daryl. *Calculating Credibility: How Leaders Assess Military Threats*. Ithaca, NY: Cornell Univ. Press, 2005.

Pugh, Michael. "The Social-Civil Dimension." In *Regeneration of War-Torn Societies*, edited by Michael Pugh, 112–33. Basingstoke: Palgrave Macmillan, 2009.

Qassem, Naim. *Hizbullah: The Story from Within*. London: Saqi, 2005.

Randazzo, Elisa. "The Paradoxes of the 'Everyday': Scrutinising the Local Turn in Peacebuilding." *Third World Quarterly* 37, no. 8 (2016): 1351–70.

Richmond, Oliver P. "Beyond Local Ownership in the Architecture of International Peacebuilding." *Ethnopolitics* 11, no. 4 (2012): 354–75.

———. *A Post-Liberal Peace*. London: Routledge, 2011.

———. "The Romanticisation of the Local: Welfare, Culture and Peacebuilding." *International Spectator* 44, no. 1 (2009): 149–69.

————. *The Transformation of Peace*. Basingstoke: Palgrave Macmillan, 2005.

Richmond, Oliver P., and Jason Franks. *Liberal Peace Transitions: Between State-building and Peacebuilding*. Edinburgh: Edinburgh Univ. Press, 2009.

Roberts, David. "Beyond the Metropolis? Popular Peace and Post-conflict Peace-building." *Review of International Studies* 37, no. 5 (2011): 2535–56.

————. "Post-conflict Peacebuilding, Liberal Irrelevance and the Locus of Legitimacy." *International Peacekeeping* 18, no. 4 (2011): 410–24.

Rubinstein, Robert A. *Peacekeeping under Fire: Culture and Intervention*. Boulder, CO: Paradigm, 2008.

Ruffa, Chiara. "What Peacekeepers Think and Do: An Exploratory Study of French, Ghanaian, Italian, and South Korean Armies in the United Nations Interim Force in Lebanon." *Armed Forces and Society* 40, no. 2 (2014): 199–225.

Ruggie, John Gerard. "International Regimes, Transactions, and Change: Embedded Liberalism in the Postwar Economic Order." *International Organization* 36, no. 2 (1982): 379–415.

Salem, Paul. "Can Lebanon Survive the Syrian Crisis?" Carnegie Middle East Centre, Dec. 11, 2012. http://carnegie-mec.org/2012/12/11/can-lebanon-survive-syrian-crisis-pub-50298.

Sartori, Anne. *Deterrence by Diplomacy*. Princeton, NJ: Princeton Univ. Press, 2007.

Schelling, Thomas C. *Arms and Influence*. New Haven, CT: Yale Univ. Press, 1966.

Schofer, Evan, Ann Hironaka, David John Frank, and Wesley Longhofer. "Sociological Institutionalism and World Society." In *The Wiley-Blackwell Companion to Political Sociology*, edited by Edwina Amenta, Kate Nash, and Alan Scott, 57–68. Oxford: Blackwell, 2012.

Seaver, Brenda M. "The Regional Sources of Power-Sharing Failure: The Case of Lebanon." *Political Science Quarterly* 115, no. 2 (2000): 247–71.

Sending, Ole Jacob. "Why Peacebuilders Fail to Secure Ownership and Be Sensitive to Context." NUPI Working Paper 755. Oslo: Norwegian Institute of International Affairs.

Shaery-Eisenlohr, Roschanack. *Shi'ite Lebanon: Transnational Religion and the Making of National Identities*. New York: Columbia Univ. Press, 2008.

Stein, Arthur A. "Coordination and Collaboration: Regimes in an Anarchic World." In *International Regimes*, edited by Stephen D. Krasner, 120–24. Ithaca, NY: Cornell Univ. Press, 1983.

Suchman, Mark C. "Managing Legitimacy: Strategic and Institutional Approaches." *Academy of Management Review* 20, no. 3 (1995): 571–610.

Sullivan, Marisa. "Hezbollah in Syria." Middle East Security Report 19. Washington, DC: Institute for the Study of War, Apr. 2014.

Tan, Alvin Tze Tien. "Sovereign Credibility in International Political Economy." PhD thesis, Harvard Univ., 2001.

Tardy, Thierry. "A Critique of Robust Peacekeeping in Contemporary Peace Operations." *International Peacekeeping* 18, no. 2 (2011): 152–67.

Thakur, Ramesh. *International Peacekeeping in Lebanon: United Nations Authority and Multinational Force.* Boulder, CO: Westview Press, 1987.

Tomz, Michael. "Domestic Audience Costs in International Relations: An Experimental Approach." *International Organization* 61, no. 4 (2007): 821–40.

Tyler, Tom R. "Trust and Legitimacy: Policing in the USA and Europe." *European Journal of Criminology* 8, no. 4 (2011): 254–66.

UNHCR [United Nations High Commissioner for Refugees]. "Syria Regional Refugee Response." http://data.unhcr.org/syrianrefugees/country.php?id=122.

United Nations. *United Nations Peacekeeping Operations: Principles and Guidelines.* New York: United Nations Department of Peacekeeping Operations and Department of Field Support, 2008.

United Nations Department of Peacekeeping Operations. *Handbook on United Nations Multidimensional Peacekeeping Operations.* New York: United Nations, 2010.

United Nations Peacekeeping. "Contributors to United Nations Peacekeeping Operations." http://www.un.org/en/peacekeeping/contributors/2016/aug16_1.pdf.

―――. "Country Contributions Detailed by Mission." http://www.un.org/en/peacekeeping/resources/statistics/contributors.shtml.

von Billerbeck, Sarah B. K. "Local Ownership and UN Peacebuilding: Discourse versus Operationalization." *Global Governance* 21, no. 2 (2015): 299–315.

Vuga, Janja. "Cultural Differences in Multinational Peace Operations: A Slovenian Perspective." *International Peacekeeping* 17, no. 4 (2010): 554–65.

Wallis, Joanne, Renee Jeffrey, and Lia Kent. "Political Reconciliation in Timor Leste, Solomon Islands and Bougainville: The Dark Side of Hybridity." *Australian Journal of International Affairs* 70, no. 2 (2016): 159–78.

Wesley, Michael. "The State of the Art on the Art of Statebuilding." *Global Governance* 14, no. 3 (1999): 369–85.

Whalan, Jeni. *How Peace Operations Work: Power, Legitimacy and Effectiveness.* Oxford: Oxford Univ. Press, 2013.

Wilkins, Henrietta. *The Making of Lebanese Foreign Policy: Understanding the Hezbollah Israeli War.* London: Routledge, 2013.

Wunderle, William, and Andre Briere. *US Foreign Policy and Israel's Qualitative Military Edge: The Need for a Common Vision.* Washington, DC: Washington Institute, 2008.

Yaari, Ehud. "Israel's Growing Role in Southern Syria." Policy Analysis, Washington Institute, Jan. 29, 2014. http://www.washingtoninstitute.org/policy-analysis/view/israels-growing-role-in-southern-syria.

Zahar, Marie-Joelle. "Liberal Interventions, Illiberal Outcomes: The United Nations, Western Powers and Lebanon." In *New Perspectives on Liberal Peacebuilding*, edited by Edward Newman, Roland Paris, and Oliver Richmond, 292–315. Tokyo: United Nations Univ. Press, 2009.

Zunes, Stephen. "Washington's Proxy War." In *The War on Lebanon: A Reader*, edited by Nubar Hovsepian, 93–118. Northampton, MA: Olive Branch Press, 2007.

Index

March 14 movement, 77, 79, 132, 188n85
Maritime Task Force, 72
Marja'youn, 72, 117, 120, 159–60
material interests, 7, 16, 22, 29, 43, 47, 53, 54, 55, 123, 164, 165, 166, 171
mayor, 117, 118, 120, 121, 122, 141, 145, 149, 150, 162, 163
Mercer, Jonathan, 28, 55
microsecurity agreements, 89, 95, 96, 97, 103
minimal use of force, 4, 25
mukhtar, 121, 138, 195n25
Multinational Force (MNF), 112, 167, 194n92
municipal government, 23, 111, 120, 115–17, 118–20, 121, 122, 123, 132, 138, 140, 141, 143, 147–49, 154, 157, 161, 163
municipalities. *See* municipal government

named parties, 3, 23, 53, 66, 82, 83, 84, 99, 104, 113, 169
Nasrallah, Hassan, 78
national level, 22, 23, 33, 52, 54, 64, 74, 114, 117, 124, 167
natural disasters, 30, 106
negative peace, 3
negotiation, 9, 11, 23, 37, 50, 82, 84, 90, 95, 100, 114, 115, 159, 171
normalization of peace, 9, 54, 56, 113, 172–73, 177n12

Observer Group Lebanon (OGL), 72
occupation, 5, 21, 59, 62, 63, 64, 68, 73, 76, 78, 116–17, 125, 128, 187n71, 189n98, 195n8

Operation Litani, 59
organized protests, 91

Paffenholz, Thania, 36
Palestine Liberation Organization (PLO), 60
Palestinians, 60, 62, 66, 73, 74–75, 76, 80, 81, 91–92, 195n8
Paris, Roland, 39
participant observation, 16, 19
peacebuilding, definition, 13–14
peace enforcement, 12, 82, 112, 167
peacekeepers, 9, 10, 11, 19, 38, 49, 56, 59, 61, 62, 78, 85, 86, 89, 92, 127, 131, 139, 141, 148, 158, 159, 171; Belgian, 10
peacekeeping, definition, 11–14
photographs, 100, 156–57
plurality, 17, 65
political affairs officers, 9, 19, 72, 95, 102, 115, 123, 124, 136, 169
positive peace, 39
predictability, 24, 51, 97, 173
predictable security environment, 9, 24, 53, 56
prevention, 76, 95, 99, 110

al-Qaeda, 10, 93
qualitative military edge, 75, 134
quick impact projects, 34, 115, 118, 120, 144, 145, 154, 195n17

Ras Naqoura, 95
rational choice, 28
reflexivity, 17
reputation, 26–27, 28, 29, 50, 103, 110, 130, 140

UNTSO (United Nations Truce Supervision Organization), 11, 178n19, 179n34

violations: accidental (unintended), 64, 71, 84, 85–89; air, 76, 81, 89, 92; deliberate (intentional), 84, 89–95; Hezbullah, 89, 112, 190n2; repeated, 84, 87–88, 89; sea, 73, 187n71

Wazzani River, 88
weapons pointing, 92, 101, 110
Whalan, Jeni, 41–44
wider peacekeeping, 13
WikiLeaks, 79
Williams, Paul, 12

zone of security, 64

Vanessa F. Newby has a BSc in psychology from the University of Westminster and an MA and PhD in international relations from Griffith University. She is an Affiliated Scholar at the American University of Beirut and a Visiting Fellow at the National Security College at the Australian National University. Her research interests include international security, peacebuilding, migration, informal institutions, and the politics of the Middle East. She is an Arabic speaker and has spent over seven years conducting research in Lebanon and Syria. Vanessa has published in international peer-reviewed journals such as *International Peacekeeping*, *Contemporary Politics* and *Third World Quarterly*.